The Art of Twentieth Century American Poetry

Blackwell Introductions to Literature

This series sets out to provide concise and stimulating introductions to literary subjects. It offers books on major authors (from John Milton to James Joyce), as well as key periods and movements (from Old English literature to the contemporary). Coverage is also afforded to such specific topics as "Arthurian Romance." All are written by outstanding scholars as texts to inspire newcomers and others: non-specialists wishing to revisit a topic, or general readers. The prospective overall aim is to ground and prepare students and readers of whatever kind in their pursuit of wider reading.

Published

Forthcoming

The Art of Twentieth-Century American Poetry

Modernism and After

Charles Altieri

Blackwell Publishing

© 2006 by Charles Altieri

BLACKWELL PUBLISHING
350 Main Street, Malden, MA 02148-5020, USA
9600 Garsington Road, Oxford OX4 2DQ, UK
550 Swanston Street, Carlton, Victoria 3053, Australia

First published 2006 by Blackwell Publishing Ltd

1 2006

Library of Congress Cataloging-in-Publication Data

Altieri, Charles, 1942–
The art of twentieth-century American poetry : modernism
and after / Charles Altieri.
p. cm.—(Blackwell introductions to literature)
Includes bibliographical references and index.
ISBN-13: 978-1-4051-2106-4 (hard cover : alk. paper)
ISBN-10: 1-4051-2106-8 (hard cover : alk. paper)
ISBN-13: 978-1-4051-2107-1 (pbk. : alk. paper)
ISBN-10: 1-4051-2107-6 (pbk. : alk. paper) 1. American poetry—
20th century—History and criticism. 2. Modernism (Literature)—
United States. I. Title. II. Series.
PS310.M57A577 2006
811'.509112—dc22
2005012328

A catalogue record for this title is available from the British Library.

Set in 10/13pt Meridien
by Graphicraft Limited, Hong Kong

For further information on
Blackwell Publishing, visit our website:
www.blackwellpublishing.com

Contents

Preface and Acknowledgments

This book was fun to write. It felt a natural outgrowth of my teaching, and it seemed license just to read poems as complex acts of thinking and feeling – what got me into this profession to start with. It is also fun to round up what are now all the usual suspects to thank for their help in working out my arguments – Charles Molesworth, Marjorie Perloff, Lyn Hejinian, Cheryl Walker, and Henry Staten in particular. There are also new subjects to thank – especially Brian Glaser, Joshua Clover, Geoffrey O'Brien, John Shoptaw, Kimberly Tsau, Charles Sumner, Jen Scappetone, Omri Moses, Margaret Ronda, and Charles Tung. I am most grateful to the writers I engage in this book for having given intense pleasure for now over forty years. But I have to apologize to the many scholars from whom I have learned a great deal that has enhanced that pleasure: the format of this series simply does not allow precise acknowledgment of one's scholarly debts.

It has been a great pleasure working with the staff at Blackwell, especially Emma Bennett, Karen Wilson, and my copy-editor Jacqueline Harvey. Everyone has proven efficient, intelligent, and affable – an increasingly rare combination of attributes. Not having to track down permissions myself will provide the impetus to write another book. Andrew McNeillie, then at Blackwell, deserves special mention because it was he who talked me into this project. Now I can be grateful.

I cannot track the lineage of the ideas presented here. Some sections derive from various essays I have written; some from dismay at what I had not written as I dealt with modernist topics. I do know the basic argument was developed in response to an invitation from the

American Literature Association to give a keynote talk at a mini-conference on modern poetry. I want to thank the organizers for their faith, and *American Literary History* for publishing a version of it. I also want to thank the several audiences who have heard arguments that eventually found a place in this book for their kindness and their patience.

The idea of patience brings me to domestic settings. It is an immense blessing that my wife Carolyn Porter is very well endowed with this virtue, as well as her more flamboyant and endearing qualities. And the idea of blessings brings me to my daughter Laura. I cannot imagine what life would be like if there were not this extremely intelligent and sensitive adult who is by nature and by culture compelled to like me, and indeed be like me. For the latter I sometimes pity her; for the former I always am full of gratitude. Dedicating this book to her is a small token of what our friendship still promises.

Acknowledgments

The author and publisher gratefully acknowledge the permission granted to reproduce the copyright material in this book:

John Ashbery, excerpt from "As We Know," excerpt from "Pyrography," excerpt from "Scheherazade," and "Ut Pictura Poesis," from John Ashbery, *Selected Poems*. New York: Viking, 1985.

W. H. Auden, excerpt from "Homage to Clio," excerpt from "In Memory of W. B. Yeats," and "The Prologue (or Adolescence)," from Edward Mendelson (ed.), *Collected Poems*. New York: Vintage, 1991. "Adolescence" copyright © 1945 by W. H. Auden; "Homage to Clio" copyright © 1976 by Edward Mendelson, William Meredith, and Monroe K. Spears, Executors of the Estate of W. H. Auden; "In Memory of W. B. Yeats" copyright © 1940 and renewed 1968 by W. H. Auden. Used by permission of Random House Inc.

Elizabeth Bishop, excerpt from "Arrival at Santos," excerpt from "Brazil, January 1, 1502," and excerpt from "A Cold Spring," from Elizabeth Bishop, *The Complete Poems: 1927–1979*. New York: Farrar, Strauss and Giroux, 1983. Reprinted by permission of Farrar, Straus and Giroux, LLC. Copyright © 1979, 1983 by Alice Helen Methfessel.

Robert Creeley, "A Song," "Joy," "Something," and "The Rain," from Robert Creeley, *The Collected Poems of Robert Creeley 1945–75.* Berkeley: University of California Press, 1982. Reprinted by permission of the University of California Press.

Langston Hughes, "Ballad of the Landlord," "Dreams," "Evenin' Air Blues," "Harlem [1]," "Little Lyric (of Great Importance)," "Subway Rush Hour," and "Young Prostitute," from Arnold Rampersad and David Roessel (eds.), *The Collected Poems of Langston Hughes.* New York: Knopf, 1994.

Robert Lowell, excerpt from "Colloquy at Black Rock," "Skunk Hour," "The March 1," and excerpt from "Waking in the Blue," from Frank Bidart and David Gewanter (eds.), *Collected Poems.* London: Faber and Faber, 2003.

Mina Loy, "Gertrude Stein," excerpt from "Sketch of a Man on a Platform," and "XXIV," from Roger L. Conover (ed.), *The Lost Lunar Baedeker: Poems of Mina Loy.* New York: Farrar, Strauss and Giroux, 1996. Reprinted by permission of Farrar, Straus and Giroux, LLC and Carcanet Press Limited. Works of Mina Loy copyright © 1996 by the Estate of Mina Loy.

Marianne Moore, excerpt from "A Grave," "An Egyptian Pulled Glass Bottle in the Shape of a Fish," "Poetry," and excerpt from "Steeplejack," from Marianne Moore, *Complete Poems.* London: Faber and Faber, 1968.

George Oppen, "Eclogue," "Poem 27," and "The Street," from George Oppen, *New Collected Poems.* New York: New Directions, 2002. "Eclogue" copyright © 1962 by George Oppen; "Poem 27" copyright © 1934 by The Objectivist Press; "The Street" copyright © 1965 by George Oppen. Reprinted by permission of New Directions Publishing Corp.

Ezra Pound, "April," "In the Station of the Metro," "The Bath Tub," "The Encounter," and "The Tree," from Ezra Pound, *Personae: Collected Shorter Poems of Ezra Pound.* London: Faber and Faber, 1952.

Adrienne Rich, excerpts from "Splittings" and "Phantasia for Elvira Shatayev," from *The Dream of a Common Language: Poems 1974–1977* by Adrienne Rich. Copyright © 1978 by W. W. Norton & Company, Inc. Used by permission of the author and W. W. Norton & Company, Inc.

Excerpt from "Heroines," from *A Wild Patience Has Taken Me This Far: Poems 1978–1981* by Adrienne Rich. Copyright © 1981 by

Abbreviations

Full details of each reference can be found in the list of Works Cited at the end of the book.

Ashbery, SP	John Ashbery, *Selected Poems*
Auden, CP	W. H. Auden, *Collected Poems*
Bishop, CP	Elizabeth Bishop, *The Complete Poems 1927–1979*
Creeley, CP	Robert Creeley, *The Collected Poems of Robert Creeley 1945–1975*
CWC	Ernest Fenollosa, "The Chinese Written Character as a Medium for Poetry"
DH	W. H. Auden, *The Dyer's Hand and Other Essays*
EK	Ron Loewinsohn (ed.), *The Embodiment of Knowledge*
Eliot, CP	T. S. Eliot, *The Complete Poems and Plays of T. S. Eliot*
Eliot, SE	T. S. Eliot, *Selected Essays*
FD	Adrienne Rich, *The Fact of a Doorframe: Poems Selected and New 1950–1984*
GB	Ezra Pound, *Gaudier-Brzeska: A Memoir*
Hughes, CP	Langston Hughes, *The Collected Poems of Langston Hughes*
LE	Ezra Pound, *Literary Essays of Ezra Pound*
LLB	Mina Loy, *The Lost Lunar Baedeker*
Lowell, CP	Robert Lowell, *Collected Poems*
MM	Henri Bergson, *Matter and Memory*
Moore, CP	Marianne Moore, *The Complete Poems of Marianne Moore*
NCP	George Oppen, *New Collected Poems*

P	Ezra Pound, *Personae: Collected Shorter Poems of Ezra Pound*
Pound, SP	Ezra Pound, *Selected Prose, 1909–1965: Ezra Pound*
Prepositions	Louis Zukofsky, *Prepositions*
Rich, PP	Adrienne Rich, *Adrienne Rich's Poetry and Prose*
Stevens, CP	Wallace Stevens, *The Collected Poems of Wallace Stevens*
TFW	Henri Bergson, *Time and Free Will*
Williams, CP	William Carlos Williams, *The Collected Poems of William Carlos Williams*, vol. 1
Williams, SE	William Carlos Williams, *Selected Essays of William Carlos Williams*

Chapter 1

Introduction
The Art of Twentieth-Century American Poetry: An Overview

Writing an introduction to modernist American poetry has proven an interesting exercise in self-definition. When I agreed to this project, I had the simple idea that an introductory book combined accessible prose on a general topic with an ability to intensify whatever interests brought readers to the book in the first place. I did not realize how many difficult practical decisions there would be about what to include and exclude; nor did I realize the range of possibilities for envisioning what audiences desired or how authors might provoke interest in the topic.

Consider the two books Blackwell has already published as introductions to twentieth-century poetry. In *21st-Century Modernism: The New Poetics*, Marjorie Perloff has chosen to be highly selective, developing a specific vision of the course of modern poetry, mostly in Europe. She makes a brilliant case that there is a direct line from the experimental spirit of T. S. Eliot's "The Love Song of J. Alfred Prufrock" and Gertrude Stein's *Tender Buttons* to Language Writing at the end of the twentieth century. World War I intervened, deadening the spirit of experiment and bringing to poetry in English a renewed ponderousness that it has taken almost a century to overcome: "Ours may well be the moment when the lessons of early modernism are finally being learned."[1]

Christopher MacGowan's *Twentieth-Century American Poetry* takes the opposite tack.[2] Rather than choose a specific path through the twentieth century, MacGowan tries to be as inclusive as possible. He writes superbly condensed, highly informative essays situating the important poets in each major development in modern American poetry; he provides instructive essays on topics like poetry's relation to the other arts and the American long poem; and he offers capsule accounts of forty-eight poetic careers before attending more closely to twenty-five volumes by some of these poets.

Having read these and other introductions to modern poetry, I cannot say I am any the clearer about what an introduction should be. But I am much clearer about how I might be fully engaged by the task and hence perhaps be of use to others without repeating work that has already been done quite well. Any student who wants basic informa-tion about the poets is likely to be satisfied by MacGowan's book. That is an enormous relief for me because I could never organize so much so well. Thanks to MacGowan, I can pursue a more idiosyncratic path through twentieth-century American poetry, concentrating on relatively difficult writers who considered their work a challenge to traditional notions of poetry. That brings me close to Perloff, although there are large differences that will soon emerge. We share a sense that once the information is available in a book like MacGowan's, a new introductory book can concentrate on enhancing the intellectual and affective pleasures available in attending imaginatively to the work these poets produce.

My title is my way of celebrating this sense of freedom to set my own purposes. I want to establish ways of enjoying this challenging material, which means illustrating one way a reader might think about what he or she is reading. As I proceed, I try not to forget that this is an introduction geared towards a literate public, especially to advanced undergraduate and graduate students studying these materials seriously for the first time. But I want to emphasize the pleasures that can be involved as readers learn to participate thoughtfully in the worlds that the works develop. And participating thoughtfully requires confront-ing substantial difficulty – both in handling the concepts that frame the issues the poets faced and in exploring how particular poems explore quite complex experiences. For me much of the pleasure in modernist poetry consists in engaging these difficult materials in a way that never quite brings peace, although it does bring increasing recognition of why the difficulties are necessary. So there will be times when this book will prove somewhat rough going. However,

I shall be careful to indicate why the difficulty is significant so that we can honor the poetic intelligence grappling with the problems.

As will be obvious, my agreement with Perloff's sense of how to present an introduction to modern poetry does not extend to sharing her vision of what matters in the story that the introduction provides. Her story is fundamentally one of loss and rediscovery based on very few exemplary figures. My story will present a more dialectical narrative emphasizing the sense of liberation provided by early modernist formal experiments, then the disappointment that followed in the 1930s when those discoveries proved very difficult to correlate with the capacity to address pressing social needs; the third stage consists of three generations of poets unwilling to reject modernist stylistic breakthroughs even though they also recognized the limitations in the rationales for the breakthroughs. Because these poets realized that they could not continue maintaining the sharp modernist distinctions between poetry and rhetoric that enabled them to subsume social into spiritual problems, they tried to reformulate their strategies to elaborate new ways for poetry to take social responsibility.

We can flesh out this dialectic a little by focusing, first, on the experimental climate of early Anglo-American modernism and the cultural needs these experiments were intended to address. In my classes I introduce this material by concentrating on what the writers are repudiating, since writers are discursively much clearer on what they reject than on the alternatives they are trying to produce. Their actual work can represent the positive side in all its complexity. Moreover, because the negative discursive statements tend to be quite general, they provide the best index of how the writers imagine they can make an impact on cultural life.

This book will stress two basic modernist refusals of basic values in the culture they inherited. The first is essentially epistemological, the second psychological. (One could call the second "ethical" if the rubric had not been horribly cheapened by overuse.) The epistemological refusal consists in the poets' turning from ideals of sensitive description and symbolic representation to pursue what they saw as links between a new realism in science and a "presentational" realism possible for poetry. In their eyes, the old realism was based on ideals of copying nature in order to disclose principles of behaviour that could be generalized. So the modernists criticized the static nature of those pictures and the authoritative position this model gave the picture-maker. Hence William Butler Yeats' influential attack on Lucien Stendhal's ideal that a masterpiece could be likened to "a mirror dawdling down a lane."[3] To Yeats, Stendhal's image suggests both a disturbing distance from his materials and a dangerously imperious sense of authority born of that distance.

The new realism, on the other hand, found its roots in the emerging scientific methods which emphasized not the copy but the sensations produced by events. The pictures produced by the mind seemed less important than the actual processes, where the relations among sensations could be seen as the products of natural and mental forces. In fact the new realism was leery of any effort to isolate a "mind": what mattered was the activity by which intensities became "realized." Ian Bell has written a terrific book outlining the various influences that such sciences had on Ezra Pound's formulation of possibilities for new modes of writing.[4] Here I will presuppose Bell's work on the scientists in order to concentrate instead on a philosopher and a painter, Henri Bergson and Paul Cézanne, who developed the conceptual and practical frameworks by which this new science entered the literary world. These were the central figures in showing how the old realism was bound to the logic of the copy and of the type, and they made striking the challenge for artists to develop what I shall call a "presentational realism," stressing not accuracy to the object but accuracy to the felt moment of perception. As T. S. Eliot said of Bergson, this new thinking used "science against science" to establish "the reality of a fluid, psychological world of aspect and nuance, where purposes and intentions are replaced by pure feeling."[5]

The second, "psychological" set of negatives was much more broad and diffuse. The young modernists acutely felt the pressure of entrenched values and, worse, of entrenched personality types that the culture established in order to preserve those values. Consider how often the early work of T. S. Eliot, Mina Loy, and Ezra Pound turned to snapshot portraits in which only a few traits sufficed to skewer representative characters embodying the "sincere" ego of romantic poetry and the "righteous ego" of Victorian moralizing discourse. Young artists in every generation probably want to treat their elders this way. But the modernists could do so boldly because they thought their art sufficiently complex to model new ways to imagine the psyche at work. The poets might not know quite what their experiments in literary psychology could release, but they knew all too well the need

[margin handwritten note: presentational realism — describe how it felt not what happened]

for some kind of relief from an over-moralized world long on opinion and short on fresh intense modes of feeling. Senses activated by the work's stress on internal relations might become testimony to possibilities of a desperately needed new psychology.

Taken together, modernist efforts to project such a psychology might be considered a new "constructivist expressionism." The old expressionism they saw as an essentially "romantic" effort to cut away every rhetorical device and ideological position that prevented the individual from articulating sincere personal responses to immediate particular situations. While the early modernists wanted to keep this sense of the intricate immediacy of experience, they felt a new expressionism was necessary in order to repudiate the postures and roles that had accreted around the notion that poetic authority depended on demonstrating capacious sincerity. For a poetics based on an ideal of sincerity simply had to ignore the many ironic factors that might undercut the pose of self-mastery. And, more important for the young poets resisting such sincerity, this stance could be seen as misplacing cultural authority because it made authority dependent on the display of character rather than on the display of what attention could see and language realize. Therefore the modernists treated expression as an ideal based not on the character of the writer but on the constructive activity giving the object a distinctive play of forces that is impossible to summarize in any discursive practice.

Consider the example of Ezra Pound's "In a Station of the Metro," a poem I shall engage later in this book:

The apparition of these faces in the crowd
Petals on a wet black bough.

There is no overt speaker here, and no scene of moralized discovery with which to ennoble sincerity. Here what matters is the audience's participation in an intricately unfolding sense of metaphoric expansiveness. This highly condensed utterance (cut down, Pound tells us, from a thirty-line poem) stresses the power of the constructive act to make such attention immediately compelling. Just listen to the range of crisp vowel sounds and the intricate shift between nature and what we might call "unnature" or myth – the apparitional quality of the underworld made even more insistent by the lack of explicit connection to the physical details of the last line.

The most important psychological feature of this new constructivism for me is its impersonality, its reliance on the expressive power of the work rather than the expressive power of the artist's meditative presence. This aspect of modernist poetry is now much maligned, but I hope to justify the emphasis by showing how it responded powerfully to social conditions that the poets felt they had to change. "Sincerity" is a tricky ideal, since, as Jean-Paul Sartre showed, being intent on sincerity focuses attention on the role one is playing and detracts from the attention to the object one is claiming to be sincere about. Therefore sincerity is a dangerous model for cultural authority because it honors the appearance of virtue rather than demanding that virtue prove itself by actually getting down to work that engages the interests of other people.[6] So the modernists tried to show that there were alternative stances that might establish strong suspicions about the power of self-consciousness to master emotional turbulence. Engendering such suspicions then might call attention to the play of desires at several levels of consciousness, and so might construct an ideal audience aware of how the experience of such subtle resonance is in fact shared – on both conscious and unconscious levels. Moreover, by occupying positions not bound to the ways society reinforces the imaginary authority of the ego, poetry could invest entirely in compositional rather than rhetorical energies.[7] As T. S. Eliot put it, by breaking down grand emotions into "very varied feelings," those feelings would be "at liberty to enter into new combinations."[8] Impersonality encouraged writers to explore those strange transpersonal sites where what seem common terms of suffering open into transcendental visions.

Modernism was immensely successful in altering taste because the new realism and the new anti-rhetorical expressionism managed to reinforce one another. The emphasis on sensation responsive to force helped break down large emotions into constituent units, and these units both required and rewarded experiments in form that could explore how the combinations of "feelings" established unique significant experiences. Rather than attribute authority to the contemplative poet, readers could attribute authority to how the poet as artificer managed to match the resources of language to these opportunities for new experiences. Pastoral traditions were the most visible victims of these new tastes. Their simplicity irritated poets eager to test their linguistic skills by rendering complex urban settings or intricate psychological studies. And pastoral typified inherited forms which relied on rhetorical traditions that the work did not examine critically or contest imaginatively.

However, the principles establishing this sense of liberation were to create major problems for succeeding generations. Writing that successfully challenged the role played by rhetoric in poetry, and writing that successfully broke down the real into sensations that could be realigned imaginatively, both ran the risk of creating a significant gap between the ambitions driving the writers and the terms by which even most highly literate people lived their lives. Poetry could do without inherited rhetorical principles since it could revel in other imaginative modes of structuring sensations and exploring the powers of language. But the separation on which modernism thrived, between the authority of the art and the presumed and problematic authority of "sincere" artists, left it with almost no means to take up the traditional roles of delighting and instructing – at a time when an emerging economic depression made the lack of overt instruction seem irresponsible.

We need this hypothesis in order to explain why almost all the major modernists experienced substantial crises about their work and about their lives in the late 1920s and early 1930s. I think the sense of crisis stemmed primarily from their growing fears that the constructivist aesthetics on which they had come to rely made it impossible to develop sufficient frameworks for identifying with those suffering from social injustice. For if poetry is to have social force beyond an elite community, it may have to develop modes of presence that depend on the activity of a positioned speaking voice as it works its way through various possible identifications and identities. Constructivist aesthetics can develop a variety of voices and can make us keenly aware of the dangerous indulgences these voices elicit, but it cannot readily have these voices form and maintain sympathies and commitments directly pursuing improved social conditions.

I am not arguing that constructivist modernism lacked a sense of history or an empathy with social conditions produced by industrial capitalism. On the contrary, it might have had too rich, or at least too fine, a sense of history because it was obsessed by a compelling need not just to account for itself historically but to find from within history direct energies and patterns which might better equip individuals to deal with what seemed inescapable dark times. But constructivist models of expression now seemed incompatible with the rhetorical stances necessary for convincing others that in fact something might be done to increase social justice. The modernists' distrust of concepts and of images, indeed their distrust of any medium not grounded in actual sensation, prevented any direct alignment of art with the sympathies necessary for social progress.

By the late 1930s the limitations I suggest were becoming increasingly obvious, and increasingly painful. So poets returned to seeking ways of dealing positively with the roles the imaginary plays in our lives. One large group of poets, typified by those publishing in *The Masses*, took the most direct path: they embraced rhetorical stances and tried overtly to provide images of just and noble behavior that a population might emulate. Those more sympathetic with modernism's critical sensibilities took a somewhat different tack. Many of the major innovations in American poetry from the late 1930s to the present were devoted to continuing modernism's reliance on objectified witnessing, but now as a witnessing that could bring the theatrical dimensions of the imaginary back into play while finessing its tendencies to sustain illusory subject positions.

This way of characterizing the historical situation enables us to honor what I think are major achievements by Wallace Stevens, George Oppen, Langston Hughes, and W. H. Auden. Each of these writers worked out distinctive ways of reintroducing the force of the imaginary identifications rhetoric fosters while using the resources of art to separate that force from the images and social roles whose authority is usually reinforced by our self-projections. Stevens tried to indulge the powers of the imaginary while orienting them toward the social on the level of process rather than on the level of images and roles. That is, he located sociality in learning to appreciate how we share investments that are grounded in the very ways we experienced their intensities. Oppen lacked Stevens' rhetorical flair, but he was a master at rendering complex situations that eliminate any possibility of self-congratulation. Hughes made realist concision a direct access to shared social investments. And Auden's deep distrust of vanity of all kinds led him eventually to a performative mode in which imaginary identities are replaced by a process of constantly testing whether one can take responsibility for the process of valuing established by poetic voice.

These poetic projects proved very influential on subsequent generations of American poets. Enormously indebted to Stevens for the necessary resources, Elizabeth Bishop and John Ashbery both tried to emphasize an imagining that was not primarily oriented to figures of the substantial ego, while also resisting the tendencies in the most dominant critical voices of the time to have imagination sustain both truth claims and moral visions. (Ashbery can be seen as bringing Auden's performative voice into endlessly intricate combinations with the depersonalized theatricality of the Stevensian imagination.) And Hughes' and Oppen's version of fluid yet critical inhabiting of social fantasies lives on in the links between Objectivist poetics and Language Writing. Finally I shall address a group of poets who frankly but inventively make the case that writers have exhausted the possibilities in modernist styles. Frank O'Hara, Sylvia Plath, Robert Creeley, Adrienne Rich, and Robert Lowell remain part of my story because the sense of exhaustion requires them to engage the force of the imaginary in quite distinctive ways. Each of these poets returns to a version of the new realism, but they alter the role the imaginary plays in relation to that realism. This realism can no longer be opposed to the imaginary. The new new realism cannot be said to provide a world comprised mostly of sensations recombined by an impersonal art. Instead these poets regarded immediacy as already suffused with the kinds of ineffable desires that made interpretation necessary, and that frustrated any effort to form interpretive judgments in so crude a medium as language. Their images did not so much appeal to the eye as project the incompleteness of vision in a world inescapably permeated with desire and so requiring and frustrating interpretation. Impersonality seems now not an alternative to rhetoric but rhetoric by other means.

This story, unlike Perloff's, attends to every generation of modernist writing until the 1980s. Then, as MacGowan's book indirectly shows, there is simply not enough agreement on the major poets, so one is hard-pressed not to portray just a wide variety of promising beginnings. I have neither the space, the talent, nor the patient optimism required for that enterprise. I will have to be content with providing one potentially representative account of why one can be excited about carefully reading and thinking about works from four generations of American poets. If I am lucky, of if the writers are lucky, the examples they provide will also provide readers with terms which they can modify in order to establish critical paths for engaging contemporary work.

A final caveat. Because I have a large stake in the intellectual ferment to which modernist poetry was responding, I will spend considerable time outlining the concepts that seem to me crucial for understanding the writers' particular projects and for placing them in historical relation to one another. This attention to contexts will exact a considerable price. To engage contexts even on an introductory level I will have to ignore several quite substantial poetic careers. And even when I dwell on specific poems, I will have to ignore other important aspects of the poet's work. The best I can do to provide coverage of the field is to take a cue from those who do political surveys. I want to adapt the principle of "sampling." But my project will not involve taking the ideological pulse of a populace. Rather I shall propose certain works as significant for how they can quicken and hence modify aspects of such a pulse. Literary sampling involves two tasks. First, a critic must seek texts, usually but not always canonical ones, that best exemplify how authors typically stage their strengths, interests, commitments, and innovations. Second, the critic has to imagine not just how the texts matter for authors but how they can matter for readers. Sampling has to include demonstrating how readers might use poems to connect with what concerns them in their extra-literary experience. In effect, sampling tests conjunctions between literary·ambitions and critical methods. But I hope readers will also be encouraged to engage the authors more fully so that my efforts at modeling become also measures of what is limited in the narrowly focused single perspective. An introductory book has to imagine its success as inseparable from its being superseded by the reader's developing ability to tell more complex stories.

Chapter 2

The New Realism in Modernist Poetry: Pound and Williams

Nine out of every ten Americans have sold their souls for a quotation. They have wrapped themselves about a formula of words instead of about their own centers.
Ezra Pound, "Patria Mia"[1]

Valid scientific thought consists in following as closely as may be the actual and entangled lines of force as they pulse through things.
Ernest Fenollosa, "The Chinese Written Character as a Medium for Poetry"[2]

Because the knife is polished they think it is sharp.
William Carlos Williams, The Embodiment of Knowledge[3]

I begin with what I am calling the "new realism" in order to track one of the major undervalued achievements by the first generation of modern American poets. This generation managed to establish significant ways of breaking from received ways of establishing "truth" by showing how poetry could be a substantial form of inquiry in its own right. But critics tend to emphasize the poets' formal innovations (as praise and, recently, as blame), without recognizing how concerns about content drive many of their innovations.[4] In fact those formal innovations were inspired largely by late nineteenth-century science's treatments of the relation between mind and body, spirit and matter. I think it fair to say that very little of this transcendental speculative science has lasted. Yet, thanks to the fine work several critics have done in tracing these scientific arguments,[5] we can see now that science at least had the effect of challenging rigid materialist causal models, and so was quite influential in shaping the more fluid notions of matter and cause governing contemporary thinking. More important, we can begin to appreciate how the poets might have responded to the general intellectual ferment produced by those discoveries. Experiment was a general cultural ideal, not a mandarin excuse for evading historical struggles.

Obviously I cannot review all this work. But by concentrating on an ideal of a new realism I hope to bring out how the spirit of science generated both a sense of challenge and a sense of permission among modern poets. Given the fact that this book is a brief introduction, I can best honor that sense of challenge by going directly to examples of work that extend aspects of the new realism beyond science – in particular to the conceptual model provided by Henri Bergson's critiques of the Cartesian tradition and to the material model provided by Paul Cézanne's painting, with its own critiques of the habits of seeing characteristic of the old realism. Even with this narrowing of the field, we have to adjust for the fact that writers by and large do not read technical philosophy and do not look at paintings as art historians do. Therefore I shall focus only on how these ideas and these paintings sponsor new modes of self-consciousness about seeing and about sensing. This focus should suffice to show why the poets rejected representational models of writing and experimented with other, more direct means of bringing force and structure to what they could make seem immediate experience.

If one were limited to a single cultural avatar of the new realism, Henri Bergson would probably be the consensus choice. His ideas were widely disseminated in the United States and in Europe. T. S. Eliot went from Harvard University to Paris to hear the great man, and his translator in England was T. E. Hulme, someone close to the major modernist writers. Perhaps the most significant measure of his popularity was that Bertrand Russell thought it worth a small book to expose his errors. (Wyndham Lewis later wrote a much larger book with the same intent but not the same clarity.) Bergson matters for my purposes largely because he adapted the spirit of the new science into a critique of scientific method and so developed aspects of the new realism with which poets could immediately identify.[6] Bergson knew his science – his early work was steeped in academic traditions in psychology – yet he insisted that only philosophy could provide sufficient critical scope to set the appropriate agendas for research.

To keep the focus sharp I will concentrate in this chapter on how Ezra Pound's work in London from 1912 to 1919 manifests substantial parallels with these Bergsonian concerns. Then I will turn from the Pound–Bergson nexus to another match, between Paul Cézanne and William Carlos Williams, this time stressing how the new realism affected artists' rendering of the powers organized by various sensations. Although I shall concentrate on particular works by these figures, my ultimate goal in discussing both Pound and Williams is to represent shifts in how all the major modernists understood the relation between describing a world and realizing it through emphasis on the powers of the medium in which it is rendered.

*description
vs.
its medium*

I

Like the poets, Bergson is probably most lucid and most compelling when he is being negative and attacking the dominant intellectual tradition. For he realized that the new realism raised conceptual stakes that extended far beyond science: all the prevailing conceptual structures that put the old realism in place had to be questioned. And, more important, these conceptual structures had to be examined for the deep cultural problems that they may have caused. One could argue that cultural critiques like Nietzsche's become especially trenchant when one can see clearly how the old ontology's divisions between matter and spirit might have produced a pervasive nihilism.

As evidence for these generalizations, consider how the following two passages from Bergson take on the entire Cartesian tradition ultimately responsible for the idealization of representation as a vehicle for knowledge. My first passage shows that both realism and idealism, the basic traditions spawned by Enlightenment thought, share one overriding and problematic assumption:

> If we now look closely at the two doctrines, we shall discover in them a common postulate, which we may formulate thus: perception has a wholly speculative interest; it is pure knowledge. . . . The one doctrine starts from the order required by science, and sees in perception only a confused and provisional science. The other puts perception in the first place, erects it into an absolute, and then holds science to be a symbolic expression of the real. But, for both parties, to perceive means above all to know.[7]

Bergson does not deny that perception is connected to knowledge but there is an intermediate step that Cartesian thinking tends to ignore, with important consequences. While knowledge seems satisfied by static pictures, perception is a dramatic event charged by its relation to other events. Knowledge then may be a secondary development created by the conjunction of events.

Hence Bergson's second, more general, passage speculating on the cultural cost when this emphasis on knowledge gets divorced from purposive behavior:

> We feel a thousand different elements which dissolve into and permeate one another without any precise outlines . . . ; hence their originality. . . . A moment ago each of them was borrowing an indefinable color from its surroundings: now we have it colourless and ready to accept a name. The feeling itself is a being which lives and develops and is therefore constantly changing. . . . By separating these moments from each other, by spreading out time in space, we have caused this feeling to lose its life and its color. Hence we are now standing before our own shadow: we believe that we have analyzed our feeling, while we have really replaced it by a juxtaposition of lifeless states which can be translated into words, and each of which constitutes the common element, the impersonal residue, of the impressions felt in a given case by the whole of society.[8]

This is at core an echo of Romantic complaints about Enlightenment culture's abstracting of images from the feelings that accompany them. But Bergson actually has the goods, in the sense that he is articulate on the cause of this haunting sense of the self as only shadowy substance. For he can show how the old realism casts the subject as a speculative witness to its body rather than as an owner capable of establishing and adjusting purposive behavior. For the old realism, the body becomes a fact in space rather than a dynamic force in time. Perception isolated from feeling can stage knowledge, but it cannot establish contexts in which the knowledge matters for the person in a particular situation. And then language becomes trapped within this theater of dispossession because it has to be on that stage without a sense that the agent is expressing and realizing some purpose. No wonder that modern culture increasingly needs shock values to feel any sense of vitality at all. And no wonder that other people seem less agents connected to our concerns than vague threats made up of bundles of perceptions with which we fear we are unfamiliar.

Bergson's positive vision can be presented as developing four basic ideas that provide grounds for a new realism. The first builds on the critique of representation that we have already considered: "The brain is an instrument of action, and not of representation" (MM 74). In the place of perception as a vehicle of timeless knowledge, Bergson treats perception as fundamentally an aspect of a process driven by the person's interests in modifying the past in relation to a possible future. That is, he puts perception primarily in time rather than leaving it isolated in space: "Images themselves cannot create images; but they indicate at each moment, like a compass that is being moved about, the position of a certain given image, my body, in relation to the surrounding images" (MM 22). This sense of the movement of the body as the "true and final explanation" of "perception as a whole" (MM 45) replaces isolated percepts by consciousness of entire attitudes (MM 100).

Second, the old realism treated sensation primarily as the body's means of registering perception. An idea is the structure representing what sensation makes possible. For Bergson there is no direct connection between sensation and perceptions or images. Perceptions are constructs that simplify sensation by giving complexly interrelated forces in time a practical role in space (MM 52). Therefore he formulates a distinction between intensive and extensive manifolds: intensive manifolds model sensations as "in one another"; extensive manifolds model perceptions "as alongside one another" (TFW 101). Extensive manifolds, then, are spatial figures where elements are distinct and assertions about causality plausible because effects and causes can be distinguished. Intensive manifolds are qualitative relations that have to be modeled in terms of the kinds of interconnection that develop over time. When Bergson turns to pain, for example, he provides a telling account of why that state is not a percept but an affect structured as an intensive manifold:

> We shall not compare a pain of increasing intensity to a note which grows louder and louder, but rather to a symphony in which an increasing number of instruments make themselves heard. Within the characteristic sensation, which gives the tone to all the others, consciousness

> distinguishes a larger or smaller number of sensations arising at different points of the periphery . . . : the choir of these elementary psychic states voices the new demands of the organism when confronted by a new situation. In other words, we estimate the intensity of a pain by the larger or smaller part of the organism that takes interest in it. (TFW 35)

We cannot separate the pain from the agent's qualitative response to the intricacy of an overall situation.

Third, Bergson makes a strong case for the importance of intuition. He has to admit that empirical reason functions well when phenomena admit of treatment as extensive manifolds. For reason has the power to isolate independent elements and test the various ways in which they interact. But the situation with intensive manifolds is quite different. These resist reason because the elements are not independent but form wholes in which various forces at play interpenetrate one another. Such interpenetration is accessible only to a power of consciousness that can take in the whole all at once. In such cases the mind must trust to intuition:

> Recognize in pure perception a system of nascent acts which plunges roots deep into the real; at once perception is seen to be radically distinct from recollection; the reality of things is no more constructed or reconstructed, but touched, penetrated, lived, and the problem of issue between realism and idealism . . . is solved, or rather dissolved, by intuition. (MM 69)

Intuition is the means of grasping how one experiences duration.

Finally, Bergson elaborates two basic practical consequences of adapting a new realism. Like William James (and like T. S. Eliot in his dissertation on F. H. Bradley) the real then need not be something thinkers picture or represent but something produced by individuals and collectivities as we test for what we can trust in our actions: "We measure in practice the degree of reality by the degree of utility" (MM 66). The emphasis on activity then provides a not implausible way of thinking about human freedom, something which is unthinkable when empirical reason is the only faculty trusted for psychological inquiry. Empirical reason will always invade "the series of our psychic states" by introducing space into our perception of duration, and hence corrupting "at its very source our feeling or outer and inner change, of movement, and of freedom" (TFW 74). Building on this contrast,

16

Bergson locates freedom as "a relation of the concrete self to the act which it performs." This relation, he adds, "is indefinable just because we are free," since "we can analyze a thing, but not a process; we can break up extensity but not duration" (TFW 219). Freedom becomes in effect a condition of expression: that self can be considered free when its actions seem to flow from concrete purposive behavior that is impossible to treat as determined by external forces. This move proves very important for artists and writers because Bergson breaks entirely from the Kantian tradition: freedom becomes less a property of rational moral action than an attribute earned by qualities of expressive behavior.

II

Ezra Pound is not likely to have read these passages from Bergson. He knew how to talk about Bergson from his extensive social relations, but did not have the temperament to read much modern philosophy. For him the new realism was less a doctrine than an attitude, less a philosophical position than a range of working principles borrowed from various aspects of the Zeitgeist, to which he was extremely sensitive. Pound's thinking could easily resemble a powerful vacuum cleaner picking up everything in the air, then sifting it in accord with a sensibility very finely tuned to what seemed new and interesting opportunities for the arts. He combined those collecting instincts with the capacity to develop and promulgate individual points with striking clarity, even if there might not be a corresponding clarity in how his ideas fit together. This clarity in turn probably posed an intriguing challenge to his peers: if his discourse could not make them better poets, at least it might open them to become more willing to articulate what they cared about in poetry.

Ezra Pound was born in Hailey, Idaho, but moved to Pennsylvania when he was 2. He was educated at the University of Pennsylvania, where he established friendships with both H.D. and William Carlos Williams. After graduating with an MA in romance languages, with an emphasis on medieval Provence, he started teaching at Wabash College in Crawfordsville, Indiana. There American writing was blessed by what at the time seemed an unfortunate incident. When a young woman was discovered to have spent the night in his room, Pound swore that he had taken her in because she was homeless, and that he had slept on the floor. He had, after all, studied a good deal of chivalric literature. But the college was unrelenting, so he went off to London in 1908 to make his career. And make his career he did, serving as W. B. Yeats' secretary for two years, becoming a mentor to T. S. Eliot, serving as editor or contributing editor for journals like the *Egoist* and the *Little Review*, and imposing his rude mark on the British establishment as the most American of the émigré writers.

From the start Pound transformed the decadent aesthete role fashionable at the time in London. He cultivated long hair and had one of the few earrings in a male ear in London. But he also pursued an exaggerated manliness in every way possible, finding that manliness even in romance traditions where William Morris had found only pale, suffering, ardent lovers. No wonder Pound's Provence combined the erotic, the violent, and an always almost ironic self-consciousness, given expression partly by a mastery of the full sonic register afforded by English.[9]

This is the earliest poem that Pound chose to collect in *Personae*:

> I stood still and was a tree amid the wood,
> Knowing the truth of things unseen before;
> Of Daphne and the laurel bow
> And that god feasting couple old
> That grew elm-oak amid the wold.
> 'Twas not until the gods had been
> Kindly entreated, and been brought within
> Unto the hearth of their heart's home
> That they might do this wonder thing;
> Nathless I have been a tree amid the wood
> And many a new thing understood
> That was rank folly to my head before.[10]

There is already a hunger for experience, a delicate and fluid responsiveness to links between the order of sense and the order of imagination, a remarkably secure ability to suspend and alter his view of his own identity, and, above all, an amazing facility with sounds. The alliteration in the first line stages the three *d* sounds, two of them internally rhymed, balanced against the glorious play of different *o*s in the third through fifth lines. Then there is the intricate sounding of all the vowels in the closing lines. This intricacy is needed to set off how strange a state and a phrase "rank folly" is once one comes to feel that this judgment blocks wisdom at its very source.

Yet there was not much possibility for Pound making his mark in London by resurrecting medieval postures, however subtle and delicately precise. But there was another route. He had learned from Yeats the possibilities of stripping down poetic rhetoric so that the lyric might become spare and precise. Then two closely interrelated events in 1913 helped him formulate a conceptual background for those stylistic changes – a background that made it possible for him to articulate a version of the new realism. He was given the notebooks of Ernest Fenollosa, a Harvard-educated philosopher who had been teaching in Japan. Fenollosa's Emersonian roots led him to develop a theory of how a sense of nature as force and process made the Chinese written character a very different medium of expression from what was available for poetry in the West. And Pound began writing in defense of Imagist poetry by attaching it to the kind of realism that characterized modern science and the "advances" articulated by such prose writers as Gustave Flaubert and especially Henry James (on whose commitment to freedom he has still the best essay). These engagements taken together made Pound's thinking the fundamental pre-text for every American poet at the time who sought to display his or her distinction as a truly modernist writer adapting to a century where the old pieties and roles might be finally buried.

In both cases Pound seems an unlikely ally of Bergson because Pound seems committed to the power of language to create pictures or images of the real. But if we read him carefully we will see that as he worked on how language provided pictures of the world, he increasingly resisted any notion of the image as static or spatial or disembodied. Pound was committed to the author's picturing the world, with a full sense of the affective duration that makes for satisfaction in the act of picturing. With Fenollosa, he received his fundamental breakthrough. A radical pictorial language like the Chinese character afforded a world very different from the old realism's representations. The Chinese character did not encourage abstract dichotomies between the act of signification and the object signified. Instead ideogrammic writing included the energies implicating the perspective by which the mind engaged the image. Chinese does not convey just nouns, but always nouns in action: "Like nature, the Chinese words are alive and plastic, because *thing* and *action* are not formally separated" (CWC 145). Armed with this support, Pound set about trying to figure out why English was so different in its treatment of the information from the senses. This resulted in a sharp critique of traditional logic and, more important, an affiliation with how modern science and, pre-eminently, modern fiction, seemed to be struggling against that logic.

He could forge this affiliation because he saw Fenollosa's notes not only articulating alternatives to Western poetry but also revealing profound symptoms that pervaded traditional Western habits of thinking. For example, Fenollosa argued that when confronted with the thought "the man runs," a Western logician makes two subjective equations, namely, the individual in question is contained under the class "man"; and the class man is contained under the class of "running things." But once these equations are in place, the logician has "no way of bringing together any two concepts which do not happen to stand one under the other and in the same pyramid. It is impossible to represent change in this system or any kind of growth" (CWC 151).

It is no accident, Fenollosa argued, that the concept of evolution came very late to Europe: "it could not make way until it was prepared to destroy the inveterate logic of classification." A new science could make progress in getting at the nature of things only if it refused to submit to the authority of classificatory logic. Then it might discover "how functions cohere in things" because it could express its results "in grouped sentences which embody no nouns or adjectives but verbs of special character." Correspondingly Chinese writing teaches us that poetry is richest when it "agrees with science, not with logic": "The moment we use the copula, the moment we express subjective inclusion, poetry evaporates. The more concretely we express the interactions of things, the better the poetry." "The true formula for thought is: the cherry tree is all that it does. Its correlated verbs compose it."[11]

Pound was writing what he would call Imagist poems well before he encountered Fenollosa's notebooks. Yet I begin with Fenollosa because it can help us see how Pound was offered a perspective that required his rethinking what an image could do. Foremost in his mind was the need for poetry to avoid both sentimentality and rhetoric while coming to compete with the precision and elegance of prose writers like James and Flaubert. But now through Fenollosa he understood that a new poetry required more than stylistic innovation. It required challenging the cultural assumptions and the logic of inquiry that Pound realized supported both sentimentality and rhetoric. So long as thing and action were kept distinct, poetry could be at best a supplement to other disciplines that provided names for those things. But if the image could display an inseparable fusion of thing and action, one could claim significant powers for poetry as a distinctive way of organizing experience. Poetry could articulate relational structures and, more important, relational activities pronouncedly too subtle for the classifying mind.

The first task of such a poetry was to defeat the blend of ornamental rhetoric and discursive argument that seemed the lot of a poetry banished by the old science from having any direct role in constituting any kind of knowledge. So there had to be new principles of craft. Pound offered three practical precepts: "direct treatment of the 'thing' whether subjective or objective"; the use of "absolutely no word that does not contribute to the presentation"; and composition "in the sequence of the musical phrase not in the sequence of the metronome." Then poetry might cultivate specific, evanescent moments, presenting "an intellectual and emotional complex in an instant of time."[12] Poetry could correlate sensation with intricacy of feeling rather than with perception.

I consider "Portrait d'un Femme" Pound's best Imagist poem because the details sustain a complex psychology while warding off any easy rhetorical judgment of the lady or heroic response on the part of the poet. All the words register aspects of the lady's presence; none are devoted to attitudinizing, moralizing, or seeking profundity on the part of the poet. But now I have to choose brief examples. This is "April":

> Three spirits came to me
> And drew me apart
> To where the olive boughs
> Lay stripped upon on the ground;
> Pale carnage beneath bright mist.   (P 101)

The intellectual and emotional complex is constructed by having the speaker invited to what initially seems a significant adventure, only to be restricted to a series of evocative sensations. Then, after the picture develops, there is superimposed a different level of sensation, a strange conjunction of abstract detail (the carnage) with an atmospheric setting that absorbs the entire scene. The effect is of moving from time to timelessness as the concrete situation generates a highly condensed figure at once characterizing the boughs and giving them the power to evoke a metaphoric equation.

It becomes impossible to tell where sensation ends and interpretation or intellection begins: everything becomes detail, yet the last line hovers over the poem in a way that almost subsumes the event into an idea of "pale carnage," building the slight details into something evoking recurrent devastation. (Pound probably settled on "carnage" because it echoes "pale" and sets the *a* sounds against the final *is*, but the word also marvelously pushes beyond the pastoral setting into a much bleaker domain.) But this turn to abstract diction is only momentary. All the connotations are reincorporated into the physical order by the figure of the mist, as if the scene could expand without losing its basis in complex sensation. In effect the poem constructs a plastic site building on these two orders of perception – the world of the mist and the strange material and abstract qualities of "carnage." Then the music of the poem expands the sensation in another direction by the extraordinarily luscious play of vowels and the intricate balancing of syntactic relations.

Now consider a quite different use of the image, here as the presentation of a psychological state that fuses a feeling for the powers of simile with intricate sensations, then places the whole in a deliciously ironic context:

> As a bathtub lined with white porcelain,
>> When the hot water gives out or goes tepid,
>> So is the slow cooling of our chivalrous passion,
>> O my much praised but-not-altogether-satisfactory lady.   (P 109)

And finally consider, "The Encounter," a self-consciously hip poem that goes perhaps as far as poetry can in cultivating what can be sensed but not subjected to moralizing discourse. The imagination of what this lady offers is inseparable from touch – text become texture:

> All the while they were talking the new morality
> Her eyes explored me.
> And when I arose to go
> Her fingers were like the tissue
> Of a Japanese paper napkin.   (P 120)

These poems seem slight vehicles on which to make significant thematic claims. Yet they are slight vehicles that make a point of how their own slightness emerges – a promising beginning. The poems might even be said to question their culture's habits for making judgments about slightness. Maybe what has seemed weightiness depends primarily on rhetorical traditions that purchase an aura of profundity at the cost of precision and subtlety. Perhaps we need new models of judgment that rely more on intricate blends of sensations and a precise ear for nuance than they do on grand gestures asserting their own significance. That may be the only way to see how nouns and verbs combine to foster an intricate sense of process. And perhaps the blend of natural diction and a sense of playful contingency may give poetry the kind of substance that one can trust because it actually connects to how consciousness engages experience rather than merely classifying it.

Yet critics persist in treating these Imagist poems almost entirely as stylistic exercises, without concern for how they might pursue a distinctive model of what perception involves and why that might matter. So I want to bring these poems into the orbit of the conceptual concerns articulated in Fenollosa's essay. The task requires emphasizing not only the statement about "an intellectual and emotional complex in an instant of time" but also the following sentence: "I use the term 'complex' rather in the technical sense employed by the newer psychologists, such as Hart, though we might not agree absolutely in our expectations" (LE 4).

The best prose writers like Henry James had already made the necessary affiliation with the new sciences of the mind. But how could poetry make the shift away from conventional lyricism without becoming just decadent artifice? How could poetry share in the new realism without being subordinated to the prose efforts that were already quite sophisticated at adapting the new methods of inquiry?

More elementally how could poetry foreground criticism of the old realism without exposing its own slightness as a vehicle for engaging cultural life? How could poetry create significant opposition to Stendhal's defining a masterpiece as "a mirror dawdling down a lane"? And how could poetry provide a means of articulating widespread resentment of younger writers against a naturalism that represented the old realism at its most blunt? For there realism as a relation to detail gave way to realism as the insistence on general laws that governed

[margin annotation: a call for nuance over the grand gesture]

even the very minds that were calling for enlightenment.[13] Finally, how could poetry forge a relation to the new realism capable of exposing how Futurism, Pound's hated competitor for avant-garde status in London, was merely an "accelerated Impressionism" fascinated by the trappings of force but blind to how science was adapting to such force.

For the old realism a literary text proposing to offer significant knowledge had to present images that represented what an audience could agree were matters of fact. Then the text had to do the work of classification, or, more generally (since we are dealing with literature and not science), to establish categorical principles so that the individual event could be considered an instance of some generalization about nature or culture. The sharper the picture, the more it could represent what is shareable about minds, and the better it could illustrate the general principle. Even when they dealt with emotions, such texts had to appeal to powers of mind that were distinct from self-reference on the one hand and from any strong emotional responsiveness on the other. One could respond emotionally, but one had to know why this response had been elicited: ultimately one had to treat subjectivity in third-person terms. One had to make judgments about one's subjectivity in the same way that one made judgments about impersonal propositions. At the extreme, art could be realistic only if it could approximate a god-like indifference – not unlike the typical attitude a poet like Thomas Hardy mixes with an all too human sense of pathos.

III

I am oversimplifying a very complex set of values and a quite diversified literary tradition. My aim is not to account for the old realism but to characterize the dissatisfactions it elicited among the young modernists. If we return to Pound's "Pale carnage beneath bright mist" or the lady's fingers with the texture of a Japanese paper napkin, we will be struck by how final these images are! This poetry resists judgment in terms of general categories because the items are intensely sensual – not symbols carrying meaning so much as details bearing witness to some kind of force impossible to generalize about. Pound's Imagist poems are certainly not as rich culturally as Hardy's, but they offer something different, something new, something worth theorizing about. They offer the possibility of romance within secular society – without

Pound's Imagist poems.

transcendental sanctions. And they offer the stimulus for further theorizing about art that would eventually transform the Imagist mode into what Pound called the "ideogrammic method" of his *Cantos*.

The way to the *Cantos* begins with these efforts to establish what kind of "truth" poetry could present. How could poetry break from both the naming and the classifying functions of the old realism and at the same time carry more complex experiences than Imagist poetry might provide? Pound began the journey beyond Imagism by elaborating two somewhat different versions of how the new realism could redo the naming function – one with historical consciousness in mind and one driven by the model of the new fiction. Considering history as the backdrop, Pound imagined poetry pursuing "the method of Luminous Detail, a method most vigorously hostile to the prevailing mode of today – that is, the method of multitudinous detail, and to the method of yesterday, the method of sentiment and generalization" (Pound, SP 21). Notice here how swiftly and precisely Pound handles what he saw as the options possible within his own culture. Then, as he elaborates his case, he shows that one can present images capable of bypassing the powers of judgment required to establish and trust in categories and laws. Luminous details expand to representative generality while retaining the status of historical particulars because the case does not develop by slowly adding facts to establish generalizations. Rather these details evoke and reward the intuitions so important to Bergson. It becomes the task of the image to "give one a sudden insight" that carries within itself "intelligence of a period – a kind of intelligence not to be gathered from a great array of facts of the other sort." The luminous details "are swift and easy of transmission. They govern knowledge as a switchboard governs an electrical circuit" (Pound, SP 22–3). (I hope my argument helps show that Pound's use of science in this last simile was carefully chosen.)

Luminous details refer to a world made dynamic for intelligence. Pound's second foray into the question of how poetry might exemplify a new realism concentrates instead on how fiction writers construct psychological traits capable of such responsiveness:

> There is the clarity of the request: Send me four pounds of ten-penny nails. And there is the syntactical simplicity of the request: Buy me the kind of Rembrandt I like. This last . . . has as many meanings as the persons who might speak it. To a stranger it conveys nothing at all.

It is the almost constant labor of the prose artist to translate the latter kind of clarity into the former. . . . The whole thing is an evolution. . . . Gradually you wish to communicate something less bare and ambiguous than ideas. You wish to communicate an idea and its modifications, an idea and a crowd of its effects, atmospheres, contradictions. You wish to question whether a certain formula works in every case, or in what per cent of cases, etc., etc., etc., you get the Henry James novel.

(LE 50–1)

If poetry is to be at least as well written, and as unsentimental and free from rhetoric, as good modern prose, then it would have to learn to serve communicative functions that could be kept distinct from rhetorical ones.[14] Such communication would have to occur on two levels, each of which evades the classifying functions of the old science and the modes of interpretive judgment based on the old realism's filiations with that science. First there is the subtlety of the material, of how ideas in effect are permeated by possible atmospheres of effect and affect. The old realism sought to characterize enduring conditions that were emblems for social life. The new realism's concern for intricate relations among details made it immensely suspicious of binary oppositions that set the head against the heart, description against evaluation. More important, philosophers like Bergson and William James were showing that classification was bound to spatial models of how the world gave itself to experience. Classification simply could not characterize interactions among states or the transitions allowing new states to emerge. Classification could capture being but not becoming, structure but not event – detail but not what made detail luminous.

Then there was the writing itself. Intricate nuance without generalization meant that neither characters nor authors could rely on any form of abstract and depersonalized understanding. Characters had to become involved as embodied subjects. They had to experience the partiality and intensity of the personal investments that made such involvement possible, and made it dangerously vulnerable to deceit and disillusion. Alfred North Whitehead was later to characterize the old realism as a case of misplaced concreteness. Observers abstracted a sharp distinction between the subject offering descriptions and the static objects necessary for judging whether the descriptions were true. But in fact we never experience pure subjectivity or pure objectivity. Those are conditions out of time, out of becoming. What we experience is becoming something or other in relation to various kinds of

Details tell
the tale, they are
not decoration

situations. In honoring this, the new realism recasts what had been
the classical subject–object problem. Details are aspects of relationships,
not independent observations that then get attached to interpretations
by articulating the appropriate categories. Even the writers' labors of
construction become inseparable from their powers of observation,
part of recognizing what can stay vital and why it matters. That is
why Pound never tires of distinguishing between an art that merely
describes or represents and an art that makes something present and
therefore vibrant, and therefore an intellectual and emotional complex
(for example, LE 6).

Many modernists would go on to make similar distinctions between
representation and presentation. But Pound is distinctive in his insistence that this demand on presentation holds no less for the scientist
than for the poet, in both cases requiring concepts of will and witness
that poets since the Renaissance have failed to acknowledge. So what
begins as a defense of the new realism expands throughout Pound's
career to become a justification for a radical individualism, in both
poetry and science. Poetry differs from science in the specifics of its
attention, but not in the sense that its work is testimony to the ways
of the world. Poetry and science are both means of witnessing to what
strikes consciousness as luminous. More precisely, both disciplines are
not just modes of description but modes of presentation. And presentation cannot rely only on the mind's depersonalized observational
powers. Pound is as insistent as Nietzsche that thinking is intimately
involved with willing, description with desire. Observation is inseparable from testimony and testimony inseparable from evidence at every
moment that there is an individual will at work.

No longer is the central concern the Enlightenment's primary question, "How do you know?" Rather the emphasis shifts to a concern
for what conditions make it possible to show what is vibrant about
a situation. Then one can also indicate how one takes responsibility
for these acts of witnessing. There become infinite paths for valuing
facts and for valuing what individuals do in exhibiting how those
values might be established: "The serious artist is scientific in that he
presents the image of his desire, of his hate, . . . precisely as the image
of his own desire. . . . The more precise his record, the more lasting and
unassailable the work of art" (LE 46).[15] Analogously, we do not have
to treat the music of poetry as an ornament or an aspect simply of its
beauty. Capturing how a sense of music informs the desire may be the

simultaneous
X
all aspects
not pointed

fullest way of rendering the relation between an "I" and the Rembrandt the person desires.

The Imagist poems we have already considered also afford good examples of Pound's sense of subject and object merging as intellect and emotion form an intricate complex in a moment of time. Try to separate the irony from the pathos from the admiration from the disappointment in the intricate attitude assumed by the single sentence comprising "The Bath Tub." The speaker's admiration that the passion cools so slowly seems inseparable from resentment and disappointment that the lady allows the passion to cool at all. Here irony is not intellectual, not a matter of appearing to say one thing while meaning another. Irony is attitudinal, a matter of disposing the will by adjusting the tone in which someone is regarded. And the willing is specific to the poem – not an expression of character traits so much as an adjustment to what language allows in the situation.

"April," on the other hand, stages the will as recognizing and affirming how the luminous detail opens a space for myth and romance within what remains faithful to observational criteria. Lines 2–4 present a very simple scene of destruction, and even the first line's reference to three spirits seems at first a periphrastic way of referring to people. The last line changes all that, mining every resource given by the rest of the poem in order to charge the empirical scene with mystery without calling on any faith beyond what the luminous detail can inspire. Just the sound patterns of this last line, "Pale carnage beneath bright mist," suggest activity more careful and more powerful than such scenes typically inspire. Two adjective–noun combinations are intricately balanced around a spatial preposition. Each combination becomes memorable because of assonance – of *a* sounds in the first, sharp *i* sounds in the second. Then we realize that the preposition alliterates with "bright," and so rebalances the line to compensate for the extra syllable in the first adjective–noun combination.

begin + end

This rebalancing is not just ornamental. These sound effects call our attention to how the last line transforms the poem from recording something seen to exclaiming something felt. That process of transformation then makes visible something approaching a permanent condition of becoming that hovers within the world observed. The last line sets in conjunction three domains of force – the stable abstraction of the noun "carnage," the strange materiality of that noun because it seems inappropriate for the otherwise descriptive and Anglo-Saxon

not a realization, or delineated

diction, and the generalized moody specificity of the slight contradiction between brightness and mist.

IV

Yet Pound was not satisfied. He had managed to develop a poetics that could merge real and romance states, but his theorizing had not dealt sufficiently with how poetry might have distinctive ways of realizing those states. The theory of Imagism turned out to be most applicable to the prosaic aspects of poetry. He could explain how images rendered complex sensations, but he had yet to face the active role demanded by form when sensations become so fluid and evanescent. So in order to explain how poetry as centaur could "move and leap" in distinctive ways, Pound turned to the visual arts. There he found young British artists embracing the slogans of Vorticist theory, and there he found what might be a better emblem than Imagism for the cultural work poetry could do. Vorticism preserves most of what Pound had valued in the image, but now the image becomes only an aspect of a more comprehensive mode of synthetic activity. Writing in 1915, Pound altered the definition from two years earlier to cast the image itself as "a vortex or cluster of fused ideas . . . endowed with energy" (Pound, SP 375). The image had been a means of rendering luminous detail; the vortex is a means of attributing luminosity to the forces of becoming achieved by the aesthetic object as a whole. The vortex could foreground complex internal relationships only implicit in Imagism's version of the poem as an emotional and intellectual complex: "In a poem of this sort one is trying to record the precise instant when a thing outward and objective transforms itself, or darts into a thing inward and subjective" (Pound, SP 89). This is no longer simply a matter of emotion and intellect being united in a timeless moment; it is now a matter of entire worlds fusing and taking on levels of possible meaning.

Unfortunately how a vortex works is not as easy to explain as how an image works.[16] Now I can provide only a very brief sketch of Pound's basic attempt at explanation by relying on his marvelous memoir *Gaudier-Brzeska*, written in 1916 in honor of the Vorticist sculptor who died early in World War I. Pound recognizes that Vorticism first took hold as a movement in sculpture. But, rather than apologizing for extending its principles to poetry, he revels in the fact that turning to sculpture requires shifting from what can be known through the image to what has to be experienced in terms of the poem's presentation of constructive energies. How the work is constructed becomes inseparable from how it can communicate.[17] More important, Pound manages to develop an account of poetry that does not simply equate form with beauty or allow the energies of art works to collapse into the vague impressions where beauty had come to reside. Form depends on the structuring of the object, and so directly tests the power of will to establish alternatives to received ideals of beauty. This awareness in the work of its own constructive power begins as a celebration of the senses, but the very idea of celebrating the senses proves inseparable from the pleasure of extending our understanding of what sense can do.

Therefore Pound emphasizes the Vorticists' commitment to the art object's expressive use of masses in relation to one another. These objects could put such expressive power to mimetic or descriptive uses. But even when the work orients us to objects in the external world, it should do so by activating the audience's sense of surfaces in tension, where edges are made to function as dynamic interventions in the composed space. Then the work would surpass the "mimicry of external life. It is energy cut into stone, making the stone expressive in its fit and particular manner" (GB 110), while preserving a sense of the implacable and unswerving in the stone.[18] Gaudier-Brzeska's marble *Cat* presents a sleeping cat with sharply etched bas-relief leg-bones and thigh muscles, pronounced facial bones, and a tail that could sweep at any moment. Everything seems coiled energy even as the cat gathers itself in compact rest. His *Red Stone Dancer*, on the other hand, is an almost abstract isolated dancer whose body forms an elaborate vortex anchored by brilliantly staged crouching legs, with each edge of the legs forming a slightly different plane directing the force. In contrast to the open base with its dynamized negative spaces, her upper body forms an intricate knot or vortex of folded forces where breast, looped arms, long dynamic fingers, and abstracted wrists all sustain one another by the tension created among the planes.

These examples do not lack for luminous detail. But the details are now elements within a pronouncedly intense overall object earning its free-standing status by its capacity to balance material forces in tension. The work lives as a formal structure making clear possible relations among forces within experience. And the formal intensity points to the synthetic constructive work of the artist that in turn challenges the audience to try out its capacity to achieve an analogous state of will. In other words, the emphasis on creativity allows Pound to claim, "Will and consciousness are our VORTEX" (GB 24).[19] Vorticist work requires not only a new realism but a new psychology and a new sense of art as ethical force. In a world increasingly marked by anxiety and restlessness, the art bears witness to a cold contemplative sense of conviction in its own power, a conviction ultimately justified by the work (not by one's discourse about sincere intentions within the work).

That sense of witness in turn brings out a new dimension of Pound's individualism. Art ultimately becomes a challenge measuring the cleanness, the lack of crippling self-doubt, still possible for a mind that itself can hold masses in taut relations. Hence Pound's paean to Jacob Epstein: "The test of a man is not the phrases of his critics; the test lies in the work, in its 'certitude.' What answer is to be made to the 'Flenites'? With what sophistry will you be able to escape their assertion?" (GB 102). Epstein's "Flenites" is not an idea to be argued about but an event demonstrating that this particular matters enough to provide a challenge threatening any lazy compromise with the powers that be.

Pound's basic example from his own poetry in *Gaudier-Brzeska* will appear almost as slight as his Imagist poems. But this time the slightness is not the point. The point is the bareness capable of allowing the force of the vortex to pervade every single element: the risk of apparent slightness becomes a measure of the quality of the poem's intricate certitude. Pound tells the story of how during the period of a year he compressed "In a Station of the Metro" from a thirty-line poem "of second intensity" to this "hokku-like sentence":

> The apparition of these faces in the crowd:
> Petals on a wet, black bough.   (GB 89; P 119)

[handwritten margin notes: subjective speaker — no speaker; all writerly energy; Two shifting plates — strength in tension between the two]

Rather than project a clear interpretive stance by which an audience can directly grasp what a speaker thinks of the subway car's arrival, Pound intensifies the pull of competing sensations as if they presented masses in intricate relation to one another. The result is a whirling set of energies that can be given stillness, but only as forces creating relations between subject and object much more subtle and mobile than ideas can establish.

Just introducing "apparition" preceded by the definite article is strange and compelling. The opening phrase becomes so much more than an initial descriptive element setting the scene. "The apparition" seems asserted as a confident description, so that expression threatens to alter the basic meaning of "apparition," namely that it is indefinite and fleeting. Now the apparition seems definite. Indeed it seems full and hefty because the Latinate word strikes out almost on its own, as if even an apparition has to be appreciated as a material substance. Moreover the implicit mind within the poem is not bothered by the apparition at all: it seems comfortable not only giving it definiteness but extending that definiteness to "these" and "the," two assertive indices of immediate presence. We enter a world with a strange ontology because what is descriptive and what illusory become inextricably joined within a process requiring the readers to adapt to the force of sensations as they form momentary conjunctions.

This hypothesis about the poem's ontology is strengthened by the fact that there is no dramatic speaker for the poem. Consciousness does not point toward a person but toward the effort to hold these various semantic pulls together. Everything depends on the interactions among a range of intricate tensions between natural and mechanical objects, between the definite modifiers of the first line and the indefinite one of the second, between faces and objects, and, most important, between intense realism and the bizarre multisyllabic call in "apparitions" to have that realism undo itself by forcing on us a simultaneously present glimpse of mythic forces.

Pound does not want to deny the elemental principles of realism. He wants only to suggest how a full realism, rather than a reductive empiricism, might engage the possibility that "apparition" can play a significant role in our functioning vocabulary for characterizing the impact of this underground crowd scene. Were this poem to call attention to the speaker's position, it would have to give the speaker a social identity or at least a way of composing a self-image. And that would mean making some kind of judgment whether or not this speaker can believe in the presence of apparitions. The poem then would risk being driven to Hardy's suspiciousness of all traces of romance. But by presenting the poem as simply writerly energies trying to be adequate to the event qualities of a given moment, Pound can let the very word "apparition" carry a much more intense and mysterious set of organizing energies than the attribution of character might provide.

"Apparition" functions as a fulcrum organizing sculptural relations among volumes and weights while refusing to let any lesser realism impose itself. Almost singlehandedly, this definite expression doubles the scene so that it ultimately carries a substantial sense of mythic presence. The faces are apparitions because they participate in an ancient ritual descent to the domain of Persephone. Technology enters an odd alliance with mythology. For how but in mythic terms are we to take in this strange ability to enter underground worlds and be transported as fluid crowds? Yet we also have to let the realism redefine the roles this mythic sense can play in our lives. Rather than relegate the world to our standard terms for self and for value, we are encouraged to let ourselves enter those hallucinatory spaces that art can treat as extensions of the senses. But it is the poet's language, not his character or his "vision," that becomes the test of what is possible. We are not told that energies rush beyond what description can handle; rather we encounter language bearing witness to how expanded fields of sensation can introduce new possibilities for being alive as humans.

I have to conclude my discussion of Pound by leaving him at the brink of greatness. After his essay on Vorticism Pound began to take for granted the new realism and to test himself by trying out various extensions of it – into the realm of cultural differences in his book *Cathay*, into the powers translation might give to establish how poets from the past could provide lasting witnesses to enduring energies derived from their encounters with historical situations (especially in his *Homage to Sextus Propertius*), and, finally, in the *Cantos'* efforts to deepen the world of "apparitions" into a permanent world of visionary possibility in tension with the domain of practical experience. For these projects there are very good scholarly guides. I can hope only to add to those a sense of how fully that work fulfills dialectical possibilities immanent in his initial efforts to equate modernism with the imperative to make it new. So I close this discussion by invoking a prose statement by Pound that clearly extends both the ideal of luminous detail and the notion of planes in relation to the project of the *Cantos*:[20]

> WE appear to have lost the radiant world where one thought cuts through another with clean edge, a world of moving energies . . . , magnetisms that take form, that are seen, or that border the visible, the matter of Dante's *Paradiso*, the glass under water, the form that seems a

form seen in a mirror, these realities perceptible to sense . . . Not the
pagan worship of strength, nor the Greek perception of visual non-
animate plastic . . . but "this harmony in the sentience" or harmony of
the sentient, where the thought has its demarcation, the substance its
virtu, where stupid men have not reduced all "energy" to unbounded
undistinguished abstraction.   (LE 154)

V

[handwritten marginalia: Impressionist painting — trigger of modernism. (new realism)]

Neither Bergson nor Pound were to be the most important revolutionary force in establishing for the arts the promise of the new realism.
That honor goes to the Impressionist painters, who initiated an enormously complex historical adventure in reinterpreting the force of
sensations and their possible impact on modern understandings of the
psyche. And Post-Impressionist painting began a major shift in artists'
understanding of the will to form that was to blossom in Vorticism and
related ideals of expressive abstraction. It is this work that established

Fig. 1.   Claude Monet, *The Bridge at Argenteuil*, 1874, National Gallery of
Art, Washington; collection of Mr. and Mrs. Paul Mellon

Fig. 2. Paul Cézanne, *Still Life with Drapery*, 1899.
Hermitage, St. Petersburg / www.bridgeman.co.uk

the range of concrete effects the new realism could generate, and it is
this work that constituted an immense provocation to the writers. It
seemed that the painters had the most secure grasp on what it meant
to be modern so the writers were eager to earn that honor for their
own work. Yet they realized that simply copying the painters would
only insure that being treated as merely imitators. The writers had to
find new ways of making it new.

Here I will present the challenges and possibilities the new paintings
posed for the poets by concentrating on two paintings. The first, Claude
Monet's *Bridge at Argenteuil* (1874), demonstrates what we might consider the initial onslaught on conventional representation (figure 1).
The second, Paul Cézanne's *Still Life with Drapery* (1899) explores the
values involved when these concerns can become the stuff of philosophical reflection (figure 2). Cézanne's career made it apparent that
what was emerging as a new realism also demanded that even visual
art had to make efforts toward a new psychology. How the world
appeared to the senses had to become inextricably linked to artists'

feelings for how their own compositional energies manifested powers fundamental to any comprehensive account of human agency.

Many features of Monet's paintings are so familiar that my remarks need only function as a reminder. Yet I think we still underestimate the eventual difference it made culturally when, after centuries of studio painting, talented artists began to work on site. Materially, painters could actually engage particular visual events, and look at their own looking second by second. They could discover that shadows had color of their own, and that color in the wild revealed itself as consisting of infinite gradations of hue rather than sharp distinctions in substance. And this prepared the way for two major shifts in value. Painting could suggest that appearance was not the pale shadow of real substance or ideal forms; how the world emerged in sight was a sufficient topic for art. Second, such a sense of discovery suggested by contrast that the very space of the studio was mired in dead conventions. Previous painters seemed blind, so caught up with drama, psychology, and tradition that they did not really look at the life of the eye among things. These painters did not see that tracing differences among various settings might be more important than pursuing the concepts that would provide stability in relation to those differences.

The Bridge at Argenteuil pulses with Monet's sense of the capacities of his new realism. Because its color is almost infinitely fine in its gradations, the painting seems to capture the shimmering effect of reflected light on a summer day. And the tonal shifts make it possible to replace Constable's heavy, imposing clouds with whispy fluid ones. (There emerges a virtual symphony in white because this lightness allows rhymes between the sails and the clouds, with contrasts to the heavier whites of the houses.) This sense of freedom is also echoed in the way that the perspective organizing the painting seems contingent rather than studied. It is as if the open air situation encouraged painting from any perspective, affording the eye immediate interest in a scene. Such interest could organize attention in more fluid ways than studio painting, since that painting seemed locked into elaborate structural planning tested by preliminary sketches.

Monet's canvas makes a dramatic show of resisting this structural planning in the service of immediacy. Notice how there seems a governing form in the painting made up of the parallelogram outlined by the two masts on one side and the bridge on the other. But the spirit of sensory event seems to overwhelm that temptation to provide traditional structure. On the viewer's left, the sails revel in their own freedom from such a logic. And on the right, there emerges a fascination with the details of light on and under the bridge, so that local detail seems at war with the demands of structure. Speaking formally, we might say that the relation between these edges, between the worlds of light pleasure and brooding shadow, simply overwhelms what provides the conventional center of the painting.

In other words, sensation and sensibility work to free themselves from conventional ideals about judgment and form. And they do so in the name of a realism requiring focus on sensations created by local details – as if to celebrate the discovery of how the eye sees when it is liberated from habit and conventional instruction. As in Monet's *Impression: Sunrise* (1873, Musée Marmottan, Paris), this life of the eye proves so intense that the world of human actions and emotional psychology is either ignored or relegated to almost indistinguishable bodies. For Monet it is as if dramatic psychology itself were so bound in conventional platitudes that it could not provide much guidance to the new realism. What occupies the stage now is sensation. One does not need to speculate about the emotions and thoughts characters within the work are experiencing because an audience can turn instead to the immediate and intense awareness of feelings composed within the eye's sense of release from constraints. So a new realism about the eye seems also to call for a new psychology about the "I" that will be responsive to this fluidity and density of experience.

VI

Cézanne: faithful to the intensity he sees and

Paul Cézanne's letters are perhaps the fullest modern discursive engagements with what sensation can become in painting. He treats "the intensity that is unfolded before my senses" as a challenge requiring him in effect to forget everything but the skill it takes not to falsify or simplify that intensity. Rather than seeking truth in some idea, painting is governed by the imperative to exhaust itself in the impossible but glorious effort to realize those sensations on canvas:

> I am able to describe to you again, or rather too much I am afraid, the obstinacy with which I pursue the realization of that part of nature, which, coming into our line of vision, gives the picture. Now the theme

to develop is that – whatever our temperament or power in the presence of nature may be – we must render the image of what we see, forgetting everything that existed before us. Which, I believe, must permit the artist to give his entire personality, whether great or small.[21]

The new realism must generate a new art of "realization."

What was an adventure of technique in Monet becomes the stuff of obsessive reflection in Cézanne. The painting is not planned; it comes as a gift to one who has prepared himself or herself to see in such a way as to get beyond habit. So for Cézanne seeing as a painter is so distinctive an event that it demands also that the painting include self-consciousness about such seeing. Consequently he begins to develop what would be fundamental aspects of a new vocabulary for the arts in general. Terms like "render" and "realize" would replace "imitate" and "interpret" for writers as diverse as Joseph Conrad and William Carlos Williams. And Cézanne would begin to fill out the demand already evident in Monet to develop a somewhat new psychology based on features immediate to perception.

Cézanne's peers acknowledged that Monet inaugurated a sense that for serious painting what happens to the eye seems more important than what has traditionally been the foregrounding of human emotions and judgments – think of how Caspar David Friedrich's landscapes almost always have an observer to focus the sublime emotions triggered by his scenes. Cézanne, however, took this innovation much further. The depopulated and de-psychologized canvas becomes a challenge to pursue an alternative presentation of how the mind actually worked in seeing. His focus is not on the visual detail or on the emotions of dramatic characters but on the artist's personality as it manipulates sensations. Yet this is no romantic fantasy of self-expression. What matters to Cézanne is not expressing the self but transcending the self by managing to absorb personality within the act of realizing what it can see.

My abstraction cries out for an example. I have chosen the still life *Still Life with Drapery* because Cézanne's differences from traditional painting are most pronounced in this genre. Three features best exemplify his version of the new realism. First, there is an amazing interplay between the overall plastic structural set of balances created by the curtains and tablecloths on the one hand and, on the other, the sense that each individual piece of fruit is a significant optical event. Cézanne was convinced that modeling by light and shadow did not adequately capture how objects emerge for the eye: the traditional model of modeling was a clear instance of habit substituting for vision. Instead, "in an orange, an apple, a bowl, a head, there is a culminating point; and this point is always – in spite of the tremendous effect of light and shade and colorful sensations – the closest to our eye; the edges of the objects recede to a center on our horizon."[22] So each piece of fruit has a distinctive way of gathering the light. In effect each could be a human character because every fruit insistently occupies its own space and makes the painting slowly unfold in time. This is Monet's attention to event grown self-conscious within the painting, as if the fruit knew that, seen properly or "realized," it could make claims on our attention.

The second Cézannian way of articulating this new realism is to challenge our traditional expectations about those very boundaries of objects that the first innovation brings to our attention. The challenge is posed by the technique of *passage*, the willingness to acknowledge the two-dimensionality of the canvas by having certain objects compete for space rather than illusionistically establish a distinctive place behind or in front of the other object. Notice how the cloth on the viewer's left becomes the dish rather than covering it, and how several of the fruits are cut into by others so that they seem to be one complex painterly object. Cézanne experimented with *passage* because he thought individual mass was an intellectual construct not given by immediate vision. Immediate vision is not attentive to weight or "objectness"; it concentrates on surfaces and their interrelationships. Everything else is literature.[23]

Finally it is crucial to see what Cézanne made of Monet's insistence that the primacy of vision warranted different psychological emphases than traditional dramatic painting. Meyer Schapiro once noted how no one would desire to eat a Cézanne apple.[24] But he suggested a psychoanalytic explanation for that, rather than speculating on how Cézanne might have explained himself (if he had trusted language). Cézanne probably thought that the desire to eat an apple is simply the wrong instinct for painting to invoke. He is not illustrating cookbooks but realizing objects visually, so the appropriate appetites seeking satisfaction in painting are visual. And one can dramatize visual possibilities only if one also frustrates more typical associations that the culture has established for the stuff of still-life.

39

Refusing these typical associations also has a more important role to play because such frustrations highlight complex relations between art and life. Cézanne wants to suggest that art can replace satisfactions based on recognition and interpretation with other satisfactions more complexly weaving thinking and feeling into our sense of objects. Notice how the fruits on the table seem to possess the power to stare at us and to demand an adequate visual response to the art – not just to the image. It seems that without the art we could not know how we see, and we could not appreciate the affective investments our personalities can make in visual realization. The strange silence established by the absence of appetite poses a challenge to bring more to the art than one's sense of the material world. This is why Cézanne calls for bringing the whole personality into play. One can fill that silence by yielding one's will to the painting, as if in realizing objects the painting also realized something basic to one's need to see how the world and the artwork can enter such cooperation. Cézanne inaugurates one of the basic gambles of modernism – that art could become not merely an accompaniment to the world but the realization of how mind and world become one dynamic field. He seeks modes of appearance capable of providing a sense of intimate dwelling for psyches that would otherwise be forced into ironic relations to their materials.

VII

Like Pound, and like Cézanne, William Carlos Williams began his career pursuing a strange, exotic beauty, and paying the price for it in a profound dissatisfaction with life outside art. For early Pound the imagination lived in the site of medieval romance; for early Cézanne it sought lurid romance along the lines of Flaubert's *Temptation of Saint Anthony*; and for early Williams the appropriate site was Keatsian romance, the domain where one could pursue a life of sensations rather than thoughts.

The story is often told, best by Williams himself, of his subsequent struggle against Keatsian ideals of beauty.[25] The problem turned out to be simple, but also fundamental. In his eagerness to pursue "beauty" he was setting that ideal against all reflective thought, and this made it impossible to escape a much too passive set of attitudes longing for escape from the real. So he had to find a way in which beauty in poetry offered its own positive form of thinking and engaging the world. He found that way by changing his fundamental attitude toward sensation, learning to treat it as an active mode of attention and apprehension rather than simply a passive register of experience: "The only human value of anything, writing included, is intense vision of the facts, add to that by saying the truth and action upon them."[26]

Such statements do not have the range or complexity of his friend Pound's fascination with the authority of science as the foundation for a new realism. But Williams did have an intensity of intellectual focus Pound lacked. So the realism he arrived at concentrated on two elemental properties which were to make his work exemplary for a later generation of American poets. He was a much keener critic of how the ego transformed fact into solipsistic illusion, and he was much more directly involved in finding ways that poetry might intensify the value of fact: "this is after all the substance, therefore the explanation of my poems and my life in which *there exists* (instead of *you exist*)."[27] Williams for the most part refused Pound's abstract discourse about form in order to emphasize how sensitivity to place and to common speech might be a sufficient source for the dynamizing of fact. And, not quite paradoxically, he was much more the propagandist for "the imagination" than Pound, and hence much more directly engaged in struggling to transform romantic values so that they might flow directly from grasping how "there exists." He wanted to combine romantic intensity with a sense of fact that could not be overwhelmed by the specific interests and projections of individual subjects.

Therefore his was also the more direct engagement with Cézanne:

> Today where everything is being brought into sight the realism of art has bewildered us, confused us, and forced us to reinvent in order to retain that which the older generation had without effort.
> Cézanne –
> The only realism in art is of the imagination. It is only thus that the work escapes plagiarism after nature and becomes a creation.[28]

Therefore I want to complete my story of new realisms available for modernism by briefly sketching how Williams worked his way out of romanticism by transforming into poetry painterly models for integrating the claims of imagination with the sense of fact.[29]

It would be an exaggeration to say that the new realism in French early modernist painting was a first step in teaching Williams how to

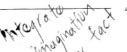
integrate imagination + fact

stress sensation as an active mode of taking up the real world in the constructive imagination. But it certainly reinforced his sense that the direction in which he was trying to work aligned him with the future rather than the past. As early as 1912, his essay "French Painting" tried to show how this line of painting did not entail formalism because it in no way sought to "escape representation." Rather this work was committed only to escaping "triteness, the stupidity of a loose verisimilitude" that made it want "to trace" scenes and thus to confuse paint values with natural objects" (EK 22). But even this sense of purpose was enough to establish a revolutionary attitude toward representation that could be "highly instructive to the writer – and has been to me" (EK 22) because it so clearly shifts the burden of writing from descriptive accuracy to evocative adequacy in bringing to facts an intensity that lives in its own right:

> Well, what does one see? to paint? [*sic*] Why the tree, of course, is the facile answer. . . . The tree as a tree does not exist literally, figuratively or any way you please . . . What does exist, and in heightened intensity for the artist, is the impression created by the shape and color of an object before him in his sensual being – his whole body (not his eyes) his body, his mind, his memory, his place: himself – that is what he sees. And in America – escape it he cannot – it is an American tree.
>
> (EK 24)

This jingoism may seem a large price to pay for a new realism. Yet it is not foolish to think that one cannot fully honor the life of the senses without establishing a distinctive sense of place. An American stimulated by Post-Impressionist painting has to realize that simply aping the "French manner is to put out his eye – then surely he has not seen the tree at all" (EK 25). By "Spring Strains" (1916) Williams' efforts to see such a tree in what he feels is an appropriately American mode of attention has enabled him to break entirely with his earlier Keatsian mode:[30]

> In a tissue-thin monotone of blue-grey buds
> crowded erect with desire against
> the sky –
> tense blue-grey twigs
> slenderly anchoring them down, drawing

them in –
two blue-grey birds chasing
a third struggle in circles, angles,
swift convergings to a point that bursts
instantly!

Vibrant bowing limbs
pull downward, sucking in the sky
that bulges from behind, plastering itself
against them in packed rifts, rock blue
and dirty orange!

But –
(hold hard, rigid jointed trees)
the blinding and red-edged sun blur –
creeping energy, concentrated
counterforce – welds sky, buds, trees
rivets them in one puckering hold!

Sticks through! Pulls the whole
counter-pulling mass upward, to the right,
locks even the opaque, not yet defined
ground in a terrific drag that is
loosening the very tap roots!

On a tissue-thin monotone of blue-grey buds
Two blue-grey birds chasing a third,
At full cry! Now they are
flung outward and up – disappearing suddenly!   (Williams, CP 97–8)

This poem does many things well, or at least earns notice in many
ways. There is first the intense commitment to sheer dynamics. For
Williams is characteristically more blunt than Pound in his evocation
of parallels between art and science: "Art is the pure effect of the
force upon which science depends for its reality" (Williams, CP 225).
Yet the substance of the poem remains quite delicate, a tissue of
subtle observations that ground the various present participles largely
responsible for the sense of energy. And while this poem is clearly
influenced by Pound's Vorticism, syntactic emphasis on masses in
relation is significantly less important than Williams' sense of the relative weights afforded by his control of line-endings. This poem creates
a powerful tension between the energies observed in space and the

work the line-endings do to embody modes of temporal suspense as we read. Notice especially how the fourth stanza holds off any substantial correlation of line and sense units until the very last line, so that this line has the effect of literally riveting the parts together for imaginative contemplation. All this emphasis on endings may then be the imagination's way of complementing natural energy with the play of human desire.

Finally there are intriguing uses of the tradition of pure lyric even as this tradition gets tied to the rendering of natural energies. Within this evocation of immediacy there emerges something like a refrain, as if the celebration of energy left to its own devices would restore aspects of song. It does not take a lyric "I" to satisfy the imagination. In fact the conclusion of this poem returns to perhaps the most classical lyrical motif, the lament for transience. All the energies gathered here turn out to disappear suddenly, perhaps because the demand for attention is so closely bound to a desperate awareness of time passing. We must attend with a Paterian sense of greed for the qualities of every moment because the scene will soon shift and make very different demands on the spirit. Yet the poem provides a significant modernist twist even to this aspect of traditional lyric because the negative conditions are not simply stages for the positive realizations; rather, the negatives are to be seen as exercising an equal energy. Hence what disappears is registered with the same participial form that bears the burden of representing the positive energies. The concluding contrast then may be less a source of lament than a Cézannian charging of negative space as also a quality made present for the imagination.

But even though this is a forceful poem, and in the conclusion an almost subtle one, it also is a somewhat embarrassing one. It is hard not to think the poem tries too hard, and impoverishes itself in the process. It almost seems Williams was playing an ironic tune on the title, or that the title was taking revenge on the poem (except that the next poem in the *Collected Poems* shares the same rush of adjectives and adverbs). Every detail strains to fill the scene, struggling for the same plane of intensity. Williams wants simple attention to suffice as a source of fully satisfying human energies without sufficiently honoring how those energies might require complications that put further demands on the resources of the maker. Ultimately "Spring Strains" offers a substantial imaginative picture of energy but it does not exhibit much imaginative energy about what the new realism might enable.

One could turn to slightly later poems on trees like "Willow Poem" and "Winter Trees" to see how Williams learns to extend his realism in order to elaborate complex states of consciousness.[31] But for brevity's sake I will immediately turn to Williams' fully developed realism in probably his best volume, *Spring and All*. There he manages to put the constructive imagination more fully into play without relying on a Vorticist language of formal relations.[32] He stresses the power of poetry to liberate from mere description, but he almost always insists that the feeling of freedom results from the sense of discovery the poem affords.

At first *Spring and All* presents a world in which no values seem to take hold. Even the chapter numbers are out of sequence and printed in various ways as the poet's prose fails to find any secure way to invest in what it is experiencing. Then in "Chapter XIX" (which is different from "Chapter 19" where the numbering actually begins) we find that spring is emerging, and with it the possibility that "the great copying which evolution has followed . . . is approaching the end." Now the poet can realize the evocative powers of poetry:

By the road to the contagious hospital
under the surge of the blue
mottled clouds driven from the

northeast – a cold wind. Beyond, the
waste of broad, muddy fields
brown with dried weeds, standing and fallen

patches of standing water
the scattering of tall trees

All along the road the reddish
purplish, forked, upstanding, twiggy
stuff of bushes and small trees
with dead, brown leaves under them
leafless vines –

Lifeless in appearance, sluggish
dazed spring approaches –

They enter the new world naked,
cold, uncertain of all

save that they enter. All about them
the cold familiar wind –

Now the grass, tomorrow
the stiff curl of wildcarrot leaf   *passive*

One by one the objects are defined –
It quickens: clarity, outline of life
But now the stark dignity of
entrance – Still, the profound change

has come upon them: rooted, they
grip down and begin to awaken.   (Williams, CP 183)

Immediately after this poem the volume announces that it has entered "Chapter 1," from which it never departs. So we have to ask why the poem has the power to invoke the possibility of perpetual beginning, even when many of the ensuing poems remain charged with anxiety. I think our answer has itself to begin with the possibility that this is a new kind of landscape poetry, a poetry that has found a way of liberating the imagination from the pain suggested by the contagious hospital because it now can fully attend to the energies present in the world of facts. The emphasis here is not on the subject's impressions of the meaning of spring but on the objectified force calling for response. The poem lacks the fine phrases of conventional pastoral, yet at the same time it is much too aware of its artifice to stand as description. But there is no promise of transcendence or self-discovery that might be capable of sustaining a romantic lyric. There is no self-consciousness apart from the awareness of how the making complements the incipient spring by turning observations into discoveries that project possible values. What matters is how "there" emerges and how the subject finds aligning with that a source of value capable of redirecting a life.

This alignment takes place primarily through two distinctive features of Williams' writing. The first is the remarkable control of lineation (the parallel to perspectival shifts in Cézanne). From the start this verse is not reporting on a scene but carving out the edges by which one takes in the energies produced by the conjunction of details. And the inventive pauses create a kind of suspense that would be appropriate for narrative, but is now adapted to poetry's commanding attention to how the natural scene discloses itself.

pauses and
suspensions
of line breaks *tension*
reflect poem

The second feature is the overt way the poem's content depends on how the syntax reinforces these disclosures (the parallel to formal activity and *passage* in Cézanne). For example, the first verb, "approaches," an innocuously abstract one, occurs in the fifteenth line – until that point there have been only adjectival phrases reinforcing the apparently timeless thereness of the late winter situation. That verb by itself does not generate any change in affect. But the repetition of "Now" forcefully introduces the sense of time, of event, into this hitherto purely spatial field of descriptions. Then the stage is set for the emergence of active verbs fleshing out the figures of birth potential in the situation. There is at first only the additional verb, "quicken." However, that is enough to charge nouns like "clarity," "outline," and "dignity" with assertiveness. And "still" seems a conjunction of several parts of speech as it beautifully spreads the "now" without cancelling the sense of event.

When the rush of verbs arrives, it does so in an ingenious way. The poem switches to the passive voice, only then to take up that passivity into active verbs. Doing that enables "rooted" to be intensely dynamic, functioning as a hinge between passive and active. The subject is only the vague "they." But here the "they" enables spring to be completely distributed. All nouns seem to share in the energy, without distracting us with a now irrelevant particularity of person or place. The scene remains general, but it is no longer bare, even linguistically. There is an intriguing redundancy in the expression "begin to awaken," as if now the verbs cannot wait to appear. The effect is to suggest a capacity for poetry to serve as witness to the life force without the turmoil of "Spring Strains." Simply rendering the verbs that dynamize the scene suffices to do the work that romance once performed.

This new world of beginnings is not confined to landscape. *Spring and All* offers social poems where the speaking voice must make adjustments more complex than those in "The Young Housewife," and there are several strange poems that I can only suggest comprise an effort by Williams to accommodate the Dada sensibility brought to New York by European expatriates.[33] Here I have space only to dwell on one other poem, so I cannot not choose the "The Rose is Obsolete," because this is the probably Williams' most ambitious foray into constructivist modernism – the domain where the activity of making must bear the fundamental burden for attributing meaning to the details. In pure constructivist modernism artists do not directly link

[handwritten in left margin: most meaning in the poem derived from its means of construction]

signs to the world as constituting illusory pictures or scenes. Rather they concentrate on how the composing activity emphasizes qualities of the signs as signs; then the work has to make those qualities the locus of our connections to the world. We do not take the apple as edible but emphasize what can be done to appreciate how formal measures make the apple appear as a distinctive force in the world.[34] Or, as Williams puts it, constructive modernism tries to have "words freed by the affirmation affirm reality by their flight" (Williams, CP 235).[35] Therefore I want to study this poem as an example of Williams at his most ambitious, most painterly, and, it turns out, most responsive to a dilemma basic to his culture.

Recall that a major aspect of the despair in the confused prose chapters was the issue of plagiarism, which for Williams was a state of cultural life shaped by quotation rather than engaged by the quest for the actual forces driving our efforts at expression. As the volume approaches "The Rose is Obsolete," the motif of plagiarism returns. Williams invokes visual work by Juan Gris[36] as an example of the challenge posed to poets that they also pursue the modern trend "to separate things of the imagination from life" so that they can take on a force all their own (Williams, CP 192–4). After the poem he returns to the contrast to resemblance by citing Cézanne, then focusing on Gris:

A CREATIVE FORCE IS SHOWN AT WORK MAKING OBJECTS WHICH ALONE COMPLETE SCIENCE AND ALLOW INTELLIGENCE TO SURVIVE – his picture lives anew. It lives as pictures only can; by their power TO ESCAPE ILLUSION and stand between man and nature as saints once stood between man and the sky. . . .

(Williams, CP 199)

So the poem itself has a lot to live up to if it is to make such prose plausible. This is its opening movement:

The rose is obsolete
but each petal ends in
an edge, the double facet
cementing the grooved
columns of air – the edge
cuts without cutting
meets-nothing-renews
itself in metal or porcelain

whither? It ends –
but if it ends
the start is begun
so that to engage roses
becomes a geometry . . .

Somewhere the sense
makes copper roses
steel roses –   (Williams, CP 195)

The rose is obsolete because it has become an instance of plagiarism,
of a "crude symbolism" that "associates emotions with natural phenomena such as anger with lightning, flowers with love" (Williams,
CP 188). Such work takes traditional sentiments for the reality that
seeks expression – and thereby falsifies experience, making nihilism a
reasonable despairing response. But modern art provides another path:
by distortion or by "the break-up of beautiful words" (Williams, SE 75),
the artist says "No" to the prevailing ideological structures, setting
against them apparently illegible objects. If we learn to appreciate the
differences such art establishes, however, we see the possibility that
the world can be remade in the imagination by testing alternative ways
of conceiving values. Perhaps the destruction of belief in love as a comfortable joyous site might make us pay more attention to what loving
actually feels like. And perhaps then art can play a significant role in
shaping such feelings because the medium itself can produce strange
but appropriate sensations, helping us realize affective states that we
typically suppress. Perhaps love is closer to how the mind engages art
than it is to the roles desire plays in nature. Because refiguring the
real is what art does, making copper and steel roses may align us with
a vision of love capable of surviving in the modern world:

The rose carried weight of love
but love is at an end – of roses

It is at the edge of the
petal that love waits

Crisp, worked to defeat
laboredness – fragile
plucked, moist, half-raised
cold, precise, touching   (Williams, CP 195)

Love is at an end of roses in two senses. The rose can no longer provide a fresh expression of what love involves. But the ends of roses might be quite a different matter, so long as the ends are edges crafted by the imagination. For then the object can recall to us everything that feeling on the edge involves, especially the longing for and appreciation of qualities of contact. The poem seems eager to take up that possibility – too eager. Its exuberant list of qualities threatens to naturalize the whole process again and subsume what makes art different into another version of sentimentality. It seems the poem has to enforce a sharp distinction between our eagerness to thematize and a willingness to let the objects speak. So it inserts a question which is set off by itself, then it changes gears, refusing to dwell in the tendency to celebrate adjectives that offer only abstract promises of renewal.

To escape this dilemma the imagination has first to dwell on what is absent rather than on what words can easily make present, and then it must return to the particulars of the art object:

> What
>
> The place between the petal's
> Edge and the
>
> From the petal's edge a line starts
> that being of steel
> infinitely fine, infinitely
> rigid penetrates
> the Milky Way
> without contact – lifting
> from it – neither hanging
> nor pushing
>
> The fragility of the flower
> unbruised
> penetrates space   (Williams, CP 195–6)

The best way to answer the question "what" is to look carefully at the collage by Gris. Then both the mode of attention and the details provide fresh metaphors for what the rose has symbolized. Or, better, in the place of the content of art as the metaphor, the figure for love lies in how the properties of the artwork realize themselves for an audience.

A plausible figure for love emerges if we forgo our desire for symbolic meaning and focus instead on what is projected by our effort to put the collage together. The details of that work, and the spaces or edges between details, are the only domain in which the fragility of the flower can re-emerge, now inseparable from what seems an exaggeratedly masculine capacity to penetrate space. Love makes itself visible finally in the object's mode of appearing. For only there can we locate the oxymoronic union of fragility and strength that recuperates in the domain of affect what the rose has been in the domain of meaning.

Williams is rarely this constructivist, but we have seen that even poems directly invoking natural scenes like "By the Road to the Contagious Hospital" manifest a constructivist interest in foregrounding the expressive use of syntax and lineation. As he was to put it in 1944, a sense of active nature depends ultimately on the poet's compositional activity:

> When a man makes a poem, makes it, mind you, he takes words as he finds them interrelated about him and composes them – without distortion which would mar their exact significances – into an intense expression of his perceptions and ardors that they might constitute a revelation in the speech that he uses. It is not what he says that counts as a work of art; it's what he makes with such intensity of perception that it lives with an intrinsic movement of its own to verify its authenticity.   (Williams, SE 257)

We will see how that sense of the "real" provides a benchmark for poetry throughout the twentieth century.

Chapter 3

The Doctrine of Impersonality and Modernism's War on Rhetoric: Eliot, Loy, and Moore

*In accordance with the slowly arising democratic order of things . . . , the origin-
ally noble and rare urge to ascribe value to oneself on one's own and to "think
well" of oneself will actually be encouraged . . . ; but it is always opposed by an
older, ampler, and more deeply ingrained propensity – and in the phenomenon
of "vanity" this older propensity masters the younger one. The vain person is
delighted by every good opinion he hears of himself . . . , just as every bad
opinion of him pains him: for he submits to both, he feels subjected to them in
accordance with that oldest instinct of submission that breaks out in him. . . . It
is "the slave" in the blood of the vain person . . . who afterwards immediately
prostrates himself before these opinions as if he had not called them forth.*
                    Friedrich Nietzsche, Beyond Good and Evil[1]

Nietzsche could be read as one of the most radical of the new realists.
He insisted on reducing will to the domain of sensation and thinking to a means by which all animate organisms oriented themselves
to their situation. More important, he challenged writers to test the
capacity of this realism to handle moral and psychological questions
with the same lucid, unsentimental attitude that the scientists were
taking toward the world of nature. Hence my epigraph, an analysis of

vanity and instinct that appealed to virtually every major poet in the early years of the twentieth century.

Here I want to emphasize the work of T. S. Eliot – not for his specific attachments to Nietzsche but for the intensity and scope with which he rose to the challenge Nietzsche posed. Eliot sought to make poetry a mode of cultural criticism that could elaborate the consequences of that traffic in good opinion, but he thought poetry could contribute to that traffic only if it turned away from philosophical argument, since the professional philosophers of his age were perhaps the most prone to every kind of vanity. He felt he had to emphasize the formal means that made poetry a distinctive mode of discourse. Then, by emphasizing the internal forces that give poetry most of its power, he could also adapt for poetry one important aspect of both the old and the new realism in science – its commitment to impersonality. That in turn would provide a fulcrum for unsettling the romantic dreams of having the lyric express individual personality, a desire that also made substantial contributions to the play of cultural vanities. By adapting impersonality as an ideal for poetry, Eliot could show how the "sincere" first-person speaker might be forced to become always conscious of an observing third person demanding ironic distance from the roles eloquence makes so tempting. And he could use the scientist's emphases on sensation in order partially to free sensations from their objects and make them dependent on the roles they play in the overall poetic structure.

Making sense of these ambitions is more than enough for a chapter. But I want to indicate the popularity of impersonal styles by also tracking quite opposed uses of this lyric mode in some poems by Mina Loy and by Marianne Moore. These poets, in quite different ways, realized that impersonality could not only free poetry from the traps of romantic "personality," but also afford an apparent objectivity that would provide substantial room for the play of the idiosyncratic. Poets might render relatively unique manners of imaginatively structuring experiences without any promise that such experiences would fit into any rhetoric of self-discovery or any claims that the poet's self was potentially representative for its audience. As Loy put it: "Not to accept experience at its face value. But to readjust activity to the peculiarity of your own will."[2] For these poets the test of will was to make one's individual concerns patent within the most unrelenting objectified social conditions.

[handwritten margin notes: "how to make social concerns into personal concerns?", "make the voice sincere + impersonal"]

Underlying these choices is my conviction that Eliot's treatments of impersonality and their subsequent roles in American poetry are vastly misunderstood today, at least by those who are not academic specialists in Eliot's work. Most people take Eliot's impersonality as a piece with his mandarin shyness, his elitist conservatism, and his tendency to withdraw from the social struggles his work revealed as obviously pressing. Such readings make it impossible to recognize how exotic and thrilling it once seemed to be responding to these pronouncements on impersonality and the poetry that embodied them. It then seemed possible to overthrow the hegemony of the romantic "I" and the Victorians' unstable "we," all the while continuing Nietzsche's war on "the *moral* interpretation and significance of existence." I want to restore this Eliot to contemporary consciousness – for his clarifying what it would take for allies of the new realism to overcome romanticism and for the greater adventure of combating what I will call the dangerously narrow and blind modes of ego-formation that were basic to elite public culture at the time. If I can do that, my readers will see how the new realism and the doctrine of impersonality inspired a vigorous body of "experimental poetry" that was in turn to create an immense problem for their heirs. Poetry could break fresh ground in exploring the limits of personality. But how could it reject the ideals of sincerity and the rhetorical modes that made this sincerity persuasive for others and still move audiences to engage issues like poverty and commodification that were causes of intense pressure on society?

I

The critic Hugh Kenner made what proved a popular distinction between Pound and Eliot: Pound was the true realist, suspicious of every mode of indefiniteness and committed to finding concrete objects adequate to the emotions the poetry elicited; Eliot, on the other hand, was a romantic poet despite himself because he remained more interested in "the art of creating with an air of utter precision the feel of concepts one cannot localize."[3] Pound was the poet of exquisite attention, Eliot of symbolist longings to transcend the mere actual world. No wonder Pound was fascinated by a pagan sense of natural plenitude, Eliot by the mysteries of religion, first from the East, then from doctrinal Christianity.

This view obviously contains a good deal of truth, especially as each poet hardened into his own projected image of himself. Pound was the practical American, Eliot the neurasthenic upper-class American, doing all the work for a PhD in philosophy at Harvard in philosophy. And where Pound was never comfortable in London, Eliot tried desperately to blend in, eventually taking British citizenship. But drawing out these contrasts too far dangerously oversimplifies both writers. Pound is as moved by the intricacies and mysteries of psychology as Eliot, hence their mutual respect for Henry James; and Eliot was almost as shaped by the possibilities of a new realism as Pound. Eliot never thought that this realism could in itself satisfy the demands of spirit, but it could free spirit to recognize needs that were suppressed by how empiricism and humanism found homes in the old realism. Ironically, the faith in representation and in material progress that this old realism had sponsored seemed to Eliot the main hindrance to any possible spiritual progress.

Eliot's early poetry was very much like Pound's complicated psychological poems such as "Portrait d'une Femme." But where Pound preferred an objectifying distance in those poems, Eliot relied on first-person speakers so self-conscious that it was impossible to tell where irony ended and the process of understanding could begin. "Opera" (1909) begins with ten lines presenting how an opera performance tortures "itself / to emotion for all there is in it / . . . flinging itself at the last / limits of self-expression." Then it is the self's turn to look at itself looking:

> We have the tragic? Oh No!
> Life departs with a feeble smile
> Into the indifferent.
> These emotional experiences
> Do not hold good at all,
> And I feel like the ghost of youth
> At the undertaker's ball.[4]

This has the exaggerated precision of Pound's "tissue of Japanese paper napkins" (P 120). But Eliot's lines do not purport to describe anything objective. Indeed they almost celebrate the impossibility of objectivity for the psyche. The speaker seems doomed to a theatricality that has to sense its own overdramatized self-consciousness, as if it were using consciousness not to engage the real so much as to deflect it. The speaker desires a pose, but he seems bound not to find satisfaction in its own cleverness because that cleverness is at best a substitute for all the intensities that the "I" cannot experience. Eliot's realism takes the French poet Jules Laforgue as a model for rendering the torments of self-consciousness infinitely evading a self-knowledge that it brings almost to hand.

Eliot's treatment of the "I" would not change until "Ash Wednesday" (1927), which inaugurated a quest for personal speech worthy of uttering fully Christian sentiments without embarrassment. But he would try different ways of contextualizing the intricate levels of irony in which the subject is trapped, and he would call attention to cultural sources, or at least cultural analogues, for the characters' malformed efforts at self-expression. These efforts modified the structure basic to poems like "Opera" in two ways. Rather than a simple speaking, the poems offered delicately rendered processes of sensation, which provide occasions for a variety of voices. And rather than a simple opposition between stanzas, the poems would take on more intricate sets of structural relations in order to reach beyond the subject to more general forces at work within the dilemmas subjects suffer.

By the time Eliot added a fourth section to "Preludes" and published the poem in 1915, he was quite a different poet from the author of "Opera." The first section (1910) had already made a significant breakthrough because it focuses on complex sensations rather than on an ideal construct like the self. In fact the sensations seem almost unmoored and so call out to be completed by something like consciousness:

The winter evening settles down
With smell of steaks in passageways.
Six o'clock.
The burnt-out ends of smoky days.
And now a gusty shower wraps
The grimy scraps
Of withered leaves about your feet
And newspapers from vacant lots;
The showers beat
On broken blinds and chimney-pots,
And at the corner of the street
A lonely cab-horse steams and stamps.

And then the lighting of the lamps.[5]

Here sensations are palpably contrasted to any ideal content: realism is never letting any value take on stability. Yet desires for value pervade this world. The "then" of the last line is especially important in this regard because it beautifully brings out the way sensations imply qualities of desire, even when the scene is carefully denied all human presence. The preceding lines had stressed the fragmentary aspects of experience, with each detail pronouncedly only a part that was visibly denied any sense of wholeness. Now there is an event that brings a minimal purposiveness into play in a world rendered otherwise in terms of a painful and pervasive passivity.

The other three "Preludes" gradually introduce human modes of consciousness so that sensation can more explicitly involve a psychology even though the poem refuses to fix on any one speaking subject. The second "Prelude" is set in the morning, where seven lines of fragmented space generate a slightly more integrative and purposive consciousness than had "the lighting of the lamps." Here at least there is a pronoun providing a human center: "One thinks of all the hands / That are raising dingy shades / In a thousand furnished rooms." The third "Prelude" shifts to a second-person center of activity. A "you" is repeatedly addressed as the poem develops a night scene of desperate inactivity.

Finally the fourth "Prelude" brilliantly ties these various pronouns together – not to provide a paraphrasable meaning but to clarify what is at stake in the way sensations have been rendered. The section begins by shifting its mode of consciousness to third-person description. "His soul stretched tight across the skies" links a series of details about the evening, all by implication "Impatient to assume the world." But this section turns out not to be trapped within only one mode of consciousness. Third-person description elicits a first-person state in which a speaker finally internalizes the condition pervading the entire four parts of the poem:

> I am moved by fancies that are curled
> Around these images, and cling:
> The notion of some infinitely gentle
> Infinitely suffering thing.   (Eliot, CP 19)

This "I" has no personal characteristics. It is less a full-fledged speaker than a grammatical position actualizing the possibility of intimate address for any first person. (It is as if the poem evoked the ability of Whitman's "I" to hear the cries everywhere emitted by the landscapes, only to remind the readers that now they faced modernity and their Whitman had to become more abstract and impotent.) Yet even this minimal first-person condition stages the possibility that all this description can lead to sympathy, and hence the image can evoke personal responsiveness.

But in this phase of Eliot's career one rests in first-person stances only at one's peril. These lines follow immediately:

> Wipe your hand across your mouth, and laugh;
> The worlds revolve like ancient woman
> Gathering fuel in vacant lots.   (Eliot, CP 20)

First-person sentiments have to be repudiated because the objective rendering of sensations, and, for early Eliot, the ironic stance will always get the last word. To celebrate the sensibility of the "I", spirit would have to be anchored in something more substantial than this expression of fancy. In Eliot's world the task of the poet is to gain sufficient distance in time and in space to put such fantasy in its place.

II

This grim imperative to "Wipe your hand across your mouth, and laugh" introduces what one could argue is a new possibility in the Anglo-American lyric. Not objectivity itself, and not irony itself – Hardy had done that. Eliot saw the possibility of staging the desire for objectivity as a conflicted stance: poetry might foreground attitudes as fundamental building blocks, putting the rendered sensations and the feelings they evoked under considerable pressure. So it should not be surprising that Eliot turned to a series of essays in order to work out what seemed the principles underlying this new work. He realized that a theatrically impersonal style could allow no surrender to the sympathies (and requests for reciprocal sympathy) so easy for the unchallenged first person, with its presumed harmony between the self imagined and the self actually determining one's actions. But he still had to work out the possible stakes in these experiments.

By 1919 he could state succinctly what ideals of impersonality might create for poetry:

> The point of view which I am struggling to attack is perhaps related to the metaphysical theory of the substantial unity of the soul: for my meaning is, that the poet has, not a "personality" to express, but a particular medium, which is only a medium and not a personality, in which impressions and experiences combine in peculiar and unexpected ways. Impressions and experiences which are important for the man may take no place in the poetry, and those which are important in the poetry may play quite a negligible part in the man, the personality.[6]

Eliot's critics love this passage because it provides *prima facie* evidence for claims that Eliot is a cold, elitist aestheticist. He seems willing to deprive speakers of their voices and the lyric of its dramatic center in order to cultivate peculiar and unexpected ways of combining impressions and experiences.[7] Giving up personal voice for impersonal renderings of impressions is, on the face of it, a bad trade, especially when the distance these renderings produce reinforces a fastidious personal conservatism in all aspects of imaginative life. Yet this critical judgment ought not to be the last word. We have to entertain, at least provisionally, the possibility that Eliot is on to something in his claims about the limitations of treating subjective voice as the central gravitational pull in poetry. The most timely poetry, then and now, might foreground what happens when the view from the distanced third person is put in tension with the perspective embodied in the speaking subject.

Minimally, treating poems as impersonal sites allows us to see them not as rhetorical gestures but as imaginative domains where "special, or very varied, feelings are at liberty to enter into new combinations" (Eliot, SE 7). And this allows emphases on modernist constructivist values where lyrics no longer become substitutes for experience (as Pound put it) but serve as combinatory structures transforming what is given in experience in order to encourage new ways of thinking and of feeling about the world. Eliot used the new science to explain the power such structures might take on:

> I therefore invite you to consider, as a suggestive analogy, the action which takes place when a bit of finely filiated platinum is introduced into a chamber containing oxygen and sulphur dioxide. . . . The newly

[handwritten margin note: remove the Personality, subjective]

formed acid contains no trace of platinum, and the platinum itself is
apparently unaffected. . . . The mind of the poet is the shred of platinum.

(Eliot, SE 8)

The elements the catalyst works upon are "emotions and feelings." The
"poet's mind is . . . a receptacle for seizing and storing up numberless
feelings, phrases, images, which remain there until all the particles
which can unite to form a new compound are present together."
Greatness in art then is not a matter of the isolated components but
of "the intensity of the artistic process, the pressure so to speak, under
which the fusion takes place, that counts" (Eliot, SE 8).

In effect Eliot proposes taking the new realism not only as a model
for what poetry emphasizes – sensations – but also for how poetry
views the rendering and organizing of those sensations. ("Intensity" and
"intensional" are very important concepts for Bergson.) Poetry does
not try to express the self or to tell the truth; it gives possible truths
intensity by putting our ways of dealing with the world under a
shared pressure. Hence the landscape in "Preludes" is not charged with
transcendental significance, but the artist brings to life <u>new objective
possibilities</u> for feeling the impact of a situation.

 ˙ The stakes here are not simply matters of poetics or aesthetics.
I think Eliot is utterly serious, and worth heeding, in his ambitious
claim that "the point of view which I am struggling to attack is perhaps
related to the metaphysical theory of the substantial unity of the soul."
So I want to approach Eliot on impersonality as trying to establish
terms by which he might struggle for the soul of Europe, much as
Nietzsche had. The best way to do that is to link Eliot on impersonality to Jacques Lacan's critique of the tasks played in psychic life by
what he calls the "imaginary" dimension of experience. Then Eliot
becomes very much our contemporary, attempting to undo claims
about deep subjectivity and to replace them by an insistence on subject positions dictated by social negotiations.[8] But drawing the parallel
will take more detail about the role impersonality played in Eliot's
thinking than might otherwise be necessary.

We must be clear that Eliot does not deny the power and pressure
of personality; he only rejects the role it traditionally plays in cultural
discourse about sincerity, confession, and expressivity. Consider another
passage where critics tend to dismiss Eliot's complexity because they

[margin note, handwritten:] Poetry - not to express self or tell truth / but to show possible truths (de-familiarize world)

notice (rightly) the snotty arrogance of ascribing to himself both the capacity to suffer and the wisdom to see his way to a possible cure:

> In fact, the bad poet is usually unconscious where he ought to be conscious, and conscious where he ought to be unconscious. Both errors tend to make him "personal." Poetry is not a turning loose of emotion but an escape from emotion; it is not the expression of personality but an escape from personality. But, of course, only those who have personality and emotions know what it means to want to escape from those things.   (Eliot, SE 10–11)

Yet to dismiss this passage because of its tone is to miss a distinctive aspect of Eliot's trenchant critique of nineteenth-century poetry. In another essay, "The Function of Criticism," Eliot takes what seems an odd angle on the same theme when he argues that "interpretation . . . is only legitimate when it is not interpretation at all, but merely putting the reader in possession of facts which he would otherwise have missed" (Eliot, SE 20). This sense of the demand for fact then affords a position from which to criticize those like Coleridge and Goethe "who supply opinion or fancy" in the guise of illuminating the meaning of a text: "What is Coleridge's *Hamlet*: is it an honest inquiry as far as the data permit, or is it an attempt to present Coleridge in an attractive costume?" (Eliot, SE 21–2). Coleridge is not just mistaken. Rather he is a corrupter of taste because he takes critical inquiry into a domain where there is no "possibility of cooperative activity" and so no hope of "arriving at something outside ourselves, which may provisionally be called truth" (Eliot, SE 22). There is instead only rhetoric, which Eliot defines as "any adornment or inflation of speech *which is not done for a particular effect* but for a general impressiveness" (Eliot, SE 30). Rhetoric becomes the vehicle by which personality extends its reach in order to build out of facts self-flattering general impressions. And then impersonality becomes a vehicle for keeping the pressure on the facts of performance. Impersonality looks at the performance from a third-person perspective so that it might establish agreement among a community of observers. Impersonality is everywhere the resistance to the self's efforts to think well of itself. ——> *But what if the self doesn't think well of itself?*

Eliot is careful to distinguish himself from Aristotelian accounts of rhetoric. For him rhetoric is not a tool for persuading others (argument *if the what is the role of the untrustworthy narrator in poetry?*

61

will suffice for that) but "any convention of writing inappropriately applied" (Eliot, SE 26). With this principle he could extend his suspicions of personality well beyond the nineteenth-century writing that elicited them in the first place, and he could thus develop a focus for his contemporary struggle to forge a style. Eliot saw that in his own time taste was turning away from "oratorical" and "frankly rhetorical" lyric in the nineteenth century to a much more "conversational . . . style of 'direct speech'" (Eliot, SE 26). But it was not sufficient to treat the rejection of the rhetoric of oratory as a mere stylistic choice. Poetry capable of facing modernity had to be able to treat such reactionary tendencies as cultural and spiritual symptoms.

That critical project led Eliot to enlist for his cause those he saw as the first writers to have to grapple with the effects of modernity, the Elizabethan and Jacobean playwrights. For all sorts of cultural reasons involving the development of modern skepticism and the economies it fostered, these playwrights were extraordinarily sensitive to rhetorical performances that sought only general impressiveness. Where general impressiveness was, there self-serving ideology would not be far behind. So when the characters in their plays turned to such rhetoric, Eliot envisioned those authors invoking another perspective beyond the subjective that would make the speaking audible in ways that the audience would have seen as fundamentally problematic.

From these dramatic examples Eliot developed two precepts that would govern his own work. The first is to make an audience hear efforts at sincere speech as if the speaker were a character in a play seeing "himself in a dramatic light" (Eliot, SE 27):

> A speech in a play should never appear to be intended to move us as it might conceivably move other characters in the play, for it is essential that we should preserve our position of spectators, and observe always from the outside, although with complete understanding. . . . In the rhetorical speeches from Shakespeare which have been cited, we have this necessary advantage of a new clue to the character, in noting the angle from which he views himself. But when a character *in* a play makes a direct appeal to us, we are either the victims of our own sentiment, or we are in the presence of a vicious rhetoric. (Eliot, SE 28)

This would go a long way toward challenging the social glue afforded by the upper class's ability to produce performances *"not done for a particular effect* but for a general impressiveness."

Eliot's second precept was more indirect because it did not so much challenge assertions of personality as the humanist values that afforded the stage for such performances. His distaste for such values became more evident as he turned to Christianity, but I think even his early flirtations with Buddhism stemmed from the same antagonism. Humanism seemed to him fundamentally a set of rhetorical postures offering impressive roles but no substance. For when humanism attempted to stand clear of religion, it betrayed the fact that it had no actual foundation for its moral claims (SE 433) and no way to engage in history in order to test what it propounded as ideals.

Among many possible illustrations of Eliot at his most vicious on this topic, I have chosen one where he is criticizing the humanist critic Norman Foerster:

> For culture (and Mr. Foerster's culture is a propagation of Arnold's), these are the sorts of authority to which we may properly look; and the man who has frequented them all will so far as that goes be a better, in the sense of being a *more cultured man*, than the man who has not. . . . But the search for an ethos is a very much more serious and risky business than Mr. Foerster imagines; and Mr. Foerster.is more likely to end in respectability than in perfection. Those who hunger and thirst after justice and are not satisfied with a snack-at-the-bar, will want a great deal more. (Eliot, SE 435)

It is not a great leap from that to the anger of James' Hyacinth Robinson, the satire of Huxley, Waugh, and Lewis, Nietzsche's seeing Christian traditions as wanting art to be "*only* moral" and so relegating that "art, *every* art to the realm of lies,"[9] and, finally, to the elegantly wrought bile of William Butler Yeats:

> I think that before the religious change that followed on the Renaissance men were greatly preoccupied with their sins, and that today they are preoccupied by other men's sins, and that all this trouble has created a moral enthusiasm so full of illusion that art, knowing itself for sanctity's scapegrace brother, cannot be of the party. . . . Painting had to free itself from a classicalism that denied the senses, a domesticity that denied the passions, and poetry from a demagogic system of morals which destroyed the humility, the daily dying of the imagination in the presence of beauty.[10]

III

I ask myself why I want Lacan to buttress Eliot here, since Eliot is the clearer thinker, if not the more profound. But with the exception of several excellent academic works which have made little impact on the poetry world, Eliot is now rarely considered as a thinker at all. One way to change that is to demonstrate how much he shares with Lacan's ideas about subjective agency, although he puts these ideas to somewhat different uses. So I need the authority and scope Lacan brings as he develops his controversial recasting of Hegelian ideas about subjectivity. Through Lacan, we can more easily put Eliot's concerns within the history of philosophical criticism. And then we are in the best possible position to understand the force the ideal of impersonality exercised on several generations of American and European poets. Without a sufficient psychological context, that ideal might seem seem like a narrow bid to distinguish one style from another rather than a serious critical engagement with a culture largely dependent on the modes of identity sustained by rhetorical roles.

I will invoke only one aspect of Lacan's complex and changing perspective on the psyche. It is his early work on the imaginary constitution of the ego that provides terms for recognizing how Eliot's critique of rhetoric fits with a much more general critique of how appeals to personality are typically founded and funded. Lacan argues that there is a fundamental contradiction between the images that provide the ego with a sense of substance and the desires that produce these images. We want the image that provides a sense of identity while also establishing an internal power that serves as the putative referent of such images. Yet the image is just that, merely an external picture only loosely correlated with any projected internal state, since that power may not in fact be susceptible to any image at all. The power of the "I" may depend on fluid and shifting desires that do correspond to anything that can be called upon by a picture. Like Eliot, Lacan challenges the very bases of "the metaphysical theory of the substantial unity of the soul." And in doing so he also calls into question our efforts to form social bonds based on ideals of mutual recognition.

Lacan bases his critique on rejecting ego psychology's view of the psyche as seeking to establish the self as an integrated being. Instead, Lacan asks the difficult and perplexing question how this desire for integration might originate. Why do persons project a version of agency at the core of their being that persists through change and has the power to control conflicting impulses? And why do we grant that agency so much authority that we feel guilt and shame when we think we have failed to act in accord with its imperatives?

Lacan's answer to these questions invokes the modes of satisfaction mothers produce for their infants when they treat them as significant individuals. Mothers (or those who occupy the mother position) perform a mirror function: they present the needy child with a form of repetitive affirmation, attached to a name, which fosters in the child an image of the self as something that can command love. This is W. H. Auden speaking of a limestone landscape compared to a granite one:

> What could be more like Mother or a fitter background
>   For her son, the flirtatious male who lounges
> Against a rock in the sunlight, never doubting
>   That for all his faults he is loved; whose works are but
> Extensions of his power to charm?[11]

Lacan makes painfully clear the problem with this love. For the mother offers something external and "unreal" – an image of the desired substance attached to an individual name – which the child projects as an internal principle establishing the source of its coherence as a psychological being. The mother's responding to the infant's needy cries by repeating a single name helps turn what is initially a disorganized desiring machine into a being with an image of itself. That image then comes to require constant nourishment, as if the agent could use this illusory substance to elicit desire from an other sufficient to guarantee that the image equates with reality. In Lacan's colorful phrase, the mother turns the omelette which takes disparate forms on the frying pans of desire into the "hommelette" which pursues the coherence it takes to appeal to another person's desire.[12]

Now imagine this hommelette negotiating adult social life. Its needs for the satisfactions of imagining the self as coherent and as loved lead it to keep casting other people in the familiar maternal role: the hommelette wants from others the same sense of reflected substance that the mother provides. So it goes through intricate dances to elicit the desires in others that will afford this sense of substance. That means the social ego is as imaginary an object as the child's fantasized self because it still depends on projections about what the other desires.

Yet the projections usually establish fairly stable roles because of what Louis Althusser called "processes of interpellation."[13] Interpellation is literally taking on states that function as the skin functions, that is, as both a protective surface and a boundary separating what is inner from what is outer. But for Althusser that boundary is established by culture, not by nature. Social life can be seen as a constant series of calls to identify oneself – in terms of sexual preference, occupation, or political and personal commitments. Agents assume that this call requires providing answers that project coherent selves capable of playing recognizable roles. And over time we do come to identify completely with those roles so that they do not seem imposed but chosen. Hence the sense that what we offer as social beings stems from our most intimate choices, where in fact we answer those calls because we need an identity that can elicit the approval of others. Such projected approval provides a sense of substance for the self since it is "I" who make the claim to be someone. And that projected approval greatly helps manage the chaotic play of desires since identity affords a means of structuring hierarchies for the self. If we can establish stable roles and treat them as extensions of a fundamental inwardness, we can offer a self desirable to others. And our identification with the roles will be intensified by the expected results of that desire.

No wonder then that the "general impressions" rhetoric produces provide such efficient social bonds. General impressions save us from having to grapple with the particular force of desires that might individuate agents and make them unpredictable. The better the particular fuses with the general, the better identity merges with the images that circulate in the society, and the greater the opportunity to find such identifications a source of reinforcement for the ego. Rhetoric is social glue.

But what happens if the agents are not similarly interpellated and so have different ways of adapting to society? Or what happens when agents are too similarly interpellated so they have to fear that they will not become sufficiently individualized to elicit desire? And what happens if the agents just fear that they are differently interpellated, so that hostility rather than desire is the resulting condition of identification? These questions introduce the bleakest aspect of Lacan's version of self-making. For they indicate how there is likely to be continual unhappiness and confusion because even the illusion of unity of the subject will come under challenge. Lacan shows us why our dependence on the imaginary is a constant source of defensiveness and compensatory violence because we always have to struggle against others for the specificity that the image confers, even though, or perhaps because, there is probably no significant difference in the competitors. Just the idea that others might be different from me and hence may have more powerful claims on the desires of the other, is enough to make me both defensive in relation to these others and embarrassingly aggressive toward the one whose desire I seek. And even when I think the other projects the desired desire, I have to know it is always possible that the other will change and I be bereft of substance. The imaginary, in other words, makes for great theater but unstable character.

Finally, Lacan's framework proves especially relevant when we adapt it to standard accounts of modern society because the greater the social mobility, the more central a role the psyche will be called on to play in the forming of identities within that mobility. Traditional societies also depend on strong imaginary identifications. But it seems likely that the principles shaping those identifications are somewhat different because for the majority there is little sense that the roles and values are chosen, and therefore there is substantially less anxiety about what one is performing so as to elicit the desired desire. And where there is not much anxiety, there need not be a great deal of defensive uneasiness desperately trying to act as if one's identifications were in fact justified.

Eliot and his peers found a culture obsessed with imaginary identifications, often serving to obscure what might be real and shareable about given situations. Take, for examples, the humanist posing in moral righteousness without substance and the bureaucrat desperate to identify with the single role establishing his function within the state. All of modernist writing had to encounter a society relatively new to mobility (or relatively new to being threatened by the mobility of others). And this instability was compounded by the nineteenth-century crises about religion because these put into doubt the most stable and apparently trustworthy model of individual substance anchored in the love conferred on us by our most significant other.

So those affected by this crisis had to seek other ways of satisfying what religion offered to the psyche's sense of available satisfaction in the domain of identity and identification. No wonder that the idea and ideal of being moral would take on an importance far beyond

[handwritten margin note: Obvious, but social climbing requires increased pressure and demands on psyche]

its actual use value in practical life. The concept of the imaginary helps us understand why the appeal of models positing autonomous strong identities might also produce a society rife with repressive and defensive modes of self-delusion. The imaginary haunts all human projects of identification. But it is especially dangerous in those areas where agents claim a lucidity which makes them able to see through everyone else's imaginary structures. And we see in the statement quoted from Yeats that the imaginary is probably most dangerous when it settles on the role of moral judge, for then it combines the blindness of those who claim to know what is right with the opportunity to differentiate an individual identity by contrasting it to those less enlightened or less than righteous. Perhaps the more abstract the identification with principle, the more dangerous it becomes because of what it leaves out, and because of the armor it easily takes on to hold all opposition at bay – think US foreign policy in the administration of George W. Bush.

IV

In the next chapter I will elaborate the situation in which Eliot's heirs found themselves. They had to find ways both to expose and to escape becoming mired in the combination of defensive and aggressive role-playing and moral posturing familiar to those who read late Victorian novels or contemporary therapeutic manuals. And they had to do so primarily without the resources of classical rhetoric, since Eliot and others had so closely bound rhetoric to problems of the imaginary that it could only be a part of the problem, not of proposed solutions. But for that story to have sufficient force I have first to provide a convincing account of how Eliot's generation made poetry a means of combating society's basic means of forming identifications.

They performed that work by establishing and exploring three basic projects they would define as fundamental to modernism. First, as we have seen Eliot propose, the new poetry would have to be impersonal or would at least have to use depersonalizing strategies. Poets had to reject the kinds of images that solicit identifications, and they had to use those rejections in order to call attention to alternative ways that consciousness might respond to values, find satisfactions in its own activities, and experience its social bonds. Second, the new poetry would resist these imaginary formations by cultivating a strong sense of the independence of the object. As we saw with Pound's Vorticist poetry, this work had to show that there were ways of making sense within language that did not derive from the discursive orientations providing society's basic means of interpellation. That is why the poets had to emphasize form – not just as a means of aesthetic organization but as a means of orienting attention to how sensations might be differently combined and imaginative activity freed from structures of self-regard. Formal emphasis on the relations among forces constituting the work could estrange the mind from its standard way of functioning while making that strangeness fascinating and evocative in its own right. Here the new realism's focus on reforming sensations merges with the poetics of impersonality. Finally, the art had to establish ways of attributing value to these distributions of formal energy, and it had to do so while resisting the general languages about values that risked being dominated by rhetorical postures. So the poets' ways of working with their materials had to replace the modes of authority based on the work's qualities as sincere expression or moral edification.[14]

Given this theoretical emphasis on concrete conditions of authorial action, I have to stop generalizing and give the poems a chance to speak. My primary focus in this chapter will be on Eliot's poetry, then I shall turn to how Mina Loy and Marianne Moore supplement his poetics. Like Lacan, Eliot's treatment of how the imaginary works takes place from perspectives that make identification problematic for both the poet and his/her speakers. Take for example Eliot's "The Love Song of J. Alfred Prufrock." Much of the energy in the poem derives from Prufrock's efforts to win a sense of substance for himself by fantasies of eliciting desire from other agents. But even though Eliot had yet to work out his theoretical stance on impersonality, he keeps sufficient distance from Prufrock that he certainly does not endorse the strategies of his character. In fact the extraordinary power of the poem resides in its devastating accuracy in rendering ways we produce self-defensive compensations for that lack of substance. Yet Eliot is not entirely ironic because the poem also elicits a sympathy for Prufrock that the reader knows he or she must both enjoy and repudiate: Prufrock so overtly stages a case for compassion that he risks enhancing his imaginary vision of his own pathos.

Let us look at three moments in the poem in order to grasp how intricately it renders and struggles with psychological tendencies Lacan would later thematize. The opening is crucial because there Eliot immediately produces a compelling strangeness in Prufrock's habits of thinking that will not sit still to allow a synthetic image to form. Instead the language takes on a partial life of its own, offering satisfactions that have little to do with character and much to do with the poet's capacities for what we might call "perverse precision" in diction, in rhythm, and in elaborate rhymes that seem utterly contingent:

> Let us go then, you and I,
> When the evening is spread out against the sky
> Like a patient etherised upon a table;
> Let us go, through certain half-deserted streets,
> The muttering retreats
> Of restless nights in one-night cheap hotels
> And sawdust restaurants with oyster-shells:
> Streets that follow like a tedious argument
> Of insidious intent
> To lead you to an overwhelming question . . .[15]

In effect we begin with the imaginary ego *in medias res*. What can be more purely in the service of the imaginary than this opening effort to implicate a "you" in one's love song. But the situation is complicated by the fact that this "you" is manifestly not a specific addressee. "You" here expresses a fantasy of three possible but unlikely ways of being heard – by the reader, by a projected lover, and by Prufrock himself – all imagined beings for the speaker from whom he can expect no response.

This opening passage is even more important for how it presents the strange workings of individual desire too mobile to establish an effective image of the self. Notice how the metaphors work, if only because that work signals a new era in lyric poetry. Metaphor does not reinforce underlying meaning but displaces it into chains of connections seemingly capable of going in any direction – more at the will of the language than at the will of the dramatic agent. "The evening . . . spread out against the sky" is the first metaphor. It presents what could be an innocuous, almost tautological, visual analogy. But one analogy quickly generates another in the simile of the "patient etherised upon a table." It is as if Prufock wanted to present himself as a potential victim but could allow himself that implication only because the figure of being "spread out" prepared the indirect path for such an identification.

We realize from his way with metaphor why Prufrock has so little substance and so much need: what drives his sense of self comes from an intricate complex of forces that simply cannot be represented in the form of an image. Rather there emerges something like tentacles of feeling eager to attach to any lurking metaphoric possibility. Consider the transitions among metaphoric registers as Prufrock tries to develop figures for the scene in which he finds himself. Tedious arguments do not normally establish fears of insidious intent – quite the contrary. So we have to ask why he interprets one figure in terms of this other one. Perhaps he finds "insidious intent" in tedious arguments because delay reinforces his sense of inadequacy and lets time emerge in all its immense indifference to his imagined purposes. Then we can say Prufrock is forced to adopt defensive and suspicious postures as the only way of holding on to any sense of identity at all. And we can say that the intricacies of poetry go a long way toward establishing how slippages occur that tear the fabric of purposive identification.

The second moment I wish to discuss is more explicit on the limitations in the images that we use to project stability for the ego. The speaker tries to produce images of the self so that his efforts to characterize his situation will establish a satisfying identity. But the images cannot in fact encompass the many possible perspectives that get elicited as we try to secure that satisfaction:

> And indeed there will be time
> To wonder, "Do I dare?" and, "Do I dare?"
> Time to turn back and descend the stair,
> With a bald spot in the middle of my hair –
> (They will say: "How his hair is growing thin!")
> My morning coat, my collar mounting firmly to the chin,
> My necktie rich and modest, but asserted by a simple pin –
> (They will say: "But how his arms and legs are thin!")   (Eliot, CP 4)

This marvelous passage is concerned primarily with the endless enterprise of self-defense that serves only to open new vulnerabilities.

Prufrock becomes aware of how he can be criticized for his bald spot, only to turn instead to what he seems able to control, his figure in his morning coat. But when bodies are reduced to parts, there are always more parts than one can suffuse with imaginary identity – hence the new vulnerability in his self-consciousness about his arms and legs. (Eliot's rhymes in this passage reinforce the psychology because it seems as if they force the body part into self-consciousness for enough time to make it subject to alternative interpretations.)

On the other hand, when some images do seem to stick, Prufrock turns out to be terrified of the self then made visible:

> And I have known the eyes already, known them all –
> The eyes that fix you in a formulated phrase,
> And when I am formulated, sprawling on a pin,
> When I am pinned and wriggling on the wall,
> Then how should I begin
> To spit out all the butt-ends of my days and ways?   (Eliot, CP 5)

In both cases, it seems that the speaker's eloquence functions primarily as a screen defending the self against the painfully inadequate details of which his life is composed. So it is not much of a leap to argue that the dynamic of the poem as a whole elaborates the painful gulf between what is absolutely crucial to individual being and what is irrelevant to other people. Prufrock fears that images will objectify him at such a pervasive level that he loses all sense of power, ironically largely because he is so desperate to have those images secure the sense of power he laments being unable to establish.

Finally I want to explore the moment in the poem when all the bills come due. This is the point where Prufrock can no longer put off treating himself as a dramatic character:

> No! I am not Prince Hamlet, nor was meant to be;
> Am an attendant lord, one that will do
> To swell a progress, start a scene or two . . .
> Full of high sentence, but a bit obtuse;
> At times, indeed, almost ridiculous –
> Almost, at times, the Fool.   (Eliot, CP 7)

It would be a mistake to see Prufrock somehow gaining self-knowledge here. It is no accident that it is Hamlet to whom he turns, and with

[handwritten marginalia:] eloquence as a screen — hide inadequacy

whose appeal he knows he cannot identify. For the choice of Hamlet reveals how much Prufrock remains the failed romantic – remember Eliot's comments on Coleridge's Hamlet. At best Prufrock is trying to cast his sense of failure in a particular light for others, as if he were an actor in a Jacobean play. Even his denial of identification is completely melodramatic, as if even negative images enabled him to deny the pain of realizing how little substance he has. At what would be the traditional climax of the poem then, Prufrock can do no better than shift from fighting off his need for others to fighting off any possibility that he will recognize in his situation what cannot be represented in images.

That is why the lines following this speech are the most fantasmatic in the poem. At the moment where Prufrock comes closest to the truth about himself, he comes under great pressure to avoid concrete identification and so escapes into a decidedly odd first-person plural. For he identifies with others only to note that it is human voices that make us drown. This "we" then does not betoken much fellowship. The "we" is in fact not exclusively human – it is born of fantasy and it flourishes in the exotic sea world between life and death. Nonetheless, in this poem devoted to the dilemmas of establishing a stable "I," the first-person plural is at least a way of looking at oneself differently, and it may be a way of actually hearing those other human voices, perhaps of understanding why the fact that they are only voices causes his drowning. But the force of the ending consists largely in Prufrock's hearing only the fact of those voices and not anything they say that might enable him to establish an identity or quit that impossible enterprise.

V

This is not a place where I can give Eliot's masterpiece *The Waste Land* the attention it deserves, but I want to address some of the features in the poem that made it seem the radical centerpiece of modernist poetics and not the conservative lament that Perloff and others see in retrospect. Much of the historical importance of the poem can be accounted for by features that strike me now as almost cosmetic. It solidified Eliot's reputation as the poet capable of bringing poetry out of pastoral settings into the city, and into the melange of voices and spiritual needs fundamental to urban experience. Eliot's peers were also taken by the poem's ability to combine these realistic textures with something like an archaeological dimension establishing permanent myths and rituals in which the particular contemporary actions seemed embedded. But this kind of praise is as appropriate for Joyce as it is for Eliot. Indeed Eliot writing on Joyce called this kind of archaeological imagination "the mythical method," thereby licensing endless readings devoted to how the allusions buttress or establish what could be called the meaning of the poem.[16]

I want instead to speculate on what causes the tremendous lyrical power of the poem, so that we can then treat it as a distinctive kind of experience possible only if we participate in the flow of imaginative energies. In my view any emphasis on lyric requires attending carefully to how voice, or in Eliot's case voices, make themselves present. For lyric is the richest phenomenology we have of the variety of effects possible by manipulating tone and degrees of distance and intimacy. Typically voice registers the manner by which an individual speaker affectively engages an aspect of the world. But Eliot does not want purely lyrical presence. He wants voices, not voice, as a means of capturing diverse intimate qualities of how public life is experienced. Hence the importance of impersonality. Impersonality creates the aura that these voices bear much more information than the subjects speaking them can bring to awareness. Impersonality here renders a level of voice where it is not quite in control since it is still grappling with what moves it to utterance. Because these are only fragments of expressions of inner lives, the poet appears to capture voices at the moments where they reveal their grounds in a seriously deformed cultural order. At one pole, the speaking in the poem presents only failures or symptoms of what is problematic in the culture's collective experience; at the other, the voices introduce religious needs and possible religious satisfactions so deeply subjective that the public order seems almost a dream life providing hauntingly inadequate correlatives for the inner drama. Ultimately this play of voices establishes a powerful tension between hopeless cries of pain and the possibility of finding in such pain access to prayer which promises redemption from the vale of tears.

Such tension makes even the opening lines open into a situation that is much deeper and more entangled than any participating individual can grasp:

> April is the cruellest month, breeding
> Lilacs out of the dead land, mixing
> Memory and desire, stirring
> Dull roots with spring rain.
> Winter kept us warm, covering
> Earth in forgetful snow, feeding
> A little life with dried tubers.   (Eliot, CP 53)

Nature here is generic and immediately allegorized: there are none of the particulars by which Williams characterizes April in "By the Road to the Contagious Hospital." What matters is not what an individual sees but what the society feels. And what the society feels is a despair as deeply embedded as the rhythm of the seasons. April is the cruelest month because it insists on stirring things to life despite the speaking's desire for the peace of winter's "forgetful snow." Yet the speaking does not have the last word. Notice how five of the six opening lines ends with a present participle. This is clearly no accident. There is a pronounced writerly presence or constructive presence that insists on our recognizing how patterns within the text open another space where dramas are being worked out that the individual characters participate in but do not quite understand. Eliot's structuring of participles sets up a distance from the speaking pain and signals that this poem will require a lot more from the reader than appreciating landscape or sympathizing with dramatic actions.

The situation set, the rest of the opening sixteen lines pronouncedly replace character with a melange of voices. I often teach this section as a radio play with the entire class reading in groups so that the class will be bodily aware of the differences in texture between passages like the collective voices of the opening and isolated voices like these:

> Bin gar keine Russin, stamm' aus Litauen, echt deutsch.
> And when we were children, staying at the arch-duke's,
> My cousin's, he took me out on a sled,
> And I was frightened. He said, Marie,
> Marie, hold on tight. And down we went.
> In the mountains, there you feel free.
> I read, much of the night, and go south in the winter.   (Eliot, CP 53)

For a poet to engage an entire society, it may take making such voices present. In them the reader sees that the welfare of the culture depends less on traditional heroic sentiments or lucid arguments than on a

Multiple voices, no decision / *how to include, not* / *banality?* / *indicators to* / *account quotidian existence* / *a distance*

Impersonality: Eliot, Loy, Moore

commitment not to turn away in disgust from such banality so one can listen for the faint symbolic whispers that indicate the sources of spiritual oppression.

The poem's second paragraph is a little clearer on how Eliot thinks these voices can be heard. If the first paragraph established the natural setting; the second paragraph expands that to establish the transcendental poles that reading will have to negotiate. We hear a voice claiming an authority that no mere human can possess:

> What are the roots that clutch, what branches grow
> Out of this stony rubbish? Son of man,
> You cannot say, or guess, for you know only
> A heap of broken images . . .   (Eliot, CP 53)

To internalize this voice at all one has to be willing to get beyond the self-protections of the imaginary order, even if the result is becoming absorbed in utter chaos. The alternatives are too petty, too caught in worlds where this level of voice is never heard. And if one can go this way, one might find a path beyond the imaginary to more stable conditions of identity, based not on images but on the conviction born of ecstatic moments. The poem's first extended allusion comes here, to Wagner's *Tristan and Isolde*, because there is something in the German that preserves an intensity of emotion and a sense of what endures through time completely at odds with the seasonal patterns comprising the first verse paragraph. Then the timeless memory of the hyacinth girl demonstrates that such grand moments are not confined to high culture but can occur within the intimate ken of most people.

There is not the space here to present an interpretation of the poem. And even if there were space, I would not know quite how to proceed. Almost certainly it will not do to interpret the poem by providing a story or an argument that substitutes for the poem's own ways of manipulating its sequence of elements. So it may be a blessing that I can only spell out how Eliot composes an extremely ambitious set of parameters within which the personal seems only an aspect of the heap of broken images. In essence Eliot acts as if the romantic lyric had trapped us into basing all our faith in poetry on ideals of personal sincerity, so that it is now important to test how far the lyric can go in providing something like pure cultural analysis. Then, because the relevant context becomes the life of the culture, religion can be presented as a pressing need rather than as a subjective wish. Eliot is not proposing his religious vision so much as trying to get us to discover how much of our lives will remain unintelligible as painfully partial unless we admit to sharing in what this April setting calls up as the pains and possibilities of rebirth. Along the same vein, Eliot's allusions become not mere elitism but efforts to populate collective cultural space with echoes that prevent any satisfaction in mere contemporaneity. The poet wants us to hear enough to indicate that our dissatisfactions may be more than a cause of grumbling: they may be the beginnings of a spiritual quest. Philosophy does not have an exclusive right to the mysterious powers of negation.

This approach to *The Waste Land* makes one passage especially important – not because that passage provides a key to interpretation but rather because it provides the most help in specifying why Eliot has so expanded the stage of lyric. The passage occurs midway through the poem's final section, as an echo of how Christ appeared at Emmaus:

> Who is the third who walks always beside you?
> When I count, there are only you and I together
> But when I look ahead up the white road
> There is always another one walking beside you
> Gliding wrapt in a brown mantle, hooded
> I do no not know whether a man or a woman
> – But who is that on the other side of you?   (Eliot, CP 67)

The concluding section had begun with a long meditation on the sterility of the rock landscape and the repeated hope that "If there were water" one might come to terms with that landscape. I think the allusion to Christ at Emmaus arrives when it does to suggest that there will never be water. Relief from conditions of the waste land requires changing our sense of need so that we switch to the purely spiritual import of thirst. There is no water, but that very fact makes all the more important people's transfiguration of that despair into figures of possible religious fulfillment. Figures for how the culture imagines its values have to replace landscape, in effect providing a "soulscape" legible to those who have reached a certain level of despair. Spirit must be born in what nature will not grant. Then we shall see that that culture has built up possibilities for meaning precisely because it has never been fully satisfied by what landscape can offer. On the basis of this sense of another world cohabiting with this one but never identical with it, one can at least understand why faith can be a plausible response to the suffering that separates us from landscape. And that returns us to the presence of the third figure in the scene at Emmaus. But we cannot speak directly with it. The most we can do is accustom ourselves to the fact that such figures appear only in forms that can be reduced to hallucination by non-believers.

This difficulty of adjusting to what can bring spirit to our lives gets played out again when the thunder speaks. The three Hindu commands are clear and simple, but one must interpret them, and for human beings this means endlessly negotiating between possible spiritual awareness and utter hallucination. The wisdom is present, but the culture does not seem to have adequate access to it, partly because the representatives of that culture have to resort to images in order to flesh out the abstractions. Perhaps Eliot's most trenchant critique of the imaginary derives from this structure of substitutions: our clearest need for something like faith is the need to approach spiritual wisdom without having to make the kind of practical images that provide for humans a pathetically impotent sense of power. *The Waste Land*'s efforts to secure such power leave on the one hand only a mad, vengeful Hieronymo and, on the other, the traces of significant religious experience almost but not quite capable of providing what April keeps calling for – the capacity to respond to what is truly other to the selves we construct in our imaginations. If one has sufficient personality, one might also see how one needs that otherness.

VI

Impersonality can sustain two radically opposed attitudes. It can continue in the vein of Eliot's withering critique of the ego, or it can celebrate the power of attention one arrives at when freed of the baggage of lyric self-promotion. One could argue that Eliot contains both mentalities, especially when with *Four Quartets* he turns from an otherness haunting the self to the possible deep sense of the personal afforded when it finds the faith to stabilize it in something other than the vagaries of images. But now I want strong and unambiguous examples of how other poets took the permissions of impersonality in different ways.

Why not follow Pound's advice? For him the most interesting of the younger poets published in an anthology edited by Alfred Kreymborg in 1917 were two women who had mastered the ways of impersonality: "In the verse of Marianne Moore I detect traces of emotion; in the poetry of Mina Loy I detect no emotion whatever." In the masculine world of early modernist writing, such sentiments constituted strong praise in discussing female poets. And once he had secured his air of superiority, Pound could be more precise and more respectful: these two poets have managed a difficult journey from a romantic poetics of personality to "poetry that is akin to nothing but language, which is a dance of the intelligence among words and ideas and modifications of ideas and characters" (Pound, SP 424). These poets certainly understand despair, but they echo the *Symboliste* poet Jules Laforgue about handling that "precipice":

It is a mind cry rather than a heart cry. "Take the world if thou wilt but leave me an asylum for my affection" is not their lamentation but rather "In the midst of this desolation, give me at least one intelligence to converse with." (Pound, SP 424)

And the mark of that intelligence is their having mastered *logopoeia*, a commitment to the internal play of language and the intelligence possible when writers will have "none of the stupidity beloved of the lyric enthusiast and the writer and the reader who take refuge in the . . . description of nature because they are unable to cope with the human" (Pound, SP 424).

Pound does not go into how strange a pairing these women form. The poet with no emotion was a beautiful, flamboyant soul characterized as the exemplary modern woman and figure for everything slightly dangerous in the bohemian life of Greenwich Village. The poet whom he granted some emotion was a quiet, witty, bashful soul who lived with her mother for most of her life. Not surprisingly Pound was better attuned to Loy's work than to Moore's, whose quietness seems to have generated resources enabling her always to take delight in the world even as she despaired of humans learning to share that delight. But he is very helpful in clarifying the role impersonal intelligence plays for both poets – since it is not the dramas of self-expression but the intricacies of linguistic structure that have to tie their poems to the world.

Loy was born in England in 1882 to a conservative Protestant English mother and Hungarian immigrant father. Perhaps not surprisingly, she turned to the arts, married an English painter, moved to Florence where she was the belle of the Futurists, and emigrated to New York in 1916. There her beauty made quite a hit, enchanting William Carlos Williams among others. She fell in love with the boxer-poet Arthur Cravan, and followed him to Mexico where he was mysteriously murdered and his body never found. She then returned to Europe before moving back to New York in the 1930s, to become an American citizen in 1946.

Loy had by far the most eventful and varied (and depressing) life among the major modernists. It seems almost a fall in intensity to turn to her poetry, but I have to do that immediately because I have space only to take up the three poems that I think best illustrate the various facets of her self-consciously impersonal poetics. She does not seem directly dependent on Eliot, yet there are many more significant parallels than he let himself notice in his 1918 short essay on her. In fact Loy offers an even better fit than Eliot with the perspective of early Lacan. Eliot portrays Lacanian psychology in a figure like Prufrock; Loy captures the underlying logic of the imaginary in her 1914 "Feminist Manifesto" with its famous assertion, "Women must destroy, in themselves, the desire to be loved" (LLB 155). Loy sees that if women seek love they will imagine themselves as men see them, and hence identify with fantasies that sustain the dominance of the male ego.

"Sketch of a Man on a Platform" (1915) provides a strong case for her wariness in regard to that male ego. The object of this poem is F. T. Marinetti, the founder of Futurism with whom Loy had had a lengthy affair. One might say that satire of the male ego does not require Lacanian analysis; common sense will do quite well. But Loy's specific strategy gathers considerable force against the backdrop of Lacanian thinking. For she does not carry out an overt struggle against Marinetti – that would only lock her in an oppositional position and create another fixed ego position. Rather Loy trusts in an exaggerated impersonal precision that allows her to present and to undermine Marinetti's ways of projecting his own nobility. His limitations seem to manifest themselves because of what he is rather than because of something she imposes. She does not have to ridicule Marinetti; she only has to let his amalgam of Futurist phrases reveal how impotent they are to realize his exalted imagination of himself.

The poem begins under the guise of adulation:

> Man of absolute physical equilibrium
> You stand so straight on your legs
> Every plank or clod you plant your feet on
> Becomes roots for those limbs. (LLB 19)

Yet limiting the context to "physical equilibrium" creates a slight doubt whether Marinetti's powerful stance will sustain equally powerful ideas. We wonder just who sees him as so powerful. Then by the third stanza Loy has sufficiently manipulated the energies of exaggeratedly precise diction to make it appear that another more critical consciousness seems to be able to penetrate Marinetti's ego:

> Your projectile nose
> Has meddled in the more serious business
> Of the battle-field
> With the same incautious aloofness
> Of intense occupation
> That it snuffles the trail of the female
> And the comfortable
> Passing odor of love
>
> Your genius
> So much less in your brain
>
> Than in your body   (LLB 19)

Now that powerful physical equilibrium gets reduced to an overactive Italian nose unable to distinguish what is called for on the battle-field from the "passing odor of love." What Pound called *logopoeia*, "the dance of the intellect among words," here manifests itself in the remarkable self-consciousness and ultimately playful effort at precision. These may be the jealous sentiments of many a frustrated lover, but they have rarely been put so carefully and made such intense use of the figure of metonomy. This treatment of Marinetti's nose even raises the suspicion that such an appendage underlies the Futurist rhetoric of "projectiles" and "concentration."

Finally the poem turns to the conceptual, only to find that the mobility prized by Marinetti may be inseparable from sheer tautology, permitting all forms of creative idiosyncrasy while only rarely making a difference in public life:

Fundamentally unreliable
You leave others their initial strength
Concentrating
On stretching the theoretical elastic of your conceptions
Till the extent is adequate
To the hooking on
Of any – or all
Forms of creative idiosyncrasy
While the occasional snap
Of actual production
Stings the face of the public.   (LLB 20)

The mode of address remains respectful, but the play between continuous syntax and sharp end-stops of the last four lines suggest how much the terms for admiration are carefully hedged to float between what he desires and what an impersonal perspective can grant. "The occasional snap / Of actual production" cannot be a judgment matching Marinetti's own ambitions. So even if one cannot stop loving men, one can at least redeem oneself by eventually exercising this kind of scrutiny of their efforts to assert their personalities.

Such satire is a good test of the psychological power impersonality can wield, but it is an insufficient test of the formal intelligence encouraged by thinking about poems as impersonal constructs capable of serving as catalysts for combining elements of feeling. To show how well Loy does in relation to that standard I have to turn to two other poems. First I shall confine myself to just a few sections of "Songs to Joannes," probably her richest blending of chilling distance and psychological intensity as she asks how sex might appear if it could shed all connections to the rhetoric of love. Then I will turn to "Gertrude Stein," a slightly later poem where Loy demonstrates how the formal relations provided by dense linguistic structure achieve a similar sense of "reality" to that produced by modernist paintings (LLB 160).

"Songs to Joannes" is a very intricate and tonally complex text of thirty-four sections exploring from an Olympian distance the various "interests" men and women have in establishing erotic connections. Its opening sets the tone by seeming to address the entire history of love poetry:

> Spawn of Fantasies
> Silting the appraisable
> Pig Cupid   his rosy snout
> Rooting erotic garbage
> "Once upon a time"
> Pulls a weed white star-topped
> Among wild oats sown in mucous-membrane
>
> I would an eye in a Bengal light
> Eternity in a sky-rocket
> Constellations in an ocean
> Whose rivers run no fresher
> Than a trickle of saliva   (LLB 53)

Without Loy's careful verbal intelligence this reversal of standard lyric sentiments would be nothing but a melodramatic gesture, the morning-after mood with which we are all familiar. But Loy's distance here beggars all such moods. And, rather than express just another fantasy, she lets concision and constructive intelligence do her talking. Notice how (again) she puts the independence of each line in tension with the desire for continuous statement. The concision then increases this tension because we have to attend to a mind continually making leaps that are barely but often gorgeously justified. For example, "Pig Cupid" makes a marvelously swift transition from the figure of "Spawn of Fantasies." It retains the abstraction of the opening lines, but at the same time offers an outrageous metonomy for the male sexual organ. And it makes see how the relation of part to whole in metonomy can stand as a figure for the basic forces involved in sexual activity. From Loy's perspective, males identify with their sex organs, and this in turn is one reason why sexuality is so rife with compensatory fantasy supplementing this reductive imaginative gesture. But females do no better. When the second stanza turns to women's interests, fantasy still dominates, but the space of fantasy itself is forced to take on Futurist speed. What begins as an ideal identification quickly collapses into a post-coital drip: women have no more power to escape the material facts of sexuality than men.

The various sections of the poem then explore what might be called the ideological landscape that we enter when we are driven by sexual desire. At one pole freedom seems to lie in dismissing all idealization so one can accept the sheer materiality of bodies. But there is a counter-pressure created by the apparent need even for the disillusioned to attach some kind of metaphoric framework to such experience: if metaphor cannot successfully idealize love, perhaps it can create a texture of constant idiosyncratic vigilance that refuses to "slip back into the turbid stream of accepted facts" (LLB 150).

For an explicit thematizing of this vigilance we cannot do better than cite poem XXIV, which exhibits Loy at her most vigilant, most impersonal, and most insistent on the capacity of sheer power over language to honor the pull of skepticism about romance while finding an alternative means of intensifying erotic experience:

> The procreative truth of Me
> Petered out
> In pestilent
> Tear Drops
> Little lusts and lucidities
> And prayerful lies
> Muddled with the heinous acerbity
> Of your street-corner smile   (LLB 62)

The "procreative truth" suggests two competing forces – the truth that accounts for how one is driven to sex by one's nature and the truth that one comes to over time as one acts out that nature. The one attitude marks a realistic acceptance, the other the awareness that whatever the effort at realism, illusion will prevail. Even the sounds get caught up in these contrasts. The alliterated *p* sounds that mark her sense of exhaustion are set against the alliterated *l*s in the fifth line that evoke the continuing appeal of romance.

The most impressive feature of the poem is its concluding image and its implicit relation to Imagism. I cannot help wondering how I would feel if I were described in terms of "the heinous acerbity / Of your street-corner smile." The figure is almost unintelligible because it too flirts with Poundian overparticularization. What is a street-corner smile, and how is that qualified by the properties of heinous acerbity? But Loy's setting is more dramatic than Pound's. The effort at precision performs at least two tasks. It clearly establishes a blend of affection and fascination, since the expression marks careful attention and considerable investment in getting the smile into language. But that attraction clearly has to be fought, or is being fought by the effort to isolate the smile and detach it from any conventionally attractive attributes. It seems then as if the exhausting effort to tell no lies about sex cannot escape ambivalence. There is no hope for removing the silt from the appraisable, yet that smile seems a sufficient reason to go on, despite her judgments.

Loy is even better when she turns her intricate intelligence to the accomplishments of other artists like Constantin Brancusi and James Joyce. Then she can get free from the all too personal (and often somewhat melodramatic) impersonality of her efforts to establish distance from her own sexual desires. Also then there is a clear warrant for her idiosyncratic precision, since registering a work of art's effects on a sensitive temperament establishes a crucial measure of what an artist has accomplished. Rather than fighting illusion, she can present an intelligence working to be adequate to truly complex objects, a labor capable of compelling conviction even in her endlessly suspicious sensibility.

I have chosen Loy's "Gertrude Stein" to represent this aspect of her work because there she concisely and imaginatively faces two challenges. She manages to elaborate precise praise distinguishing Stein from other modernist writers, and she takes the further step of using constructivist strategies to produce a formal equivalent for the imaginative sites achieved by Stein's art:

Curie
of the laboratory
of vocabulary
  she crushed
the tonnage
of self-consciousness
congealed to phrases
  to extract
a radium of the word.   (LLB 94)

It is crucial that the poem is one sentence, consisting only of a pure act of naming. Nothing happens in the world; a great deal happens in the mind as the naming process works out intricate equivalents for Stein's art without in any way offering an imitation (which would be bound to be vulgar). The demands on the mind begin with the pressure of each word: it cannot simply convey sense but it is also called upon to make reflective use of its grammatical properties. Take for example the simple preposition "of." "Of" is emphasized as a crucial relational operator in this poem because it is our basic means of attaching properties to nouns. ("Of" in English is a rough equivalent for compound words in German.) Loy then wants to have each "of" phrase build a new aspect of a name. That way she can honor Stein's obsession with names, and justify the link to Curie, while establishing a different model of naming from those regularly used by Stein. And the richer the link between the laboratories of Stein and Curie, the more the metaphor of Curie's work functions as almost a literal name for Stein's.

Notice how manner and matter are brilliantly fused by having the two main verbs set off within different spacing so that they can acquire something like a weight equal to the nouns as they establish substantial transitional force. One might even say that the placement of these verbs establishes a sense within the entire poem of each line as a kind of mass that then other lines have to balance. Then there is the play among three verb forms – transitive, participial, and finally the infinitive, the closest verbs can come to the timelessness of names. Loy realizes that for Stein effective naming cannot be accomplished by metaphor alone. Naming is a largely a matter of adjusting verbs to supplement description, for verbs prevent names from being static, and they transform what could be only things into events in process. (The concern for nouns doing the work of verbs brings Stein and Loy close to the editor of "The Chinese Written Character.")

All these effects are intensified and the expectations they establish fulfilled by the utterly brilliant, apparently flat last line. This line completes the metaphor proposed in the first line by establishing just what Stein and Madame Curie have in common. But it uses the model of "dim lands of peace" so offensive to Pound (that is metaphor followed by allegorical abstraction), and the line does not evoke the same intensity as the sharp diction of the previous lines. This final "of," however, has the benefit of completing the other "of" expressions, as if Loy were saying to Pound: I can even bring life to the kind of statements you abhorred. And the calm of the line, connected with the satisfaction of making explicit the basic concept linking Curie and Stein, makes it seem that the labor of crushing of the tonnage of self-consciousness brings a well-deserved resolution. By securing the sense of the underlying metaphor the poem completes its experiment in making character seem timeless: that release of discovering the underlying connections between the women can be repeated as long as the names it honors endure. By carefully weighting her lines, Loy affords a transcendental objectivity that might be the poem's best indication of what drove both Curie and Stein, and what links them still.

VII

"Gertrude Stein" is superb evidence that Loy eventually learned to use impersonality as a means of access to values as well as a critical stance. But for sustained modernist uses of impersonality as means of focusing attention outward rather than providing distance on the self, there is no equal to Marianne Moore. Moore's best poems are rather long, so I cannot represent the fluidity and scope of her imagination. (My favorite is "An Octopus," which takes as its subject how Mount Rainier in Washington forms a very complicated habitat for different modes of dwelling.) However, even focusing briefly on a few of her shorter poems will indicate how effectively Moore distinguished herself.

Moore's shortest poem, "Poetry," is one of her richest interpretations of what impersonality makes possible:

> I, too, dislike it.
>> Reading it, however, with perfect contempt for it, one discovers in
>> It, after all, a place for the genuine.[17]

There are two other much longer versions of this poem (one of which is given in the notes to the *The Complete Poems*, pp. 266–7), so we have to ask two questions: why did she settle on this version as the most satisfying, and why does she still want the other version in the background? The most obvious reason is that the longer version is quite verbose, perhaps deliberately contrasted to the genuine as a recipe is to the meal. Having this in the background makes the short version a critique of the temptation to rhetorize, and provides a stage for simply trusting to the object as "a place for the genuine" rather than laboring to establish a context. Let the poets construct the places or sites and the architecture will make visible what is "genuine" in the work. Any more talk presupposes or fills that space with something other than the genuine, since it would be illustration and not presentation. More important, further talk runs the risk that the "I" with its likes and dislikes will impose on the "one" who is given the task of discovering the genuine. The impersonal "one" can bring complete attention and appreciate idiosyncrasy without having to be faithful to any self-image or responsive to the pressures of past and future.

Marianne Moore was born in St. Louis in 1887, the year before Eliot's birth in the same city. She studied biology at Bryn Mawr, taught stenography at the government Indian school in Carlisle, and moved to New York in 1918 where she did various jobs until she became editor of the *Dial* in 1926. Like Loy she was a regular on the literary scene in New York, but there all parallels end. Where Loy was obsessed with diction as the means of giving her impersonal surfaces a dramatic charge, Moore tended to rely on intricate and shifting tones that play on and in precise description fused with complex formal patterns. Take for example another short poem, "An Egyptian Pulled Glass Bottle in the Shape of a Fish" (1919):

> Here we have thirst
> and patience, from the first,
>   and art, as in a wave held up for us to see
>   in its essential perpendicularity;
>
> not brittle but
> intense – the spectrum, that
>   spectacular and nimble animal the fish,
>   whose scales turn aside the sun's sword by their polish.
>
> (Moore, CP 83)

Moore loves the voice of tour guide. But very few tour guides have such care to make their discourse about objects like the Egyptian bottle at least be as well made and alive as the bottle. In Moore's poem the most obvious sign of care for the status of the object is her scrupulous control over rhyme and rhythm. Each of the four rhymes is a different use of the relevant resources. Exact strong rhyme prepares for an exaggerated feminine rhyme consisting of a monosyllable and a six-syllable word. Then there is a monosyllabic slant rhyme followed by another feminine rhyme where the key syllable would receive very little stress without the rhyme. When we turn to the rhythm we see how the syllabic structure (4, 6, 12, 12) enables her to play with varied line length while offering almost equal weight and duration when one speaks the lines.

But what is most important in the poem is the way the intensified object dimension of the text functions thematically. The poem becomes itself sufficiently intricate and polished to turn aside the sun's sword. And the poem becomes a powerful example of the cultural work an "essential perpendicularity" can perform by dramatizing how the mind can inhabit what otherwise would be mere description. Perpendicularity is essentially that mental attitude capable of continually creating new possibilities in the real precisely because it does not claim to picture the world but only to differ from it in illuminating ways. That is why it matters that the description of the bottle manifests an intelligence capable of holding the different registers elicited by "thirst" and "patience" in the same thought. The art of the glass bottle makes it attractive and so reminds one of its functions to carry liquids capable of relieving thirst. But one would be hard-pressed not to take "thirst" as also metaphoric, suggesting both our thirst for experience and the bottle's thirst for the world. And then "patience" also starts to move around. It refers to the care with which the bottle is constructed, but it also can refer to the endurance that the bottle has exhibited while nothing has been happening to it. Moore felt that these possibilities brought a new significance to both the object and the life with which it intersects, so long as the object is free from the obligation to mean in an unequivocal manner.

The second stanza then elaborates this power of perpendicularity by shifting from our looking at the object to our looking with eyes sharpened by the object to explore certain imaginative possibilities. That is why the poem makes the distinction between brittleness as a condition of the object and intensity as a condition of the viewer attracted to the relationship between the bottle and the fish it represents. The powers of the subject and powers in the object seem increasingly to flow into each other until ultimately the play of light on the object allows a glimpse of how the subjectivity of the fish might engage the world. More generally, turning aside the sun's rays is testimony to polish of every kind – the life in art trumping the realist's desire to capture that world by acts of lucid description. Perpendicularity becomes a desperately serious form of playfulness. It dramatizes the power of polish while also reminding us that such polish is by no means innocent. Readers have to ask what lies behind the polish and what creates the interest in resisting the light. Yet the poet cannot quite answer, since the poem shows us that the Egyptian glass bottle takes on what power it does precisely by maintaining a perpendicular relation to the appeal of discursive statement.

"The Grave" is not so formally intricate nor so "witty" in the use of that play, but it is one of the most bleakly intense and intelligent poems written in the twentieth century as it explores just what might lie beneath surfaces. Here I shall try to capture those qualities by focusing on the poem's opening and closing moments. It begins with a sense that there is no effective perpendicularity in relation to the sea because the sea so dramatically invokes a death that brooks no opposition:

> Man looking into the sea,
> taking the view from those who have as much right to it as
> you have to it yourself,
> It is human nature to stand in the middle of a thing,
> but you cannot stand in the middle of this;
> the sea has nothing to give but a well-excavated grave.
>
> (Moore, CP 49)

Moore's usual witty perpendicularity is now only the effort to maintain calm impersonal distance as she records this horrifying sense of the sea as grave of all. That distance at least establishes a human focus or angle of vision not quite absorbed by despondency. Notice how important seeing becomes from the start, largely because humans are not able to exert any more active powers, like standing, in relation to the sea and what it has come to represent. To become aware of any powers in confronting the sea is also to become aware of how limited they are. The poem tries to focus on particulars by turning from the sea to the fir trees at its edge. Yet the sea in effect returns that glance, since it is characterized as a collector "quick to return a rapacious look." Blocked in the effort to isolate human seeing, the speaker now can only succumb. That voice thinks of humans now as having shared that rapacious look, but only for a brief moment because "their bones have not lasted," and therefore their "expression is no longer a protest."

After this realization, the poem shifts inward, contrasting its concern for sight to a fascination with what might lie beneath the surface
that the sea is so eager to hide. It seems then the sea and humans
are in agreement after all, since men want desperately to respect that
surface so that they can proceed "as if there were no such thing as
death":

> men lower nets, unconscious of the fact that they are
> > desecrating a grave,
> and row quickly away – the blades of the oars
> moving together like the feet of the water-spiders, as if there were
> > no such thing as death.
> The wrinkles progress among themselves in a phalanx –
> > Beautiful under networks of foam,
> and fade breathlessly while the sea rushes in and out of the
> > seaweed;
> The birds swim through the air at top-speed, emitting cat-calls
> > as heretofore –
> the tortoise-shell scourges about the feet of the cliffs, in motion
> > beneath them;
> and the ocean, under the pulsation of lighthouses and noise of
> > bell-buoys,
> advances as usual, looking as if it were not that ocean in which
> > dropped things were bound to sink –
> in which if they turn and twist, it is neither with volition nor
> > consciousness.   (Moore, CP 49–50)

The initial figure in these lines tells the whole story: as the men try
to ignore their lowered nets they take on the substance of mere water
spiders free of what the depths might hold. With the fourth line in
this passage, the poem returns to pure seeing, as if consciousness
too could be absorbed by the fullness of the apparent scene, and so
successfully put off interest in what might lie below. But that sense
of visual plenitude cannot survive the "as if" in the penultimate line.
Human consciousness has other powers than sight, has the power
of making hypotheses that strangely bring to self-consciousness what
consciousness has been trying to deny. The awareness of death returns
with the force of a series of negatives that ironically make present
just the destructive force from which consciousness has been trying
to hide.

Impersonality here is crucial because, rather than sympathize with a lament and so partially hide from absolute bleakness, we have to work out how something like pure consciousness is operating as it struggles with the horrors of mortality. The absence of personal lament becomes a vehicle for intensifying profound anxiety. Even more important, impersonality ultimately allows a capaciousness of mind that at least partly overcomes the pathos of lament.

The long lines reaching beyond the limits of the page seem to be the struggle of consciousness for an expansiveness that can rival the sea's control of time and of space. But even that effort at capaciousness only gradually arrives at the negative contrast on which the poem ultimately turns in the final two lines – between the sea that appears and the sea that seems almost deliberately to mask the brutal necessity in which "dropped things are bound to sink." That sea is quietly sadistic, enjoying how these things "turn and twist" and become absorbed in a world that can claim "neither . . . volition nor / consciousness." Yet there is a curious sense of release accompanying this consciousness of unconsciousness, probably because the poem can so uncomplainingly come to terms with how it intensifies all that we cannot control.

Moore's "Steeple Jack" (1932) may be an even greater poem, partly because this text manages both to honor modernist impersonality and to project beyond it to a new experimental condition. Moore had not published for seven years when this poem appeared and announced a more populist voice that was willing to restore the rhetorical enterprise of moving audiences to embrace relatively specific values. Like Stevens and Auden, she explores ways of actualizing an imaginary domain of identifications while resisting the structure of identification vilified by Eliot, Pound, Williams, and Loy.

I can only call attention to some significant moments within this lengthy poem. Notice how it does not begin with Eliot's abstract shared cultural plight but with a specific situation provoking direct address that then becomes the focus for lyric investigation:

Dürer would have seen a reason for living
    in a town like this, with eight stranded whales
to look at; with the sweet sea air coming into your house
    on a fine day, from water etched
      with waves as formal as the scales
    on a fish.

One by one in two's and three's, the seagulls keep
    flying back and forth over the town clock,
or sailing around the lighthouse without moving their wings –
rising steadily with a slight
    quiver of the body – or flock
mewing where

a sea the purple of the peacock's neck is
    paled to the greenish azure as Dürer changed
the pine green of the Tyrol to peacock blue and guinea
gray. You can see a twenty-five
    pound lobster and fish nets arranged
to dry. The

whirlwind fife-and-drum of the storm bends the salt
    marsh grass, disturbs stars in the sky and the
star on the steeple; it is a privilege to see so
much confusion. Disguised by what
    might seem the opposite, the sea-
side flowers and

trees are favored by the fog so that you have
    the tropics at first hand; the trumpet-vine . . .   (Moore, CP 5)

This is certainly not modernist compression. But the poem's leisurely way with details does make an important modernist point: landscape is not something one describes so much as something one inhabits by virtue of those elements of the poem that go beyond representation. That is, the leisure is the point. The poem enacts a specific attitude in order to define how this given site might be inhabited. If we acknowledge this, the otherwise strange initial reference to Albrecht Dürer makes good sense. This poem is also full of references to acts of seeing and to what attracts sight. One might even say that the basic action in this part of the poem is acknowledging the pleasures of sight and how they generate a sense of privilege because sight affords a power which enables us to share the delight in confusion offered by the scene. Sight itself becomes an active, empathic mode of understanding how lives can be organized in terms of motives for living among quite simple pleasures. And sight here allows a very concrete understanding of the otherwise portentous phrase "reason for living." If one cannot find reason for living in the sight and sound of the elegantly

simple complexity of "One by one in two's and three's," one is not
likely to find it in the recesses of philosophy.

The next part of the poem (not quoted here) introduces the stuff of
philosophy in order to expand the motif of reasons for living, but it
does so by a philosophical consciousness attuned to minute differences.
Then Moore introduces a particular figure whose modes of seeing might
justify the investments the poem is making. The course of his seeing
and the thinking that produces is worth citing:

> . . . The college student
> named Ambrose sits on the hillside
>   with his not native books and hat
> and sees boats
>
> at sea progress white and rigid as if in
>   a groove. Liking an elegance of which
> the source is not bravado, he knows by heart the antique
> sugar-bowl shaped summer-house of
>   interlacing slats and the pitch
> of the church
>
> spire, not true, from which a man in scarlet lets
> down a rope as spider spins a thread;
> he might be a part of a novel, but on the sidewalk a
> sign says C. J. Poole, Steeple-Jack,
>   in black and white, and one in red
> and white says
>
> Danger. The church portico has four fluted
>   columns, each a single piece of stone, made
> modester by white-wash. This would be a fit haven for
> waifs, children, animals, prisoners,
>   and presidents how have repaid
> sin-driven
>
> senators by not thinking about them. The
>   place has a school-house, a post-office in a
> store, fish-houses, hen-houses, a three-masted
>   schooner on
> the stocks. The hero, the student,
>   the steeple-jack, each in his way,
> is at home.

It could not be dangerous to be living,
   in a town like this, of simple people,
who have a steeple-jack placing danger-signs by the church
while he is gilding the solid-
   pointed star, which on a steeple
stands for hope.   (Moore, CP 6–7)

It is very difficult to get the tone right here. This closing segment of the poem can be read as the construction of an emblem establishing something like an Andrew Wyeth hymn to a rural America whose freedom from danger is in danger. But the poem can also be read as an Eliotic demand for the audience to hear the speaker as if he or she were in a play. Why is the speaker so much concerned with danger? Why is there so much reaching for moral sentiments like "Liking an elegance / of which the source is not bravado"? Why is the speaker's language so dependent on conditionals like "would" or "could"? How do these hypotheticals correlate with the theme of comfort and stability? And, finally, how do we read "the pointed star, which on a steeple / stands for hope"? What is the force of "stands for" in this poem? Are we to believe that this sign should induce hope just because it is often a conventional symbol of that state? Perhaps we should be more suspicious of the signs here, especially since the danger sign turns out to suggest the opposite: "It could not be dangerous to be living, / in a town like." Perhaps the danger consists in the agent's desire to believe such emblems, to submit to hope, and to give up the wariness that all the conditionals suggest is a basic trait for the speaker?

The poem does not answer these questions, but it poses them in such a way that we come to appreciate both what the world of this small town affords and what it conceals or occludes. I think we have to grant that the poem is sincere in its praise, since the text is very careful to have us learn to see as the townspeople see. In this respect the sympathy the poem tries to elicit by projecting a collective citizenry clearly resists modernist critique of rhetorics born of imaginary identifications. Rather than being suspicious of sentiments that forge specific communities, the poem embraces them. And it does so by what one could argue is a strategy that has learned the lessons of modernism, since Moore carefully expunges any righteous ego to reinforce or needy subject using the experience to provide illusory substance. There is a just a basic shared need concretely satisfied.

And yet we also cannot dismiss the possibility that Moore wants us to regard this hopeful resolution for the poem from a sufficient distance to think that on balance it is a dangerous fantasy. We have to grant that the emblem of the pointed star on the steeple stands for hope. But "stands for" is so troubling a phrase, so non-committal in its implicit divorce of intention from consequence. Who gets to inhabit a town like this, except in the needy imagination? And even in imagination there must be some worry about going from the construction of emblems to the testing of their support in any practical domain. It is important to see how the modern world still provides emblems for hope, but it is also important to remember why the modern world became suspicious of such emblems: modernity can almost be equated with the awareness of how much we may need illusion to live well, or at least to live confidently. Perhaps the steeple can legitimately stand for hope for the denizens of this place. But the observer fluent in conditionals and learned in Dürer's practices may have to keep her distance – while recognizing that distance need not entail outright rejection. For one rare and almost impossible moment the needs of the public and the impersonal poet's critique of the needy imaginary enter a stable yet fragile coexistence.

Chapter 4

How Modernist Poetics Failed and Efforts at Renewal: Williams, Oppen, and Hughes

Already in the preface addressed to Richard Wagner, art, and not morality, is presented as the truly metaphysical activity of man. In the book itself the suggestive sentence is repeated several times, that the existence of the world is justified only as an aesthetic phenomenon. Indeed, the whole book knows only an artistic meaning and crypto-meaning behind all events – a "god," if you please, but certainly only an entirely reckless and amoral artist god who wants to experience, whether he is building or destroying . . . his own joy and glory – one who, creating worlds, frees himself from the distress of fullness and overfullness and from the affliction of the contradictions compressed in his soul. . . . You can call this whole artists' metaphysics arbitrary, idle, fantastic; what matters is that it betrays a spirit who will one day fight at any risk whatever the moral interpretation and significance of existence.

Friedrich Nietzsche, The Birth of Tragedy[1]

Nietzsche is our greatest philosopher of aesthetic experience – primarily because he is not interested in what people typically understand as the aesthetic domain. Rather he takes the aesthetic as a model of value to be fought for in every domain of experience. Accordingly, he seems to think he has to combat the efforts to establish morality as the paradigmatic model of value in all of those domains. Moral thinking claims to know how to represent "the significance of existence," while the aesthetic domain can be characterized as the continual process of producing that significance. No wonder then that so many modernist writers treated Nietzche as a prophet as well as a philosopher, since these sentiments might serve as emblems for the commitments being forged by the arts shortly after the turn of the twentieth century. The various aesthetic movements early in the century were by no means formalist, nor were they purveyors of a distinctive ideology masking actual interests. Rather they were the allies of a new realism that imagined fidelity to sensual experience might bring to the culture a new sense of freedom and a new model of responsibility. Freedom became an arena in which each individual could establish what counted as the terms by which the person could live the most intense and self-aware life; and responsibility took the form of having to resist the normative powers transmitted by the culture's rhetorically sanctioned stances and values in order to "realize" the individual temperament. As Nietzsche predicted, the intensity produced by an art devoted to "experience" could be marshaled against the conceptually driven strictures of morality, and an ideal of individual creativity could serve as a rallying point for resistance against efforts to build communities based on shared abstract notions of responsibility and commitment.

But by 1930 such optimism seemed impossible. Eliot had converted, admitting that impersonality was at best a pale substitute for personal commitment informed by faith. Pound had finished *A Draft of Thirty Cantos* and was about to renounce modernist compression and suspicion of rhetoric for the elaborate discursive passages of his "Adams Cantos." Worse, there were lengthy silences from Loy, Moore, and, especially, from Wallace Stevens, who had made such a promising beginning with the inventive impersonality of his *Harmonium* (1922). What had happened? The worldwide Depression and resulting need for artists to confront economic issues was an obvious factor. But while elaborating social contexts obviously clarifies the situations of writers and artists, that mode of criticism has not offered sufficiently fine or intricate explanations of what those figures felt and thought as they confronted those situations. So we have to clarify how the poetry itself seems to stage the challenges. And we have to ask how the poets could find ways of facing those challenges that still promised them the right to treat their work as pursuing significant social values. Modernism had established high expectations for what an "experimental" art could contribute to social life. To maintain that level of commitment the poets would have to transform the versions of realism and impersonality on which those expectations were grounded.

I

Consider the case of William Carlos Williams as an example of how the limitations of early modernism became painfully evident. There had been no more confident modernist, reveling in how his lyrics might draw "many broken things into a dance giving them thus a full being." Dance was the means to fullness of being because this ideal for poetry freed the poet from depending on any "logical recital of events" or fidelity to the events themselves (Williams, SE 14). Poetry did not have to copy the world in order to have the effects and affects of a new realism because it could model new modes of attention, putting language and the real into elaborate consort. And because the new realism freed poetry from generalized argument and reliance on character types, it correlated beautifully with the cult of idiosyncrasy, making it possible in fact to treat this cult as a means of celebrating freedom from the constraints of authority.

Williams in particular was as devoted as Wordsworth to figures on the margins of society – not so much because they had special access to wisdom but simply because their lives were not primarily devoted to the getting and spending that were fundamental to bourgeois life. His early poems like "Tract," "To Elsie," and "Dedication for a Plot of Ground" presented an image of individual agency so bound to actual circumstances that the characters' imaginations of their own value did not seem to be dependent on the desire of others; nor did they pursue ideas of themselves that were divorced from the flux of experience. Thus "Dedication for a Plot of Ground" can present the voice of a funeral speaker convincingly insisting that "If you can bring nothing to this place / but your carcass, keep out." The praise is not for any abstract ideal the person met but for the series of concrete traits memorialized in the poem. So this poem encourages us to distinguish between work honoring an imaginary dimension bound to rhetorical ideals and work evoking an imaginative dimension capable of eliciting our empathic participation in the distinctiveness of that person's life.

Yet by *Descent of Winter* (1928) Williams seems to have felt a change in his internal balance. Constructivist poems and celebrations of individualism remain, but it seems that he had become increasingly dissatisfied with the ability of modernist methods to provide means of transforming the discipline of prose description into the intensities of lyric poetry. In 1922 *Spring and All* had managed to weave together prose and poetry by progressing from a hellish rush of associations to a triumphant constructivism in which poetry could manifest its capacity to make concrete sense of assertions that in prose bordered on gibberish.[2] *Descent of Winter* would have to pursue a very different course, because Williams seemed increasingly to distrust his capacity to align prose description of an increasingly corrupt social order with the dance promised by a vital and self-aware poetry. The opening two poems of this later volume offer celebrations of poetry's playful reconfigurations of that prose world into an evocative strangeness given vitality by intricate internal balances. But soon the poems become overburdened as the facts they want to make socially significant seem unable to satisfy a sensibility formed on constructivist values. Fact will not prove responsive to what imagination desires:

10/9   And theres a little blackboy
        in a doorway
        scratching his wrists

        The cap on his head
        is red and blue
        with a broad peak to it

        And his mouth
        is open, his tongue
        between his teeth

10/10   Monday
          the canna flaunts
        its crimson head
        crimson lying folded
        crisply down upon
          the invisible
        darkly crimson heart
        of this poor yard
        the grass is long   (Williams, CP 292–3)

These two, along with one other longer poem, force the book into a prose that has to grapple with the contradictions involved in the ambition to make a big serious portrait of my time (Williams, CP 295). For the ideal of portraiture challenges the poems to reach beyond notions of vibrant realization so that they can also express a love for the shoddy world that they address. Williams' text, however, cannot quite make sense of his conflicting passions. It can only mutter without punctuation: "and that is love there is no portrait without that has not turned to prose love is my hero who does not live, a man, but speaks of it every day" (Williams, CP 295). As what had been a poetics of presence becomes more ambitious about embracing social life, Williams finds his imagination haunted by the absence of what might transform making into loving, seeing into compassionate identification (see especially Williams, CP 298–301). Consequently this poet so absorbed by modernity now reaches back to Shakespeare for an image of what the poet can do, and for a nostalgic means of dignifying what he cannot quite accomplish in the present:

> Shakespeare had that mean ability to fuse himself with everyone which nobodies have, to be anything at any time, fluid, a nameless fellow whom nobody noticed, much, and that is what made him a great dramatist. Because he was nobody and was fluid and accessible.
>
> (Williams, CP 307)

But Williams' book cannot muster much drama. It barely breaks out of prose because the only world it can embrace turns out to be the evocation of moments from his own family history.

Williams' next book, *An Early Martyr and Other Poems* (1935), is even more bleak because the sense of limited powers intensifies into a pervasive self-disgust. The volume opens with a poem on the need for social testimony. Then it vacillates between lovely moments of lyric objectification and anxious efforts to face up to how his society was making mere objects of many of its citizens. The concluding poem "You Have Pissed your Life" turns that objectifying glance on the poet, and perhaps even on the history that initially shaped his confidence, until he has to face the possibility that his work offers nothing more than a texture of lies:

> Any way you walk
> Any way you turn
> Any way you stand

Any way you lie
You have pissed your life

From an ineffectual fool
butting his head blindly
against obstacles, become
brilliant – focusing,
performing accurately to
a given end –

Any way you walk
Any way you turn
Any way you stand
Any way you lie
You have pissed your life   (Williams, CP 401–2)

With the ambitions of poetry so emptied, the poem can offer only a series of infantilizing repetitions that virtually call out for the comforting female assurance to which he would turn in his late poems to Flossie.

II

Ultimately Williams' frustrations in 1935 cannot be separated from the hopefulness shaping the sense of perpetual beginning presented in *Spring and All*. He, like his fellow modernists, had reaped the consequences of two beliefs that had proven shaky at best. The new realism had come to seem almost indistinguishable from the old aestheticism: the cult of sensation could not satisfy the poet's desires to engage what had gone wrong in his society. And, even more disturbing, the critique of the imaginary and the rhetorical flourishes it encouraged had perhaps worked too well, since poets seemed to have rejected most of the verbal and psychological resources that might make them capable of directly rallying an audience in relation to these social issues.

We can work out the specifics of how the new realism now seemed a failure by returning to Williams' "The Young Housewife" (see p. 219, n. 31). Then we can explore the intimately related problems with modernist critiques of the imaginary through another despondent poem from a little later in the Depression, Wallace Stevens' "Cuisine

Bourgeois." "The Young Housewife" opposed both argument and narrative in order to develop what Williams thought were richer models of implication. He could refuse the categorical frameworks and habits embedded in narrative and argument by trying to capture the intricate, contingent sensations and feelings that bound housewife and observer in a distinctive event. There need be no moralizing about the event because the poem's energies were devoted to releasing the woman from bondage rather than repeating the structures that secured her husband's domination. More important, the attunement that was necessary to align the observer's smile with the woman's situation was inseparable from how the poem invited us to read it as an aesthetic object. To appreciate the situations of both agents, readers had to overcome traditional habits of judgment and fully engage in particular interactions that held out a promise of overcoming that entire logic of ownership. Poetry seemed to have an epistemology of its own that reinforced what the new science was teaching about replacing substance by event, matter by manner.

The young modernists did not see that a poetry so free of traditional argumentative and narrative modes of judgment could be very easily marginalized, even by those who accepted the claims of the new realism. Sensations were easy to separate from objects, and, more important, from the historical situations that gave weight to the objects. When poets cannot trust narrative and argumentative forms of coherence but turn instead to the capacity of juxtaposition to hold together the poem's subtle and diffuse sensations, coherence in fact depends completely on the agency that confers distinctive aesthetic form on those materials. But then the more individualist the sources of coherence, and the more complex and delicate the sensations foregrounded by poetry, the easier it was to doubt whether such work was sufficiently serious and sufficiently worldly to engage the kinds of suffering that were the daily bread of the mass media. As we see now in many poets' reactions to the 2003 war in Iraq, the intricacies of subjectivity can pale in significance in relation to quite public shared emotions of outrage and helplessness.[3]

A poetry responsive to such public emotions probably requires strong rhetorical traditions. But poets had learned too well the lessons taught by Eliot, Pound, and Loy. They had developed sensitive ears painfully aware of the false notes played by most discourse that turned from private meditation to public address, so the most intense public passions seemed the most dangerous. They wanted to adapt the resources rhetoric provides for lyric poetry, but they could not escape accompanying feelings of self-disgust. Yet Eliot's critique of imaginary identifications seemed now to fare no better. There seemed no valid way to distinguish between what was genuinely impersonal or transpersonal and what was only a desperate mask in which the impersonal only staged another version of the individual will to power. Poets could easily imitate Eliot's excessive self-consciousness. But they could not keep this self-consciousness from devouring the very stances that Eliot thought could provide an alternative to rhetorical appeals idealizing communal values.

This devastating self-consciousness was nowhere more striking than in the disgust Wallace Stevens soon came to feel towards his *Owl's Clover*, a set of poems invoking all the resources of rhetoric to address the crisis that the Depression posed. He would not reprint those poems, probably because he thought the work was too direct and too moralistic in invoking a collective identity, without a sufficient ironic distance and speculative self-questioning. Or so I argue in my *Painterly Abstraction*. Now that argument will become a backdrop for the discussion of a much shorter poem expressing a similar attitude toward idealization. This poem is "Cuisine Bourgeois," written a few years after *Owl's Clover*:

> These days of disinheritance, we feast
> On human heads. True, birds rebuild
> Old nests and there is blue in the woods.
> The church bells clap one night in the week.
> But that's all done. It is what it used to be,
> As they used to lie in the grass, in the heat,
> Men on green beds and women half of the sun.
> The words are written though not yet said.
>
> It is like the season when, after summer,
> It is summer and it is not, it is autumn
> And it is not, it is day and it is not.
> As if last night's lamps continued to burn,
> As if yesterday's people continued to watch
> The sky, half porcelain, preferring that
> To shaking out heavy bodies in the glares
> Of this present, this science, this unrecognized,

This outpost, this douce, this dumb, this dead, in which
We feast on human heads, brought in on leaves,
Crowned with the first, cold buds. On these we live,
No longer on the ancient cake of seed,
The almond and the deep fruit. This bitter meat
Sustains us . . . Who then are they seated here?
Is the table a mirror in which they sit and look?
Are they men eating reflections of themselves?[4]

That distance between what self-consciousness projects and any independent content that might sustain significant values generates a profound sense of disgust with everything human.

The modernist dream of composing expressive particulars now becomes a nightmare in which those particulars offer only the feeling of disinheritance. The "this" so triumphant in early Williams now presents a world haunted by what cannot find expression in the present. For here particularity offers nothing but a sense of distance between these pure objects and the humans aware that they have only been projecting versions of themselves onto the objects they care about. The present can appear only in terms of what is not, what mocks it by contrast. Even when the speaker tries elaborate rhetorical similes, the figures do not create new meaning but waver between locations and become reabsorbed into the past. No wonder the present is reduced to the "bitter meat" of having to sustain the self on mere reflections of what proves merely fictive. Figurative speech comes down to recognizing the impossibility of any imaginative figure bringing a mode of sustenance that is not a reminder of human impotence. The heads become objects eliciting disgust for all they cannot produce as subjects.

My efforts to paraphrase this poem cannot capture its remarkably straightforward bitterness and unrelieved bleakness about human creativity. But I can help contextualize the poem by suggesting that we think about the four "Worthies" on the mantle of Thomas Jefferson's study in Monticello. Jefferson said he wanted to imagine those figures – Aristotle, Plato, Voltaire, and Benjamin Franklin – looking over everything he wrote so that he would try to live up to the expectations he projected upon them. This faith in the embodied force of personal example is humanism at its most potent. In contrast, if we were to imagine Stevens writing this poem in his study, the four heads would be without identities and so incapable of providing inspiration.

Yet their presence would be strongly felt – as reminders that he too is probably bound to illusions constitutive of humanism. So their presence would embody the poem's frustratingly empty "this" that registers only facts in a series of other mere facts. The only imagination these heads can foster is a sense of lack, a gulf between the image and the mere fact that serves mainly to represent the neediness of the believer.

III

"Cuisine Bourgeois" marks the same kind of dead end as Williams' "You Have Pissed your Life." Both poets never stopped trying other modes. But this despondency is distinctive, and I think haunts even their more positive efforts at reasserting modernist values. For they indicate a fear that when the new realism could no longer produce a fresh sense of experience, the lyrical situations staged by intricate sensations began to seem unnecessarily precious. Poets had to look on the investments formed by modernist values with an increasingly jaundiced eye: lyricism itself could be seen as offering little but fantasized escapes from the literal and figurative poverty that surrounds us. Most of the poets responsive to this situation explored three basic options. They could repudiate the example of Eliot and Pound to pursue a more populist poetry oriented toward social issues; they could readapt the new realism to serve as an instrument capable of addressing specific social conditions; or they could shift focus by concentrating on articulating the powers and the limitations of speaking voices that had been oppressed in their society.

Obviously these are crude categories, so there will be difficulties placing particular poems in any one set. But they serve my purposes in two ways. They acknowledge the rationale driving many poets to return to the old representational and typological realism in their effort to engage social injustice. And they do so in a way that enables me to make distinctions between that kind of poetry and poetry more responsive to modernist innovations while also addressing the social crises made pressing in the 1930s. I desperately need this distinction because I have nothing useful to say about the first group of poets. They do not engage my hunger for philosophical resonance or my interests in the display of distinctive writerly intelligence. Nonetheless it would be remiss of me to ignore this aspect of American poetry entirely, so I will begin by addressing contemporary scholarship that makes a heroic case for their significance. Then I shall turn to the poetry that I think pursued much the same politics by absorbing and transforming modernist principles so that the resources of the lyric might be adapted to those political commitments. These poets morphed the new realism in two directions, each offering a way to provide a figurative conscience for sensation by reorienting the satisfactions possible from an emphasis on the poet's constructive activity. One direction consists of the Objectivist poets' efforts to make the ideal of "measure" derived from Pound and Williams implicate social sympathies without the aid of conventional rhetorical gestures; the other is evident in Langston Hughes' distinctive and exciting insistence that realism can focus less on what is described than on the social forces shaping the voices that do the describing. In the relevant poems by Hughes, "measure" emerges in how agents come to terms with their intense and sharp awareness of social reality.

First, then, a few words on the kind of poetry on which I have to be silent and on Cary Nelson, the most powerful critic attempting to do justice to this work. Not only is Nelson a learned and passionate advocate of this work, but his writing is also so capacious and intense that it virtually demands a response from those critics who persist in the hierarchical models he condemns.[5] For Nelson and those sharing his views, the influence of high modernism has produced a canon that smooths out diversity and marginalizes twentieth-century poetry's attempt to address mass audiences.[6] This influence leads us to ignore how traditional forms became employed for "sharply focused social commentary", especially in the work of Harlem Renaissance poets like Claude Mckay and Countee Cullen, and we therefore do not take seriously how a populist art can clarify judgments about social life and muster support for particular values. For example, Nelson shows how this song by Joe Hill developed the subversive aim of emptying "out the conservative, sentimental, or patriotic values of the existing songs while replacing them with radical impulses":[7]

Long-haired preachers come out every night,
Try to tell you what's wrong and right,
But when asked how 'bout something to eat
They will answer with voices so sweet:

You will eat, bye and bye,
In that glorious land above the sky,
Work and pray and live on hay,
You'll get pie in the sky when you die.[8]

More generally, Nelson argues that critics should keep in productive tension the historical impulse to document the various ways poets have used their art, and the canonical impulse to make hierarchies in relation to idealized functions that it thought art should provide. Then in his later book *Revolutionary Memory* Nelson specifies two basic appreciative approaches for "thinking about American poetry of the Left": the combination of biography and history to clarify the situations poems were intended to address, and the values of "community and continuity" as the explicit goal of much of that work: "A collective literature is a destination and an overriding value; it triumphs over the individual voice."[9] Ultimately, disputes about aesthetic matters are a basic means of carrying out fundamental conflicts over cultural values.

I grant that no responsible critic now can make a convincing case that the hierarchies of literary values produced in the triumphant years of the New Criticism are somehow "natural," and so grounded in human nature or in how particular poets manage to realize some essential literary properties. I even agree that many contemporary readers will prefer this populist poetry. But the case that arguments cannot be sanctioned by nature does not mean that they cannot find support in other ways, and popular taste need not determine the values of those with professional commitments to shaping that taste. And, more important, the shape of popular taste is a fact that has to be taken into account, but the accounting need not contour itself to the dominant values – especially when critics are teachers and so charged with modifying that taste, if only by explaining alternative values. In particular I want to elaborate two ways in which I can contrast my own modernist values to this populist work. First I think Nelson is dangerously sanguine about the possible balancing of the claims by literary historians and by those devoted to forming canons that idealize individual insight, capaciousness of imagination, and mastery of the medium – perhaps because he seems to think that just recognizing the nature of the cultural struggles involved would make primarily aesthetic arguments for poetry crumble, trumped by the obviously superior social consciousness of their opponents. Second, I will pose the more concrete argument that Nelson's expectations about the cultural force poetry can wield seem to me both limited and askew.

The rhetorical weight is on his side. It is difficult to oppose values like "balance" and giving history its due. Yet I cannot avoid the conviction that in this case the impulse to literary history and the impulse to canonization are contradictories, not contraries, so they can never be reconciled. This obviously does not mean that either mode of work should be somehow disqualified. It only means that each is best done when it keeps its independent focus. Literary history seeks inclusion, seeks to bring awareness to the range of writing at a given time and to effects that work has within this time period. The canon-making impulse, on the other hand, has to view texts for their significance beyond the time in which they were produced. For the historian what matters is preserving what is otherwise lost to the long view; for the canon-maker what matters is the little that may survive. The two stances should interact but we cannot expect them to agree or even hear one another very well. One could of course argue that the canon-makers should be governed by the capacity of texts to bear witness to a given historical time. But even then it is difficult not to ask how the text bears witness, or how the witnessing is distinctive. And with these questions again come issues of what deserves to survive and how that survival is involved with the ability to develop the art of poetry.

More concretely, I think the best literary work not only documents historical interests but provides plausible models for how to understand and respond to the structures of experience basic to a given period of time. The works Nelson praises rely for the most part on traditional rhetoric for their control of affect, and on representational realism for their social content. Poems like Joe Hill's can do a good job of mobilizing social energies at a given time, but very few of those poems show how the resources of the lyric can help produce models of social agency capable of challenging the modes of identification sustained by traditional rhetoric. There is an important difference between poetry that addresses society by articulating attitudes towards social agendas and poetry that addresses society by experimenting with what in this chapter I will call "providing measures for experience." If the critique issued by the poets I have been trying to represent is telling, the poems Nelson praises are dangerously retrograde in their ways of addressing modernity, despite their obvious good intentions. A spirit of experiment matters in poetry because a healthy society has to worry not only about negotiating direct claims concerning social welfare but also about the best way of securing the instruments by which we think about that welfare. That securing process may well involve cultivating individual abilities to make complex judgments that challenge communal values and try out alternative ways of modeling how agents might enact commitments to social welfare. This period provided strong examples of such writing in the work of the Objectivist poets because, while they considered themselves communists, they worried that poetry and society would suffer if poets simply identified with populist judgments of contemporary society. In their eyes politics seemed to make demands that lyric could not meet, and the lyric proved too distinctive in its intricacies to be an adequate tool for political change. So they built their poetry on a critique of the rhetorical principles that in Hill's song sought to foster collective interests. The Objectivists relied less on the specific political values called for by the represented situation than on the way the author could emphasize the capacity of a particular stance to foster concrete sympathies and to forge surprising angles on causes of suffering.

The label "Objectivist" was first offered by Louis Zukofsky in a famous 1931 essay "Sincerity and Objectivity." He was thinking of his own poetry as well as that of Charles Reznikoff, George Oppen, and Carl Rakosi, with Lorraine Niedecker soon to join the group. No one was completely happy with the term, but it provided a very useful way of blending a Marxist sense of materialist inquiry with a commitment to modernist realism averse to the temptation to allegorize endemic to the social realist writers. As Oppen put it, Objectivist poets "attempt to construct meaning, to construct a method of thought from the imagist technique of poetry – from the imagist intensity of vision."[10] That intensity of vision could become politically forceful because, in Zukofsky's terms, sensation then could be charged with "honesty and intelligence."[11] Poets could build sensation on sensation so that they did not have to represent or narrate the social scene. Rather they could try to evoke charged moments that provided a "measure" embedding political judgment within the sense of event created by the particular poem. "Measure" was the product of a will to form that was also a will to justice, to weighing particular sensations so that they established complex experiences that might serve as testimony to the difficulties of living under what capitalism had become.

Zukofsky attributed two significantly new shared traits to how Objectivist writing pursued this sense of measure. The first principle was "sincerity," the second "objectivity."[12] Those principles are quite general, but it took this combination of precision and vagueness to establish a common vision among practitioners with quite diverse talents and interests. (Zukofsky had not studied the Talmud for nothing.) "Sincerity" for Zukofsky is decidedly not the promise of authentification by a personal voice, where poetry's claim to truth is in the intensity of belief.[13] Etymologically "sincere" refers to a condition of being without wax, so the Objectivists understood that term to provide an emblem for unadorned writing that resisted all overt rhetorical gestures. That resistance meant the Objectivists would insist first of all on poetry acknowledging the manifest labors of writing and not giving the illusion that poetry captured living speech. Sincerity is not primarily a property of the psyche or "beautiful soul." Sincerity is manifest in how writing manages to establish "the detail not the mirage, of seeing, of thinking with things as they exist, and of directing them along a line of melody" (*Prepositions*, 12). As Oppen put it, sincerity was a commitment to making the "substantive" articulate so that the poet would not rush "over the subject matter to make a comment about it."[14]

"Sincerity" mattered as an ideal then because it seemed to establish practical principles that clearly involved moral commitments. Even though the term for Zukofsky was resolutely resistant to psychological concerns about the expressive ego, it retained the force of Pound's insistence on the character of the speaker as someone willing to stand by his or her word. "Sincerity" did not have to call up a domain of inner truths because it could refer simply to a person's manifest willingness to accept responsibility for a particular way of rendering the world. How the world is presented defines what matters about the subject. Peter Nichols expands this point beautifully by connecting it to Emmanuel Levinas on ethics. "The ethical subject" becomes someone dialectically situated in a relation where "one is exposed to the claims of others"[15] and responsible to those claims. There is more to the fabric of realism for social life than social realism dreams on because claims about the truth are less important than working out how one will regard the agents attempting to make such judgments.[16]

Zukofsky on objectification nicely complements this vision of the subject's responsibilities:

> An objective; (Optics) – The lens bringing rays from an object to a focus. (Military use) – That which is aimed at. (Use extended to poetry) – Desire for what is objectively perfect, inextricably the direction of historic and contemporary particulars. (*Prepositions*, 12)

All three of these meanings are crucial if we want to distinguish how the Objectivists understood the possibilities of transforming the new realism without falling into the traps of Imagism.[17] The metaphor of the lens ties the poet's truth claim about what is seen to a specifiable way of seeing. Yet this emphasis on perspective does not entail subjectivism. Quite the contrary, since the lens is itself a material object as determinate and determining for individual subjects as the most obdurate fact. So the figure of the lens is both liberating, since there can always be new angles of vision, and constraining, since the poetry must testify to what other agents can replicate if they occupy the proposed perspectival position. The military meaning reinforces the idea that focusing through a lens has a purpose beyond the display of a poet's sensibility. There is something to be known. In a 1933 letter to *Poetry* Zukofsky defended his "Objectivist Anthology against the charge of cultural elitism" by proposing that "the poem is 'the strictly objective estimate' of social forces" – hence his claim about the direction of historic and contemporary particulars. However, that objectivity is fully realized only if the poet can make subjects feel the satisfaction of achieving knowledge – hence the distinctively poetic meaning. The poems afford complex "linguistic 'inter-relation'" intended to make readers work hard before they see how the object takes form.[18] The objective in poetry manifests "a desire to place everything – everything aptly, perfectly, belonging within, one with, a context" (*Prepositions*, 15).

For Zukofsky the ultimate measure of this perfecting of the object becomes the poem's capacity to establish musical form – as if the poem could reveal historical truth made singable by the intensity of its apperception. Other poets would take "measure" in a more ethical or political sense. For Reznikoff measure became the capacity to treat facts as testimony. Niedecker never entirely renounced her interest in surreal means of staging those relationships.[19] And Oppen gave "perfection" a constructivist reading consistent with his desire to build a method of thought from Imagist practice. For him the poem constructs "a meaning . . . from moments of conviction," in such a way that the poem also manifestly stands by itself as a composed and measured object.[20]

It may be perceived as an odd choice to cite Zukofsky almost exclusively in setting up Objectivist theory, then to demonstrate the power of the theory by concentrating on three poems by Oppen. But Zukofsky's intricate poetry is an acquired taste and difficult for me to deal with in a concise way. Oppen has proved the more interesting poet to most contemporaries, partly because his commitment to "historic and contemporary particulars" provides a more obviously social sense of measure than the one driving Zukofsky's poetry.

Born in 1908 to a successful family, George Oppen grew up in a different class from the other Objectivists, most of whom shared typical immigrant circumstances. He and his wife, Mary, lived a vagabond life, George working mostly as a carpenter. After *Discrete Series* (1934), he published no poetry until 1962 because he felt that he had to choose between political action and the life of a poet. (Being a "Marxist poet" seemed for him an impossible choice because the domains involved in each name were utterly different from each other.)

Oppen considered *Discrete Series* distinctive because it combined the formal structure of sequential analysis with an insistence on evocation by careful description. A pure mathematical series derives its particulars from formal structures, but in a discrete series each particular must function on its own while still forming an element in a coherent whole[21] (John Shoptaw offers the example of the street numbers of stops on a New York City subway[22]). So the series can offer a complex image of social relations that can speak for itself without any interpretive rhetoric. Poem 27 seems to illustrate this ambition by providing an especially keen act of attention, very simple yet generating considerable thought:

> It brightens up into the branches
> And against the same buildings
>
> A morning:
> His job is as regular. (NCP 31)

At first the sun's regularity may seem reassuring, and ultimately that reassurance will matter even more as we also come to appreciate the dark side of this regularity. For the poem also measures an important difference between recurrence in nature and the pain of "regularity" in human lives.

The affective force of the poem depends on small observations establishing significant differences between recurrence in nature and the pain of "regularity" in human lives. First, we have to notice that the human presence occurs only as a reference to his job, not to any feature of consciousness or subjectivity. The subjectivity can be inferred, but only because we realize that the regularity of the job and the path to work is precisely what excludes any more elaborate sense of self. This person is mired in routine. The second observation is more formal, more clearly a relational "measure" for assessing the lives that the poem may represent. Oppen wants us to notice that what seems the least important word in the poem, "same," actually is not filler but establishes the poem's dramatic fulcrum. In one sense "same" is almost an afterthought, registering satisfaction with the sun's daily arrival. But when one adds the perspective of the person for whom "job is as regular," the recurrence is a basic feature of the oppression, all the more painful because "same" now forces us to treat the social as swallowing nature and shaping the feelings associated with it. This appropriation in turn makes compression itself a powerful alternative to rhetoric. So much depends on so little, on merely what "same" can mean from two different perspectives. There emerges then a third perspective when one realizes ironically that at least the protagonist can rely on nature's recurrence, so this regularity may be an important value in a world where one can easily lose one's job.

For more elaborate versions of Oppen's sense of "measure" at work, one has to turn to his poems published in the 1960s. "Street" establishes a complex grasp of social situations that goes a long way toward explaining why the Objectivists rejected the more rhetorical statements of sympathy typical of the social realist poets:

Ah these are the poor,
These are the poor –

Bergen Street.

Humiliation,
Hardship . . . ,

Nor are they very good to each other;
It is not that. I want

An end of poverty
As much as anyone

For the sake of intelligence,
"The conquest of existence" –

It has been said, and is true –

And this is real pain,
Moreover. It is terrible to see the children,

The righteous little girls;
So good, they expect to be so good . . .   (NCP 127; ellipses original)

This poem addresses the fundamental question of how one can speak about poverty without displacing the narrative of one's pity into a mode of self-congratulation for one's own sensitivity. That is why the tone is so intricate and subtle. The poem begins by facing the opposite problem: how can one continue to sympathize with the poor if one actually concentrates on the lives they lead. The poor are probably not even very good to each other, so why should an observer want to be good to them? With this realization, the speaker's desire for self-congratulation seems frustrated and he just stops looking at particulars. He shifts to trying out for himself the postures that comprise the middle of the poem. But fleeing the reality of poverty turns out to lead the speaker to a more acute rendering of the situation, making possible what we might call a "responsible pity."

That responsible pity depends on appreciating a remarkably apt observation about the poor: "The righteous little girls; / So good, they expect to be so good." The female children of the poor share with the better-off the dream that they can be good and that the goodness will somehow be rewarded. This is the mark of their irreducible humanity. But this optimism is doomed to fail, for the poor are not sufficiently in control of their own lives to realize such dreams. The girls will soon be among those who are not very good to one another. That is the mark of their existence under capitalism, a mark so visible that the poem need not even mention the economic realities.

Yet that sense of inevitable failure also frames the possibility of a speakable sympathy that does not ignore the reality and does not settle for piety. To develop this sympathy Oppen makes distinctive use of a means of realization basic to modernist visual art. He makes us cut through the level of illusion or scene, the level in this poem of trying to find a way to speak, so that we feel ourselves identifying not with the speaker but with how the authorial process deploys its constructive energies. Oppen's first step is to invite our realizing that our empathy with the girls is based on our knowing what they do not know. We know their fate, know that most of them will not be able to be "good," at least by bourgeois standards. We also know why Oppen singles out the girls: the older people and young males have already internalized the despair that the reader comes to feel. So the more we let ourselves explore what our own understanding of expectations brings to this poem, the richer our sense of its political urgency.

But even that evocation of political urgency is not sufficient to exhaust the poem's power. For Oppen is not simply interested in his audience's recognizing the plight of the poor. He is also concerned with the problems of finding an adequate way to render sympathy and so dispose the will of those who find themselves in the observer position. That disposing of the will is the work primarily of the form that establishes a verbal means of "measuring" poverty. Our first observation about that form is that it seems to exhibit its own mode of poverty, at least if one measures it by conventional rhetorical effusions. Oppen wants us to realize that saying more about the girls would risk returning to the world where their concrete differences from us either dispel sympathy or allow us to be patronizing. More speech here would cover over the poem's painful realization of the gulf between how easy it is to sympathize with the girls and how hard it is to turn that sympathy into any kind of political action. And more speech would risk repeating social pieties and producing a self-congratulation that blinds us to the realities. So he has to take the chance that the reader will recognize that by refusing to offer more speech the poem defines a significant mode of agency. By feeling the limitations of speech, the audience is in a position to take on a kind of responsibility for the painful knowledge they encounter. Recognizing the limits of "sincere" speech is a first step toward an effective sympathy with the kinds of constraints inescapable in a warped social order. And because the poem provides terms for understanding the very situation the reading produces, we have the consolation of hoping that, in sharing the intricate form of frustrated sympathy produced by the reading, we are at least glimpsing the prospect of how the social group formed by the readers might not hide from the reality as the speaker initially tried to do. Measure establishes a formal order that seems to emerge not from some imposed framework, some generalizing interpretation, but from the specific ways that the poem brings into an internal balance the range of perceptions, desires, and the contradictory impulses with which the readers have to deal.[23]

Oppen is a powerful social poet, but he is not only a social poet. Objectivist realism cuts two ways – toward contextualizing social situations and toward treating the "real" as an independent ontological value to be celebrated in its own right. This second dimension is striking in Oppen's "Eclogue," the first poem of *The Materials* (1962):

The men talking
Near the room's center. They have said
More than they had intended.

Pinpointing in the uproar
Of the living room

An assault
On the quiet continent.

Beyond the window
Flesh and rock and hunger

Loose in the night sky
Hardened into soil

Tilting of itself to the sun once more, small
Vegetative leaves
And stems taking place

Outside – O small ones,
To be born.   (NCP 39)

Thematically and performatively this poem faces the challenge of attributing significant power to the smallness with which it concludes.[24] So Oppen from the start establishes a fundamental opposition between the boasting talk that the poem describes and the specific process of concentration that it eventually embodies. Confronting the arrogant male imaginations with which it begins, the poem has to define values available in the space beyond the window that confines these imaginations. But Oppen also has to be careful not to transcendentalize that beyond. His beyond is not sublime, not the space of the infinite other, but of concrete potential to be born if consciousness learns to attend to something occluded by rhetorical performance.

This interest in what can be present at the margins of the room is far too narrow to satisfy the expansive speakers who open the poem. That expansiveness is blind to the values framed by the scene and visible to the reader, who is invited to shift attention to what does not speak. This shift then opens the reader to the poem's final paradox, that only what does not speak can in fact bear the multiple meanings of that final phrase: "To be born" functions as a future indicative, as an exclamation, and as a punning participial phrase indicating the pain inseparable from this kind of birth.

This, one might say, is the story presented by the poem. But we have not read the poem carefully until we can also say how the actual utterance, or the performance, provides an embodied formal measure concretely establishing the force for that story. In effect form is a crucial element in resisting the tendency of thematic criticism to seek a place near the center of the room where the men can keep talking. There are two distinctive formal patterns at work. At the center of the poem, the fourth stanza establishes the poem's basic transition from the room to what lies beyond the window. However, were Oppen to rely on only this one structural principle, the poem as measure would be too pat. It would capture a basic opposition but not give dynamic force to the sense of release promised by the concluding figure of birth. So he also composes a very different formal dynamics based on stanza lengths. The first and the sixth stanza are three-line units; the other stanzas have only two lines. Semantically this pattern allows the two stanzas presenting different modes of expansiveness to echo one another. But the more important effects of this pattern redistribute the energies of the poem as a whole by countering the force of the central fourth stanza. The longer sixth stanza seems to provide another pivot by setting up an apparent closure that in fact turns out to guarantee the final stanza its own place beyond the frames. This formal device highlights the liberating effect of the multiple meanings and so provides concrete sustenance for the conclusion's sense of new beginnings available within the natural world.

IV

Langston Hughes was born in 1902 in Missouri (apparently *the* birthplace of major modernist poets). Eventually he moved with his mother and stepfather to Cleveland, then enrolled at Columbia in New York City. There he became a leading figure in the Harlem Renaissance, but one could argue that he did not develop a fully distinctive lyric style until about 1940. His early work relies on a public sententiousness made lyrical by somewhat stagey concluding images. This is "Dreams" (1923):

> Hold fast to dreams
> For if dreams die
> Life is a broken-winged bird
> That cannot fly
> Hold fast to dreams
> For when dreams go
> Life is a barren field
> Frozen with snow.[25]

Even when he turns to race, for example in "Young Prostitute" (also 1923), the poetry tends to emphasize figural description:

> Her dark brown face
> Is like a withered flower
> On a broken stem
> Those kind come cheap in Harlem
> So they say. (Hughes, CP 32)

As is typical in Hughes' early work, this poem relies on conjoining the richness of figural presence with a tone that is pervasively ironic and distanced in relation to white culture. But there is no active principle capable of reversing the judgments typical of this culture. The issue of who measures "cheapness" is clearly raised here, but there is not much indication that there can be significant other voices capable of reinterpreting the dominant values. Notice the very different attitude toward language and toward action in his later work like "Evenin' Air Blues" (1941):

Folks, I come up North
Cause they told me de North was fine.
I come up North
Cause they told me de North was fine.
Been up here six months –
I'm about to lose my mind.

This mornin' for breakfast
I chawed the mornin' air
This mornin' for breakfast
Chawed the mornin' air.
But this evenin' for supper,
I got evenin' air to spare.

Believe I'll do a little dancin'
Just to drive my blues away –
A little dancin'
To drive my blues away,
Cause when I'm dancin'
De blues forgets to stay.

But if you was to ask me
How de blues they come to be,
Says if you was to ask me
How de blues they come to be –
You wouldn't need to ask me:
Just look at me and see!   (Hughes, CP 225)

Hughes gets better at a black idiom, but that concern with idiom was there from the start. The big difference is in how he creates an aura of realism sustaining the call for alternative value frameworks. Like the Objectivists, he now does not rely on elaborate analogical images. And there is no effort to establish depth of feeling by relying on conventional sentimental gestures or on straightforwardly ironic treatments of public language. Nor is there any of the Objectivist's effort to intensify his experience by relying on intricate and subtle patterns. Hughes feels he can distinguish himself from the social realist poets simply by the way he presents the activity of his speakers. These presentations are not quite ironic, except in relation to how a white audience might hear the speaker. But the speaker is not exposed as having false consciousness. Quite the opposite actually. The poem depends on our seeing how effectively and precisely the speaking captures an experience and avoids any escapist tendencies. The speaking as performance provides a measure of both social need and social possibility. Because there is no self-staging on the part of the poet, no effort to make judgments of those speakers, the work does not have to worry about the pressure of the imaginary. In fact what is not said, or not able to be said, is often more evocative than the images that can enter speech.

The conclusion of "Evenin' Air Blues" is so compelling because it explicitly repudiates any interpretation not focused on the conditions of the speaking. The old realist would have to provide directions about what to see; the modernist new realist would demand a special kind of attention to an object that rendered complex relations among aspects of the object. Hughes, too, has his complex relations, but the speaking of them is almost the entire point. There is the speaker's sense of what his poverty and hunger make obvious. And the ending reaches out to include the fact that the speaker is dancing despite that poverty – that is how the blues do cultural work and how they last as a cultural institution.

For Hughes then this reliance on sight is not a failure of language nor evidence of some presence with a sublimity beyond language. Constantly refusing the temptations to say more than what the poem can show becomes a means of convincing us that the poetry has direct access to truth. Invoking plain sight in a poem stems from a confidence that one has got the situation right, and from a sense that the situation matters sufficiently to make one resist any straining to make things poetic. The combination of seeing accurately and speaking concisely triumphs over any need for rhetorical supplements. That is why Hughes is such a master of the very short poem, despite his refusal to imitate Pound's elegant Imagistic jewels. It is as if what had been lacking in Afro-American culture was primarily a faith that such speaking could make visible its vitality and its hard wisdom.

As evidence of my claims about the power of Hughes' realism I offer two superbly concise, yet resonant, lyrics. The first is "Little Lyric (of Great Importance)":

I wish the rent
Was heaven sent.   (Hughes, CP 226)

Part of the little drama here is finding a rhyme for "rent" that will keep the two-beat rhythm and still say something significant. The rhyme Hughes comes up with manages at once to capture the constant pressure of having to pay the rent and the wistful self-awareness that help is not in the offing. Heaven is the least likely source of relief, and that, we realize, is a measure of hopelessness handled without lament. Additional words might bring more pathos but no greater clarity and considerably less strength of character in the speaking.

"Subway Rush Hour" is more complex:

Mingled
breath and smell
so close
mingled
black and white
so near
no room for fear.   (Hughes, CP 423)

Here the poetic economy emphasizes the internal assonance of the move from "so" to "no," combined with the sudden emergence of rhyme, as if once the line expanded to four syllables there had to be some kind of anchor. Again more words would substantially decrease the tension. On one level the poem is an effort at optimism. By stressing sensations of proximity between the whites and blacks in this situation, the poem seems to provide evidence that there is "no room for fear" on anyone's part. But "no room for fear" is not exactly an equivalent for "no reason for fear." Even the mention of "no room for fear" can be taken as a reminder that fear is almost inescapable when such culturally charged differences are forced into spaces where the agents cannot express negative emotions.

These motifs of seeing and speaking take on more of a political and moral charge when they are seen against the backdrop of Hughes' concern for the parties that can and cannot exercise the power of language. (Rhetorical poetry then becomes a white indulgence to be combated by the leanest possible oppositional writing.) Consider the range of speaking positions asserted and implied in "Ballad of the Landlord":

Landlord, landlord,
My roof has sprung a leak.
Don't you 'member I told you about it
Way last week?

Landlord, landlord,
These steps is broken down.
When you come up yourself
It's a wonder you don't fall down.

Ten Bucks you say I owe you?
Ten Bucks you say is due?
Well that's ten bucks more'n I'll pay you
Till you fix this house up new.

What you gonna get eviction orders?
You gonna cut off my heat?
You gonna take my furniture and
Throw it in the street?

Um-huh! You talking high and mighty,
Talk on – till you get through.
You ain't gonna be able to say a word
If I land my fist on you.

Police! Police!
Come and get this man!
He's trying to ruin the government
And overturn the land!

Copper's whistle!
Patrol bell!
Arrest.
Precinct Station.

Iron cell.
Headlines in press:

MAN THREATENS LANDLORD

TENANT HELD NO BAIL

JUDGE GIVES NEGRO 90 DAYS IN COUNTY JAIL.
                                        (Hughes, CP 402–3)

There are four modes of language striving for power. Two occupy the consciousness of the black speaker – first the statement of complaint, and then his actual silencing as the poem turns to a third-person rendering of the facts of his arrest. The other two modes of language evoke the sites of social power – the landlord's own ability to call the police to his aid in a civil dispute, and the newspaper's erasure of all psychology and most of the facts as it reduces the event to a completely generic story. The triumph of that story, unalloyed, becomes the best possible evidence of pain caused by society's inability to hear the voices of those that differ from the dominant order.[26]

For my last poem from Hughes I have chosen an example that I hope integrates my various themes. "Harlem [1]" establishes a particular situation in which the "I" becomes a collective "we" and the speech distinctive to that "we" requires a frightening awareness of what can only be shown but not said. What makes Harlem a coherent speech community is largely the self-awareness that consists in recognizing that it is only the others in America who can speak with any confidence about the future:

Here on the edge of hell
Stands Harlem –
Remembering the old lies
The old kicks in the back,
The old "be patient"
They told us before.

Sure, we remember.
Now when the man at the corner store
Says sugar's gone up another two cents,
And bread one,
And there's a new tax on cigarettes –

We remember the job we never had.
Never could get,
And can't have now
Because we're colored.

So we stand here
On the edge of hell
In Harlem
And look out on the world
And wonder
What we're gonna do
In the face of what we
We remember.   (Hughes, CP 363–4)

The convincing use of "we" here might be the envy of most white poets, although none of them probably would be willing to pay the price of entry to such community. But Hughes has no choice – that is another feature of his "we." To speak poetically as a realist in Harlem is to confine oneself to what will bear witness to such memories. One has to find strength in the willingness, not pretend to know anything more than will sustain living speech. Such speech is the only way Hughes can establish how poetry can measure some of the consequences of oppression driven by racial prejudice.

Chapter 5

The Return to Rhetoric in Modernist Poetry: Stevens and Auden

Instead of allegory,
We have and are the man
Wallace Stevens, "Examination of the Hero in a Time of War"[1]

Any realist aesthetic, old or new, must rely on some notion of representation, some notion of how the given work stands for something important in the world where we must act. But there are two entirely different paths for representing representation, with very different implications. One lineage emphasizes a pictorial sense of "represent" by which a realist text functions almost in the same way a proposition does: it holds a verbal picture up to the world and tests its adequacy. The other lineage comes from politics, where representation is not a matter of truth at all but of function. In this domain successful representation is a matter of managing identifications with the interests of a given constituency.

When we recognize these alternative paths, we also are in a position to recognize why issues of rhetoricity plague efforts to establish a stable and effective realism. For it is very easy for writers and artists to think they are providing pictures of the real when in fact they are relying on rhetorical devices that facilitate identifications with specific constituencies. The problem then is not just blurring a distinction between what we might call science and politics, but also confusing what rewards impersonal seeing and what depends on efforts at manipulation, however well intended. As we have seen, the felt need to avoid such confusion led the first generation of Anglo-American modernists to try the radical alternative of insisting that art did not refer to the world but made worlds that could exemplify significant values. These writers thought they could escape the temptation to confuse rhetoric with description by insisting on an impersonality that evaded palpable designs on an audience or projections about authorial identity.

I think Oppen and Hughes worked out a powerful alternative by imagining how the picturing function and the efforts at political representation could be fused. The key concept for both figures was an ideal of "measure." In Oppen's social poetry the sense of picturing the real is supplemented by occupying the will with producing the internal balances that establish possible significance for a community. The rhetorical interests of the will are not denied but redirected. The value of one perception is measured not by how the writer describes the world but by how various perceptions are made to fit with other perceptions. Then the fit among perceptions can provide a sense that seeing and evaluating are completely congruent activities. The care exhibited in rendering and fitting perceptions flows into a concern for what they compose. So Oppen's realism can be sharply distinguished from the social realism of the poets in *The Masses* because the use value of the text is not as a picture made socially relevant by invoking something approaching allegorical typologies. The use value has nothing to do with conventional pictures of villains and heroes, suffering maidens and noble knights. Rather the text approaches the real because the readers can see how it can be continuous with their efforts to evaluate as they perceive.

Hughes makes the conditions of speaking play the same immediate evaluative role that measure provides in Oppen's work. One could say that all poetry shares to some extent this emphasis on speaking. But Hughes is distinctive in his manifest care both for erasing everything that cannot be the focus of speech and for having that speech clearly align with the life of a community. In effect he does not have to provide rhetorical reasons why his realism matters because the speaking itself establishes significant uses for the perspective involved.

But even the most capacious and most "measured" realistic mode can be criticized because it ultimately must make its claims in terms of what is rather than because of what might be possible. That is why every realism tends to produce in reaction a version of romance or idealization of the imagination for its powers to develop alternatives to the "real" world, or at least to how models based on common sense cast the real world. Recall Yeats' critique of the mirror dawdling down a lane and Pound's critique of Futurism as merely "accelerated Impressionism." These idealizations of powers of imagination, however, are not without serious problems of their own. How can writers construct a poetics that pursues the values basic to these powers of imagination without succumbing to a dependence on merely fictive images? Worse, how could writers go where imagination leads without proliferating imaginary rhetorical identities modernism fought so hard to repudiate?

I am not sure that any poetic project can overcome these difficulties. I am sure that some struggles against them can be quite compelling. During the Depression and in the years immediately following it, the most intense of those struggles in American poetry probably took place in the work of Wallace Stevens and W. H. Auden. Both poets accepted the challenge of returning rhetoric to the lyric because they thought neither the old nor the new realisms could fully embody the resources of lyric poetry. So they both tried to elaborate uses of rhetoric that could restore a vital sense of what the imagination contributes to society. But they were also convinced that this fascination with the rhetoric of lyric had to be accompanied by heroic efforts to distance themselves from conventional rhetoric's tendency to use the limitations of realism as an excuse for projecting imaginary substance for individual agents and roles. They looked to how the constructive and performative aspects of rhetoric might make that process transparent, so that they could invite their readers frankly to participate in the distinctive energies that the rhetorical impulse could gather. Rather than use rhetoric to persuade, they would use rhetoric to establish identifications with what it feels like to construct possibilities for changes of heart.

I

Wallace Stevens was born in Reading, Pennsylvania in 1879. Educated at Harvard, he became a lawyer, and from 1916 until he died worked for the Hartford Accident and Indemnity Company. Stevens was notorious for rigidly separating his work life from the world of imagination he entered when he left work. Analogously, his poetry has been criticized for not being sufficiently dialogical and for imposing a dense level of abstraction on the actual world. But for Stevens the primary need in poetry was to make articulate the rhythms and powers of his individual mind: he had to do that convincingly before he could trust any claims by or about other people or other phenomena.

Stevens' first volume, *Harmonium* (1922), is to me a brilliant experiment in impersonality in service of a constructivism based on reducing the world to sensations in intricate combinations. His constructivism was different from that of the new realists like Pound because he did not care much about connecting sensation to testable perceptions. He was more abstract; his concern was not for perception in itself but for the feel of a mind resolutely committed to the material world in all its elemental transformations. And he was more abstract because he saw that an impersonal distance seemed necessary for grappling with two aspects of the imaginary – its reliance on images as substitutes for an ungraspable reality and its basing identity on desires produced by others and negotiated by habit rather than on some more performative possibility. Ultimately the poet of *Harmonium* cared less about what was real than about how an author might render investments in one's own states of mind: one does not describe the self but one enacts it, or carefully observes how it enacts itself. This commitment put him at odds with what he saw as the romantic spirit hungry for belief and eager to celebrate abstractions about the power of mind. Where claims to lyric wisdom had been, Stevens offered only the playful philosophical music played by a harmonium or hand-held organ.

I cannot here represent the range of sensual effects or the intricate ironies of this volume,[2] but I cannot resist the short poem "The Snow Man," which illustrates most of Stevens' intellectual commitments at this time:

> One must have a mind of winter
> To regard the frost and the boughs
> Of the pine-trees crusted with snow;
> And have been cold a long time
> To behold the junipers shagged with ice,
> The spruces rough in the distant glitter
> Of the January sun, and not to think
> Of any misery in the sound of the wind,
> In the sound of a few leaves,

Which is the sound of the land
Full of the same wind
That is blowing in the same bare place
For the listener, who listens in the snow,
And nothing himself beholds
Nothing that is not there and the nothing that is.   (Stevens, CP 9)

The most striking feature of this poem is also the most generative. The poem is all one flamboyantly gorgeous sentence stretched out to cover five stanzas and numerous dependent clauses. That sentence virtually becomes a character in a drama where the turns and twists are based on syntactic surprises. There is irony aplenty as the speaking presence seems not to express fixed opinions but to try out possibilities as thoughts unfold. But readers are not encouraged to hear the speaking as if it were governed by the needs of a specific character willfully blinding himself to his situation. In Stevens' poem the speaker has no character apart from being a vehicle for extending that marvelous sentence. Therefore the potential for irony does not so much undercut meaning as allow meaning to be suspended among various stances without quite committing to any one. Consider the first line. In one register, the line contains a warning: one must have a mind of winter or one will lapse into the romanticism of hearing misery in the sound of the wind, and projecting all the melodrama that follows. But in another register, the "must" has only the force of a hypothetical: one must try out a mind of winter in order to experience one of the ways the world offers itself. In this case, a mind of winter is not bitter about romantic illusion but simply aware of itself as one of the ways that we recognize the various possibilities for assessing experience.

This ambivalence, or perhaps just multivalence, stems from the difficulty of taking up a position that can assess so general a thing as a mental disposition. How can one stand outside the mind of winter to judge it? Does it make sense to ask if it is good thing to have a mind of winter? Is that mind something to be pursued or only something to be endured? Stevens seems to have thought that there is no empirical basis for deciding such questions. But one can approach answering them anyway if one pursues further the work performed by the single sentence that is the poem. For by 1920 Stevens had internalized the modernist constructivist principle that the poem should embody what it claims. That means it would be a mistake to treat it as simply describing this mind of winter. Stevens apparently wants not just a description but a demonstration that possesses and displays the fundamental features of such a mind. After all, we can know whether it is good to have a mind of winter only if we can see how a mind of winter works – how minding details characteristic of winter and elaborating winter's ways of providing structures among the details manage to adapt to this barren environment. Such minding might even sharpen our awareness of how it might be valuable to be able to see the world in the key established by that barrenness.

The first two stanzas beautifully suggest what it means to have a mind at all: the mind makes certain "regards" possible, and its dispositions are capable of attuning to natural conditions so that being cold a long time leads to certain distinctive perceptions. These perceptions in turn demonstrate the self-awareness possible when one's extended sentence does not entail any of the old romantic idealizings about the transcendental powers of mind. Here one simply looks at the mind's capacity to respond to its place; there is no speculating on the possible metaphysical role one might attribute to these powers.

The center of the poem, the third stanza, marks a major shift in activity. The first two stanzas demonstrated the mind attuning to nature. Now that mind exercises its own powers to surpass description and bring negatives to bear. With these negatives comes a peculiar image of secular heroism – consisting not of what the person can do so much as what the person can manage not to think (not a minor achievement in our media-dominated world). The speaker worries that the influence of Romantic poetry leads us to put our own emotions into the natural scene, so that if the wind "moans," that will elicit a sense of misery. By the middle of the poem the sentence asserts an independence from this notion of sympathy. But it does not idealize a conventional form of the mind's independence. The mind remains bound to nature, bound to analogues, only not on the level of nature's details. As W. S. Merwin was later to write, "May I bow to Necessity, not / to her hirelings."[3] For Stevens the poem's ultimate celebration of the mind, of its sentences, is in breaking through to that sense of force or necessity and finding it gorgeously intricate. There is now no escaping skepticism: the mind must set itself against the temptations of the romantic by insisting that it propose "Nothing that is not there," no metaphorical additions to bare nature. But one need not find that nothing completely alienating. There is the strangely comforting possibility that the mind's need to affirm something can be satisfied with the bleakness of "the nothing that is." A mind so attuned needs no illusions, so that it can almost revel in the mental processes that frame and purify this discovery.

Harmonium explores the many forms afforded by this conjunction between expansive mind and nature stripped to its metaphysical essence. The mind has to accept a complete naturalism in which it is bound to nature's energies: "Passions of rain, or moods in falling snow; / Grievings in loneliness, or unsubdued / Elations when the forest blooms; gusty / emotions on wet roads on autumn nights" (Stevens, CP 67). But these strange affinities were not sufficient to prevent ten years of silence after the volume was published. The major reason for this silence probably had nothing to do with lyric styles. Stevens was a cautious man building a career and a family (not unlike the poet-academic who is relatively silent until he or she gets tenure). But since the styles Stevens did produce later are so different from the styles of *Harmonium*, I think we have license to speculate that Stevens was unsatisfied by what he took as modernist impersonality and Laforguian sense of ironic play.

Certainly when Stevens returned to poetry he adopted very different voices. He retained his skeptical side, but now it was less concerned with accommodating nature without romanticism than with adapting consciousness to what seemed an inevitable self-deluding romantic impulse within the psyche. Ironies about truth were giving way to a decidedly new concern for what Stevens called "nobility," the possibility that attending to the lyric impulse could restore a sense of dignity and capacity impossible in a pure naturalism:

> The nobility of rhetoric is, of course, a lifeless nobility. Pareto's epigram that history is a cemetery of aristocracies easily becomes another: that poetry is a cemetery of nobilities. For the sensitive poet, conscious of negations, nothing is more difficult than the affirmations of nobility, and yet there is nothing that he requires of himself more persistently, since in them and in their kind, alone, are to be found those sanctions that are the reasons for his being and for that occasional ecstasy, or ecstatic freedom of the mind, which is his special privilege.[4]

This pursuit of nobility would result in Stevens' poems exploring ideas that might seem anachronistic for the twentieth century, ideas like major man, the supreme fiction, and the "hero." But Stevens thought that the fear of idealization was one basic way his intellectual culture was succumbing to what he called "the pressure of reality." So he felt he had no choice but to accept the risks involved in finding a rhetorical means to project these idealizations without incurring the price that early Eliot and early Pound thought inescapable once one chose that path.

II

Here I will concentrate on a few poems that exemplify some of the styles by which Stevens sought to establish modes of imaginative activity that take on nobility by virtue of the qualities they muster against this "pressure of reality." "The Idea of Order at Key West" (1934) is too long for thorough treatment, but the poem simply cannot be overlooked because it so perfectly represents Stevens' basic attitude toward rhetoric – at once celebrating effulgent rhetorical gestures and seeking to overcome the invitation to imaginary identity that rhetoric offers by securing through the poem's action a collective sense of the needs it may satisfy. Stevens begins here with a speaker reflecting that the woman he is observing sings "beyond the genius of the sea." She proves so powerful a presence that he must treat her as exemplary maker, that idealized romantic figure, while the sea becomes merely a place affording her this possible identity. Because her voice approaches transcendence, it makes the natural scene a terrifying other to the qualities of human voicing.

By the end of the third stanza the series of assertions about her genius modulates to a question important both for its content and for the collective subject it postulates:

> Whose spirit is this? we said, because we knew
> It was the spirit that we sought and knew
> That we should ask this often as she sang. (Stevens, CP 129)

Then the mood of inquiry turns subjunctive as the poem tries to articulate possible connections among spirit, song, and sea. The links become possible because of a version of "measure" quite different from Oppen's:

It was her voice that made
The sky acutest at its vanishing.
She measured to the hour its solitude.
She was the single artificer of the world
In which she sang. And when she sang, the sea,
Whatever self it had, became the self
That was her song, for she was the maker. Then we,
As we beheld her striding there alone,
Knew that there was never a world for her
Except the one she sang, and singing, made.

Ramon Fernandez, tell me, if you know,
Why, when the singing ended and we turned
Toward the town, tell why the glassy lights,
The lights in the fishing boats at anchor there,
As the night descended, tilting in the air,
Mastered the night and portioned out the sea,
Fixing emblazoned zones and fiery poles,
Arranging, deepening, enchanting night.

Oh! Blessed rage for order, pale Ramon,
The maker's rage to order words of the sea,
Words of the fragrant portals, dimly starred,
And of ourselves and of our origins,
In ghostlier demarcations, keener sounds.   (Stevens, CP 129–30)

This sheer weight of the phrasing presents Stevens at his most con-fidently rhetorical: these are the aural resources of poetry wrought to its uttermost. But what impresses me even more is how the complex intellectual framework here provides a foundation for the rhetoric with-out bringing the self of the rhetorician to center stage. It helps that the primary rhetorician in this case is a musician and not an orator: it is she who establishes the powerful impression and the speaker who is in effect assigned to make sense of the power she has exhibited. At first the impression is romantic in the full sense: the speaker casts the woman as making an order that captures the scene at its most acute, while she also absorbs the scene into the terms that honor her wish and will. But what follows is not romantic lyricism, not quite.

As in Wordsworth's "Tintern Abbey," the poet tries to secure his vision by bringing an audience onto the stage. However Stevens' sense of audience is quite different from Wordsworth's, as is his stress on purely visual powers rather than symbolic moral ones. Wordsworth invokes his sister Dorothy so that he can project his own rhetoricized memories into the future: what she learns will confirm what he claims. Stevens goes directly to a collective audience by the strong rhyme of "we" with "sea." This invocation shares with the structure of Wordsworth's poem the desire to shift from a self-reflective encounter with the sublime to a concern for what a representative community might gain from such experience. Yet, crucially, there is in Stevens no mention of any moral improvement or political wisdom. He moves from the "we" to a particular representative, the little-known philosopher Ramon Fernandez. And he follows the assertion about the woman's making with a further question about the result of the singing that organizes the rest of the poem.

Stevens' question does not elicit a direct answer: poetry makes nothing happen in the domain of marketable ideas. Rather the question becomes its own answer as it sharpens the auditors' appreciation of how the fiery poles arrange, deepen, and enchant the night. Then, because the woman's voice modulates into transforming the objective scene, what had been private hearing and wondering becomes an intricate series of linked perceptions open entirely to the public. The scene is no one's possession and it sustains no particular ego – a point reinforced by the insistence on present participles characterizing how the evening seems transformed.

Stevens cannot stop with this concrete moment. He shares the Romantics' interest in building from meditation to a sense that the poet can bless his community that has shared his vision. Yet this blessing is strangely poised between the actual maker and a more metaphysically charged supplement to the natural scene. This charge is not transcendental. Rather it depends on how the language picks up intensity as the scene deepens: thinking moves quickly from posing questions, to the observation providing one kind of answer, to sheer exclamation, all without the intervention of any reasoning at all. Reasoning is not needed because it is the impression left by the woman's singing that matters, not any conclusion about what the song means. So Stevens can treat the rhetorical process itself as sufficient to take the place of reason. That process of tracking the effects of making brings out relations hovering at the margins of the scene and enriching what the audience can share.

The words now are not primarily descriptive. They are words "of our origins," asserting and providing "ghostlier demarcations, keener sounds." By eliciting those sounds, the words bring spirit (or the "geist" in "ghostly") from the domain of the single maker into what seems the activity of the scene trying to reveal the forces that the singing opens into. After all, "keener" sounds are also the sounds of "keening." Her song, tracked with such intensity, may ultimately be the expression of something ineffable, something beyond words that makes the present both absolute and ultimately inadequate.

III

I think these last lines give "The Idea of Order at Key West" a complexity that outweighs the tendency in the poem to think well of itself, to require a hushed and reverent voice as it works out the content for its "we." Stevens would never quite overcome this tendency toward piety. But his struggles to overcome it make fascinating reading. In part he would rely on his linguistic and metrical deftness so what seems pious (especially by the standards set by *Harmonium*) also engages quite complex states of mind. And in part Stevens would struggle against piety by using constructivist techniques to explore how he could find more direct ways of establishing the sense of community created by the questions to Ramon Fernandez.

It is difficult for a critic to demonstrate how details invoke this sense of community. So, ironically, the closer Stevens comes to the concrete life psyches share, the more abstract I will have to be to clarify what is going on. In general one can say that in many of Stevens' later poems the lyric becomes a site where the writer does not persuade others to act but enables them to see how they share interests in the sources of action. Whitman is my model here. For his "I" is less the empirical ego than the imaginative force by which we all become first persons: farmers, nurses, and soldiers all share the orientation of desire by which they care about being as fully as possible the individuals they are.[5]

Whitman browbeats us into making such identifications, but Stevens is much more subtle. He often bases identification not on specific desires agents display but on how they can share concrete activities of mind and feeling. Consider, for example, what I call the "aspectual" dimension of Stevens' poetics based on manipulating the many meanings of "as."[6] "As" can function to emphasize temporal equivalents

("This is happening as that is also happening"), qualitative equivalents ("This as dark as I have felt since last year"), modal equivalents ("Speaking as a liberal") and identificatory equivalents ("This joy is what you must have felt as you got the good news"). Aspects break the world into moments or modes that then each become possible ways of exploring how intimate states might also be "parts" of shared worlds. We attend self-reflexively to how our own sensibilities focus on an event, but we also know that our activity is entirely available to anyone else who can make use of the grammatical resources that "as" affords:

> The instinct for heaven had its counterpart:
>   The instinct for earth, for New Haven, for his room,
> The gay tournamonde as of a single world
>   In which he is and as and is are one.   (Stevens, CP 476)

Imagining "as and is" as being one both expands the world for imagination and socializes that imagination at the same time because we have to reflect on the structures of concern informing our descriptions. (Stevens has a long, beautiful poem entitled "Description without Place.") But attributing social force to the grammar of "is" and "as" would be a dangerously abstract means of proclaiming a sense of community. So it is best not to base our claims only on grammar but to realize how attention to the working of grammar clears the way for mobilizing a distinctive direction of lyric force. For the other relevant feature of "as" is its capacity to call attention to the intensity with which we care about the identifications we can make. One can bring out this dimension of possible force by emphasizing the term "exponent," a term Stevens sees as crossing sheer exposition with a mathematical figure for how intensification might operate:

> The major abstraction is the idea of man
>   And major man is its exponent, abler
> In the abstract than in his singular,
>
>   More fecund as principle than particle,
> Happy fecundity, flor-abundant force,
>   In being more than an exception, part,
>
> Though an heroic part, of the communal.   (Stevens, CP 388)

"Major man" is exponent, first, because it gives a concrete figure for how poetry idealizes and projects common interests. Second, Stevens hopes that the idea of major man can tap into or create a form for interests that make the contemplative object gather and focus our energies, as if language could be raised to higher powers in the same way that numbers can.

Nobility after all does not have to be only an idea at the mercy of rhetoricians. It can take hold as a mode of force creating and qualifying identifications without depending on the manipulation of images:

> The subject matter of poetry is not that "collection of solid, static objects extended in space" but the life that is lived in the scene that it composes; and so reality is not that external scene but the life that is lived in it. . . . It is hard to think of a thing more out of time than nobility. Looked at plainly it seems false and dead and ugly. . . . But as a wave is a force and not the water of which it is composed, which is never the same, so nobility is a force and not the manifestations of which it is composed, which are never the same.[7]

So it makes sense to envision the poet wielding this force by the sheer intensity he can evoke as an audience participates in the acts of naming that he performs.

Look at how Stevens uses that idea of major man to produce a version of self-consciousness that does not depend on images but on feelings engaged by the processes of simply naming precisely what can be experienced:

> It is not an image. It is a feeling.
>   There is no image of the hero.
> There is a feeling as definition. . . .
>   The hero is a feeling, a man seen
> As if the eye was an emotion,
> As if in seeing we saw our feeling
>   In the object seen and saved that mystic
> Against the sight, the penetrating
>   Pure eye. Instead of allegory,
> We have and are the man, capable
>   Of his brave quickenings, the human
> Accelerations that seem inhuman. (Stevens, CP 278–9)

Because there are no images, there need be no isolation among the various parts. Feelings can blend in many ways. Each part can feel itself distinctively individual and still find that investment in singing something the entire communal takes up each in its own way. And because Stevens projects the communal as not held together by argument or by belief, he can instead envision it as entirely depending on the qualities of consciousness we bring to our doings. The exponential relation makes visible a fundamental interchange between what language provides as exposition and what it provides as "brave quickenings," allowing us to identify with modes of will and affirmation as if they embodied ideal characters.

IV

This project of equating nobility with the intensity of reflective experience governs much of Stevens' poetry in the 1940s and 1950s. To demonstrate how such poems work I want to turn now to two poems that represent opposite ends of the spectrum established by that work. The first, "Poem with Rhythms," relies on elaborate rhetorical figures to defeat the standard uses of rhetoric as means of producing identifications with specific social roles. Stevens' lyrical rhetoric aims not to convince but to produce dynamic self-reflexive energies dramatizing what readers share as they participate in the poem. More important, poems like this one model how the readers might care about that sharing because of who they become as they experience the states the poems compose.[8] At the other extreme, poems like "The Plain Sense of Things" flirt with prose as they present quite simple, almost discursive statements that challenge the imagination to establish the intensity capable of transforming these apparently objective conditions into modes of spiritual nobility.

"Poem with Rhythms" works very hard to have its rhetorical energies provide intensities that simply cannot be located if one postulates any empirical situation. The poem presents the mind's conversation with itself, and is willing to be quite enigmatic in order to keep that conversation the only route of reference to the world. Consequently Stevens can foreground the will, as if it, and not any concern for knowledge, were the ultimate locus for these intensities. It is the will that emerges as the focus of the poem's exponential energies, and it

the will that must seek concrete definition as the reader fleshes out
the figures offered:

> The hand between the candle and the wall
> Grows large on the wall.
>
> The mind between this light or that and space,
> (This man in a room with an image of the world,
> That woman waiting for the man she loves,)
> Grows large against space:
>
> *There the man sees the image clearly at last.*
> *There the woman receives her lover into her heart*
> *And weeps on his breast though he never comes.*
>
> It must be that the hand
> Has a will to grow larger on the wall
> To grow larger and heavier and stronger than
> The wall, and that the mind
> Turns to its own figurations and declares
> "This image, this love, I compose myself
> *Of these, I wear a vital cleanliness,*
> *Not as in air, bright blue-resembling air,*
> *But as in the powerful mirror of my wish and will."* (Stevens, CP 245–6)

Stevens stages the importance of will by asking how there can be
significant subjective states that are not bound to practical images and
the modes of identification they involve. Why can simply this hand
project qualities of human agency? How can wish and will function as
mirrors without simply replicating parts of the mind devoted to pars-
ing representations? And why does the mind addressing its figurations
find itself taking on a distinctive kind of vital cleanness?

It will help in addressing these questions if I clarify what I mean
when I say that this poem tries to avoid the attachment to images
that is typical of standard rhetorics intended to change minds and
solicit particular actions. Stevens' poem certainly relies on images, but
it apparently does not want us to put these images together into a
narrative or even into a sense that the poem is referring to any empirical situation that could sustain practical identifications. Stevens wants
the images to float somewhat free of anything more than nominal

reference: it is what is said about the images that replaces their referring functions and specifies how they can live for the mind. The rhetorical energy of the poem abstracts the details so that the only form of coherence can be the reader's active effort to make the connections, allowing the imagination to feel its own power. Then the reader's activity can be what mirrors the wish and will, in a world where that activity clearly leads beyond mere perception to much more dynamic modes of self-awareness.

I speak of abstraction here for two reasons. I need a way of opposing our usual practical ways of developing concreteness but at the same time I want to raise the possibility that there is another route to concreteness. Stevens envisions abstraction achieving another kind of concreteness because the poem articulates such intimate levels of relationship between mental acts. And I need the concept of abstraction to foreground how this poem elicits a sense of the active force of love even though it refuses to provide dramatic scenarios and modes of thematizing that establish typical images of love behavior. For Stevens the force of love begins in the very concrete repetition of "the" so that it can proclaim a strange combination of familiarity and absoluteness. The poem asks the readers to ask: Why does it speak of "the" hand rather than "a" hand or even "this" hand, "the" wall and "the" mind rather than "a" wall and mind or "this" wall and mind? "A" hand, wall, or mind would be far too contingent – the scene would be only observation without any specified investment. "This" hand, wall, or mind, would assert that specificity but the specificity would be located entirely in the object as somehow distinctive. By stressing "the," Stevens manages to keep the objects generic while also focusing on the force that desire here makes visible. ("This" and "that" soon emerge, but do so primarily to reinforce the contrast between the objects we desire and the force desire brings in relation to those objects.)

This emphasis on the elemental operators that frame images becomes even more intense and ambitious in the final stanza. For it is there that the speaking must establish how wish and will can function as mirrors. But now the syntax does not stress simple connectives. Rather it raises the stakes by turning to "It must be," an imperative capitalizing on the enigmatic forces already established by the poem. Concretely, "It must be" seems at the same time to offer a total interpretation of the scene and to redistribute the energies gathered by that interpretive effort. Now hand and wall and image all seem participants in some force of necessity, some fatality driving will and pushing it to this level of visibility for the mind seeking to find some kind of substance in this process.

Speech then does not quite issue from a particular subject. It issues from what allows the mind to envision itself visible in the force of its own figurations – a creature composed of its own rhetorical effusions. Wishing and willing can take on exponential force for individuals when the reflection process concentrates entirely on the energies they deploy. For then we can fully appreciate what we bring to images. Given such energies, it may be possible for us to enjoy our own particularity solely on this imaginative level, even if the referents in the world of fact may never appear. The "I" speaking in the last utterance of the poem approaches the status of pure force, given substance not as an image but as specifiable activity. The "I" is what can give the poem's intensified "the" and "this" the qualities of clean, self-aware focus. The "I" here is what makes visible both the particularity and the potential generality of *"my wish and will."* And the "I" here is what ultimately responds to what remain at best enigmatic sources calling up this entire process of reflection. Our capacity for filling out the figurative nature of our desires proves inseparable from realizing our vulnerability to forces these desires cannot control.

Most of Stevens' last volume turns away from such absorption in the figural in order to emphasize what seems a clear, fundamentally discursive mode. This poetry approaches prose in its chaste relation to figurative speech, even as it seems always aware of a lurking theatricality. So, rather than rely on images, it attempts to purify the discursive until what approaches prose can still sustain an exponential intensity, now as an aspect of that respect for clarity. In fact this poetry goes even further than the more sensual and figurative mode toward making the conjunction of value and fact not a consequence of our explicit judgments but a simple corollary of how consciousness finds itself attached to its worlds. Our wills can maintain imaginary investments without projecting interpretations of the self or the world and without demanding the desire of others. Where human values are at stake, the mind's role may be less to analyze arguments than to magnify our awareness of the permissions and liabilities that emerge from what elicits our participation.

"The Plain Sense of Things" offers a powerful and succinct example of this imaginative orientation:

After the leaves have fallen, we return
To a plain sense of things. It is as if
  We had come to the end of the imagination,
Inanimate in an inert savoir.

  It is difficult even to choose the adjective
For this bleak cold, this sadness without cause.
The great structure has become a minor house
  No turban walks across the lessened floors.

The greenhouse never so badly needed paint.
  The chimney is fifty years old and slants to one side.
A fantastic effort has failed, a repetition
  In a repetitiousness of men and flies.

Yet the absence of imagination had
  Itself to be imagined. The great pond,
The plain sense of it, without reflections, leaves,
  Mud, water like dirty glass, expressing silence

Of a sort, silence of a rat come out to see,
  The great pond and its waste of lilies, all this
Had to be imagined as an inevitable knowledge,
  Required, as a necessity requires.   (Stevens, CP 503)

The best way to see what is distinctive in this poem is to contrast it
to "The Snow Man." That poem had two basic commitments, starkly
realized. One was to define as cleanly as possible a world reduced to
what demands "a mind of winter." The other was to make manifest
the continuing presence of some kind of synthetic force that in fact
could serve as the minding of that winter because it has the power
to contain the entire scene in an elaborate single sentence. "The Plain
Sense of Things" offers neither that concentrated reduction of the
scene nor that particular model of compositional power. Instead the
pacing is much slower, the language no longer driven by a single syntactic structure. Why? What about the absence of imagination can
Stevens render in this mode that he could not in the earlier poem?
  Both poems treat the "inert savoir" as if it reflected the failure of
adjectives: being seems deprived of any qualities that relieve its absolute
thereness. Yet "The Plain Sense of Things" is not content with the pure
sense of the present that allows "The Snow Man" its single synthetic

sentence. History enters the later poem, so that it has to deal not only with the blank present but also with the fact that "A fantastic effort has failed." Here the mind keeps on doing the work of comparison, unwilling or unable to give up on the possibility of still being able to choose adjectives even if they have to take negative form. For even when the adjectives fail, the mind seems capable of varying the modes by which it views this bleakness. At this negative center, even the silence turns out to elicit analogies.

None of these analogies has transformative power. Yet the entire series makes the absence of imagination less a fact to be registered than a condition to be inhabited by observing what it elicits. After choice is mentioned, the poem turns swiftly to the transformation of a "great structure" into a "minor house," a measuring of loss that soon generates a strange form of negation: "No turban walks across the lessened floors." Then there is a second comparison based on physical observation, and finally a bleak generalization about failure that in its turn generates another metaphor. This measuring is so quiet that its strangeness only slowly dawned on me. Why should one register there being no turban when no one would have expected a turban in the first place? So the sense of absence is not really retrospective. It derives from the need for imagination to describe the negative – that is why the absence is less a feature of the scene than of the mind's feel for its present situation. Negatives populate scenes so that we can feel a non-presence within them. Then with the abstract statement that "the absence of imagination had / Itself to be imagined," the mind tries to articulate its own heightened response to what turn out to be its own figures.

By the time the poem utters this abstraction it is putting into the mode of necessity what it had already discovered on the order of simple description. Yet this abstraction makes a major change in the poem. It challenges the discursive mode to handle a shift from describing a situation to describing a mental state while maintaining the same distance and flatness it maintained toward the scene. Stevens' response to that challenge is magnificent. He turns to "The great pond, / The plain sense of it," even though no pond has been mentioned. Consequently the pond hovers between one imagined as actual and one that exists primarily as part of a metaphor for how the absence of imagination can be imagined (not unlike the projected atmospheric conditions that John Ashbery uses simultaneously to present and to interpret mental states). Projected description and self-referential meta-phoric reach become strangely identical.

The entrance is prepared for the great figure of the "rat come out to see." Again the rat could be part of the imagined scene. But it also could be the mind's figure for its own pushing itself on the scene so as to find ways to figure the absence of imagination. The rat parallels the mind's uncomfortable but somehow fated presence as witness to this desolation, and as one more feature of the desolation that has to be imagined. Imagination is no longer an abstract term. (Perhaps imagination no longer exists only for imagination.) It becomes just what can encompass an identification with how this rat emerges in this situation.

Appreciating the rat requires recognizing why any analogue with a human observer would limit the poem. Confronted with this scene, the most the mind can do is compose a figure for its own estrangedness in a bizarrely intimate way, as if responding to this non-identity with the self provides sufficient means for adapting to it. Yet for this know-ledge to take hold the poem also has to go beyond the figure of the rat. That figure binds the mind to pure contingency: the poem gives no reason why the rat emerges, nor does it explain why the figure seems so apt for the situation. Nonetheless the bond to that contingency seems not contingent at all: all this *had* to be imagined. *As* the mind seems forced to confront absolute contingency, it reaches also for a corresponding sense of necessity.

The daunting nature of that task becomes the poem's richest evid-ence for why it has to call upon imagination. Only imagination could establish the theatrical terms by which there can be figures for the viewing of this poverty. And only imagination can bring to bear on this poverty a sense of it as inseparable from our destiny as human beings. Needing to pursue a plain sense of things in this most unplain way is the price we pay for having the investments we do in recogniz-ing and appreciating our situations. But it is also our glory, so long as we can imagine imagining a quasi-identification with this rat as a basic aspect of that glory. That imagining provides an instrument for coming to terms with a fatality too comprehensive and abstract to be engaged by discursive reasoning.

"The Snow Man" could rely on its single sentence in order to estab-lish how the mind might be adequate even to this bleak situation. Ultimately lucidity is possible. Here the situation is quite different.

There certainly can be a parallel movement toward containing and recasting the series of reflections elicited by the plain sense of things. But even a mobile Stevensian sentence is not the appropriate vehicle. Rather than rely on a single sentence, this poem can prevent the absence from dominating the sense of imagination only by bringing to bear an even more plastic power, the power provided by the "as." That power brings to bear a range of interpretive contexts that seem inseparable from the process of self-reflection, even as they prevent any single image of the self from taking form.

First, there is the simple assertion of what we might call a mode of vision: all this had to be imagined in the mode that necessity requires. All this has to be attuned to the contingent emergence of the rat as the locus for realizing a bleakness that itself may be elemental rather than contingent. However, we cannot stop with this interpretation. The contextual force that the "as" affords has itself to become the object of reflection so that we can treat the imagination of the absence of imagination as a basic process that enables us to give a concrete dimension to the idea of necessity. Our thinking and our figuring all become aspects of recognizing that we are not so much describing the absence of imagination as ritually manifesting where we are positioned when we make that attempt. We have to align entirely with necessity, but at a distance, in another tree, provided by everything that our ability to use "as" makes visible. Such use proves most important for its giving sharp content to the "we" that begins as only a hopeful assertion in the poem's first stanza. This "we" eventually takes on definition because the readers come to appreciate who they become by participating fully in the journey the poem composes.

V

In a casual remark Douglas Mao suggests that, rather than worry about whether Pound or Stevens are the primary influences on contemporary American poetry, we might explore the idea of an "Age of Auden."[9] Certainly Auden is cited at least as much as the other writers by the younger poets writing at the time, yet critics for the most part ignore the formative role he may have played in shaping possibilities for those poets. There is excellent criticism on Auden, but it too much heeds his spirit of humility and rarely generalizes. I can't promise to match the excellence, but I certainly am eager to provide some of the missing generalizations. I think Auden played a central role in showing American poets how they might develop rhetorical stances that can finesse imaginary identifications. The best way to make my case is to return to the now standard division between his earlier work written in England and the poetry he wrote on coming to the United States.

Born in 1907 and educated in private schools, then at Oxford, Auden early on had to contend with the genius syndrome, the imposition by adults of extremely high expectations that tend to deny a youth the right to make the standard mistakes involved in growing as an individual. Auden was barely 30 years old when the first of "Age of Auden" began to be proclaimed. So it should not be surprising that this early work is steeped in an almost unbearable sense of unnameable pressures. Auden's overt ambition was to establish a lyric speech capable of addressing what the worldwide Depression was revealing about capitalist economies. He thought he could do that by generalizing from a sense of various private discomforts largely generated by his homosexuality. But generalizing of private anxieties seems to have made the actual private anxieties recede even further into an ineffable background. Auden must have felt as if everyone was attending to the public Auden's version of the private Auden, and so was also painfully aware of how much he had to conceal if he were to protect and project the person in everyone's mirror.

His poems written in England are marvelous testimony to how he could turn those private anxieties into a measure of a public world gone terribly wrong. Auden would forge the conscience of his race, and find it woefully inadequate. For everywhere the very project of forging a conscience threatens to collapse into Eliot's alternatives – the cry and the prayer. Let us begin with *The Orators*, Auden's scathing account of the status of public rhetoric written in 1931. Were this poem not so complex, I could just cite it for every claim I make about the imaginary in public life. Here one section will have to suffice – the "Prologue," re-titled "Adolescence" in collections after 1945.[10] This section presents an adolescent's imaginary investments being formed under the guidance of the assumptions shaping the prevailing rhetoric, then forced to confront a reality for which it has not been prepared:

By landscape reminded once of his mother's figure
The mountain heights he remembers get bigger and bigger
With the finest of mapping pens he fondly traces
All the family names on the familiar places.

In a green pasture straying, he walks by still waters;
Surely a swan he seems to earth's unwise daughters,
Bending a beautiful head, worshipping not lying,
"Dear" the dear beak in the dear concha crying.

Under the trees the summer bands were playing;
"Dear boy, be brave as these roots," he heard them saying:
Carries the good news gladly to a world in danger,
Is ready to argue, he smiles, with any stranger.

And yet this prophet, homing the day is ended,
Receives odd welcome from the country he so defended:
The band roars "Coward, Coward," in his human fever,
The giantess shuffles near, cries "Deceiver."   (Auden, CP 64–5)

Auden learned how to handle narrative distance from Hardy's "hawk vision";[11] the poem's psychological distance from the boy's ego probably stems from Eliot. Whatever the source, the distances are withering. The boy begins by using writing to secure his place in the family; then, when he enters the world, he imagines himself as the swan bearing an innocent nobility that makes possible an exchange of "dear" with these daughters of earth. Yet even in the beginning the reader suspects how desperately these gestures reveal the boy's needs for love. These needs will not be satisfied because the boy cannot live up to his self-image, or find a path to the rewards his relation to this mother makes him think he deserves. We cannot know why he is a coward – society perhaps does not make such distinctions easy, especially to an idealist like him. Nor can we know clearly why he is a deceiver, but the poem depends on our offering speculations about this. Probably he is a deceiver, first, because he does not represent to himself the degree to which his mother is a demanding giantess. Then, more important, he is a deceiver because he trades on the illusion of innocence born of the confidence that he is loved, so that he does not even see how the world might take him as a coward or know anything about him that he does not control. Then there is probably the most personal level of deceit, the unacknowledged fear that he is not a "real man" and so must fail to live up both to his public image and to his mother's private demand.

It is tempting to treat these early poems as interpretive puzzles demanding that readers invent plausible hypotheses for piecing the work into a unified whole. This view is unavoidable, but it is also incomplete. It is as important to understand why the difficulties arise as to speculate on resolving them. For then we see that Auden's English poems do not so much raise puzzles for their own sake as put the mind in situations eliciting various kinds and degrees of discomfort with the frameworks available for explanations. However we interpret "Adolescence," the primary matter is to recognize how the difficulties are created by the shock to the boy's narcissistic impulses.

In general we can say that in these early poems Auden finds himself in an impossible position. The poems cry out against their modernist heritage because it has failed to foster a sufficiently public side, failed to provide a plausible general audience with an accurate vision of what society has become. But the poems also seemed condemned to relying on those very modernist strategies, or at least on the heritage of Hardy reinforced by modernism. Impersonality reigns; anxiety and irony seem the only plausible human stances toward that society; and, rather than trust rhetoric, the poems insist on the constructivist mantra that they must not refer to situations but embody spiritual conditions.[12] The poems only intensify the exiled consciousness that society attributes to modernism. Then irony piles on irony when it proves real exile to the United States that begins to offer Auden new possibilities as a poet. To define those possibilities I will first leap ahead to "Homage to Clio" (1955) because I think this is his fullest lyric realization of a spiritual attitude capable of rejecting modernism and projecting an alternative set of values. Then I will loop back to Auden's first poem written in the US, "In Memory of W. B. Yeats" (1939), in order to illustrate the basic imaginative stance that was to act as the enabling permission for this later work.

"Homage to Clio" ought be fundamental to contemporary literary education because there is simply no richer rendering of how a historical sense can provide antidotes to the values articulated by romanticism and modernism. The poem is based on a conflict between how specific gods represent totally different attitudes toward experience. Worship of Aphrodite and Artemis idealizes a life devoted to the perfections of the present moment. Under the auspices of these goddesses, "flowers duel incessantly, / Color against Color, in combats / Which they all win." Clio, on the other hand, matters because of her power to remind us of the claims of what is absent. Aphrodite's and Artemis' domain is space, their power the dynamizing of what can appear. Clio's domain is time, her power the intensity with which we recognize what must always appear incomplete or lacking within our sense of the present. By honoring Clio Auden can still emphasize his sense of the unknowable within history, but he can now turn it into a positive principle.

To express this honor, however, we need a radical change of heart. Pictures and images can no longer suffice. We have to cultivate a silence attentive to what in the present remains withdrawn and impossible to assert. Thus at the end of the sixth stanza there emerges a problematic "we," not sufficiently anchored by what is present:

Why nothing is too big or too small or the wrong
  Color, and the roar of an earthquake
Rearranging the whispers of streams a loud sound
  Not a din: but we, at haphazard

And unseasonably, are brought face to face
  By ones, Clio, with your silence. After that
Nothing is easy. We may dream as we wish
  Of phallic pillar or navel stone

With twelve nymphs twirling about it, but pictures
  Are no help: your silence already is there
Between us and any magical center
  Where things are taken in hand.... (Auden, CP 611)

Clio's power does not depend on the intensity of vision but on qualities of retrospection that keep us open to a sense of mystery. She is the goddess whom we worship when we look beyond luminous particulars to see what they obscure. So where the cult of Aphrodite and Artemis culminates in awe, the cult of Clio demands the kind of love that commits to what it cannot understand. And that demand effectively defines why love matters. The two goddesses of the present exist only to be observed; Clio exists to be addressed in second-person terms. Those terms require not just knowledge but also the forming of an attitude or will in relation to our necessarily incomplete understanding of particular situations. Because Clio remains silent, she requires our coming to appreciate the place played in our lives by leaps of faith. We have to enter domains where presence simply cannot satisfy our needs for knowledge and for connection. And we have to be open to what dwells on the edges of knowledge, especially to what connects us to what is doomed to die because of that incompleteness:

> But it is you, who never have spoken up,
>   Madonna of silences, to whom we turn
>
> When we have lost control, your eyes, Clio, into which
>   We look for recognition after
> We have been found out. How shall I describe you? They
>   Can be represented in granite . . .
>
> You had nothing to say and did not, one could see,
>   Observe where you were, Muse of the unique
> Historical fact, defending with silence
>   Some world of your beholding, a silence
>
> No explosion can conquer but a lover's Yes
>   Has been known to fill.   (Auden, CP 612)

This "lover's Yes" must involve more than the present because it promises commitment beyond the moment, even beyond what we can see or control. And the lover's "yes" cannot take place when we are driven by the desire to think well of ourselves (hence the critical comments on poetry at the poem's conclusion). Auden never forgets that "Every man carries with him through life a mirror, as unique and impossible to get rid of as his shadow" (DH 93). But the mirror is committed only to presence, albeit the illusory presence of images. Love is a force that must refuse mirroring relations. Love has to postulate an otherness that gets agents beyond mirrors. To accept love requires trust in versions of causality that honor mystery and acknowledge feelings that the agents can never quite explain. For Auden this means he can accept uncertainty rather than treat it as a symptomatic sign that he is avoiding some harsh truth. What had been a source of pain in his earlier work becomes now the very possibility of commitment and of faith.

Thematic statements can only realize a part of what this lover's "yes" demands. That is why Auden also provides an intricate drama on the formal level of the poem. But again he must win a version of form that is not the domain of Aphrodite and Artemis who reign over the intricacies that can be rendered as aspects of the present tense. Auden has to recognize in formal terms the limitations of purely formal structures. Form approaches Clio's domain when it too submits to time and bases its intensities on indirection. In this poem, that aspect of form gets played out by the poet's pronouncedly playing syntax against the structure of the verse, as if what the sentences could not possess were far more important than what they could make manifest. The long opening sentence establishes the key because it works itself into the middle of the opening line of the third stanza. The next sentence extends into the third line of the fifth stanza; the third to the middle of the seventh stanza; and the fourth, brilliantly, to the last word of the eighth stanza. Sentences are driven beyond obvious stopping points because, in deference to Clio, they are committed to pursuing what has to remain incomplete. By their capacity to extend into the silence, the sentences offer themselves as aspects of the life of the mind that thrive on this very refusal to accept the authority of the drive to spatial order.

In effect performance has to resist restriction to "form"; manner to becoming a mere supplement to the matter of insistent thematic argument. Notice how Auden offers an avuncular voice that could appear both wise and intimate without exhibiting much anxiety about how he is heard or reflected. There is none of the modernists' efforts to counter the rhetorical impulse; nor is there much trace of early Auden's desperate efforts to align private and public anxieties. Now Auden can be frankly rhetorical, can frankly ask poetry to speak to and speak for a public, without the flaccid generalizations in which the ego can hide. He shows how rhetoric can become so self-conscious and visibly playful that it can bear even our imaginary investments with a lightness that simply forecloses any effort at "sincere" identification.

This characteristic voice of Auden's later poetry often seems as if its self-conscious rhetoric accomplished a version of impersonality less antagonistic and less bound to irony than Eliot's. He defines the poet's task as transforming "the crowd of recollected occasions of feeling" into "a community by embodying it in a verbal society" (DH 67).[13]

And he is quite serious that words can form societies just as people do, since they too can come together to constitute wholes characterized by distinctive interests and methods. More important, the words need not implicate specific personal needs and investments: they can appeal directly to audiences willing to try provisional identifications with what gets expressed, without bringing to those investments the burden of personality. The words establish an articulate voice testing for possible exchanges with other voices so that the emotions involved may get beyond fantasy to the expression of collective need and the articulation of possible collective wisdom. Rhetoric is the public side of what for the private self takes form as religious commitment to a life depending on shared ritual forms.

Thus Auden could provide a very different critique of the imaginary than constructivist modernism proposed.[14] One might say that constructivist modernism needs Aphrodite as the only possible alternative to what would become the nightmarish realm of Circe. And Auden would have to admit that it is not impossible to treat works of art as if they have reality as objects. One need only pay attention to non-iconic sculpture and much of expressivist painting – Aphrodite has her claims on us. But he wants his readers to wonder if these models were the most appropriate ones for dealing with language, especially with the ways in which silence tends to be folded into the differential textures that give language its meaning and tone its affective force. So, rather than rely on setting the real work the medium does against claims about the sheer imaginary status of the text's rhetoric, he could play two different aspects of rhetoric against one another – the effort to foster positive identifications against the effort to establish the sense of potential community founded on need rather than on projections of power. Then there would be good reason to believe that what makes writing distinctive, what gives it the possibility of modifying how agents act in the world, is precisely its performative dependency on the rhetorical space where social significations struggle to solicit belief and so to survive. If the poet is to reach beyond the elites, he or she may have to risk the labor of making clear how identification need not be tied to fantasies that the mirror preserves.

"In Memory of W. B. Yeats" brings all this abstract theorizing into the domain of concrete practice. Instead of emphasizing how the object takes on reality, Auden puts at the center of poetry the forms of presence that the subject could establish by struggling with all the silences constituting historical existence. This mode of presence would borrow from rhetorical ideals: Yeats is treated as a person speaking to other persons and seeking ways to make present for them different ways of taking stances in relation to modern experience. But Yeats the poet did not quite seek persuasion and did not quite use linguistic resources primarily as means for moving audiences toward predetermined agendas. More important, the voices with which Auden chooses to address Yeats do not identify with the standard ethos or standard roles by which rhetors have won over their audiences. The various voices in the poems all seem born of the agency of poetry, not of speakers conforming to social codes. It is as if poetry itself could honor one of its masters by taking on itself the task of performing a sincerity distinctive to the genre. Poetry invites attention to how fully and how well language is brought to the pressures of experience. So the poet's task is to explore the degree to which a speaking voice can work its way through all the ironic gestures modernism encouraged without losing the urgency of its conviction. If it could accomplish this, then it made something happen within the language that is worth audiences trying out its voices rather than imposing their own.

Consider how the various modes of speaking are staged in "In Memory of W. B. Yeats." The opening section of the poem assumes the mode of third-person speech because that is the most basic framework within which we encounter death: the world becomes object and the voice has to orient itself by utilizing whatever descriptive resources it can:

What instruments we have agree
The day of his death was a dark cold day.   (Auden, CP 248)

Then the final two sections take on the task of establishing modes of speaking capable of providing other, more sensitive instruments for probing what the author's commitment to poetry might make of this situation. First the poet tries second-person address in order to enter intimately into the strange gulf between the poet who dies and the poetry that lives. Here we find Auden's famous anti-modernist statement that "poetry makes nothing happen." But we also find him elaborating what poetry can accomplish because it makes nothing happen:

For poetry makes nothing happen: it survives
In the valley of its making where executives
Would never want to tamper, flows on south
From ranches of isolation and the busy griefs,
Raw towns that we believe and die in; it survives,
A way of happening, a mouth.   (Auden, CP 248)

So long as poetry keeps the effect and the affect of happening, it gives the mouth a substantial place in the world – not by invoking images but by dramatizing processes within which various dialogues can take place.

The third section of Auden's poem embraces an even more challenging task. In order to explore his possible bonds with Yeats, he actually assumes the formal tone and drum-like rhythm of poems like "Under Ben Bulben." This becomes Auden's most daring transformation of the imaginary: rather than projecting roles for himself, he explicitly tries to identify with Yeats' own self-projection. Then this Yeatsian voice can offer a series of imperatives that define both a legacy and a continual challenge. But the challenge seems manageable precisely because the material voice thrives on identifications, especially those that can be put to work in the reader's own performative theater. These final lines offer no specific image of Auden as poet or as moralist. They are entirely an implicit dialogue between what can survive from Yeats and what must emerge from the poet if that survival is to have social significance:

Follow, poet, follow right
To the bottom of the night,
With your unconstraining voice
Still persuade us to rejoice;

With the farming of a verse
Make a vineyard of the curse,
Sing of human unsuccess
In a rapture of distress;

In the deserts of the heart
Let the healing fountain start,
In the prison of his days
Teach the free man how to praise.   (Auden, CP 248–9)

Speaking in a Yeatsian mode allows Auden to put on stage two basic human situations – the historical framework of needs, hopes, and desires to which Yeats was responding, and the ability of voice still to make things happen because of how it also demonstrates capacities to hear and to project.

The Yeatsian legacy becomes a challenge to future poets to keep the responsiveness of the human voice a vital force in the present. To do that, ironically, that voice also has to hear the past and make the hearing fundamental to the desires it forms. That is why both Yeats and Auden emphasize the power of quite conventional rhetorical figures. Poetry has to respond to what seem collective desires; its originality is largely a matter of applying them in ways that focus the identifications they make possible. Anything less, anything more idiosyncratic, would not count as either listening well or speaking responsibly.

Chapter 6

Modernist Dilemmas and Early Post-Modernist Responses

I would love to be able to bring this book up to the twenty-first century, but several factors make that impossible. Introductory surveys seem a foolish enterprise when canons have not settled at all. And contemporary poetry in the United States has become extraordinarily diverse and decentered, so even the effort to establish a teaching canon seems unlikely to sponsor anything more useful than competing lists of writers. More important in this case, I simply do not have a clear view of whether younger contemporaries enter into substantial dialogue with the modernists on either of my two basic themes – developing the new realism and resisting the temptations of imaginary identity and the righteousness to which such efforts at identity are prone.

Therefore I have decided to stop where there has emerged a fairly clear canon, and where I am fairly confident that the poets are still engaged with the issues posed by the major modernist poets. The poets I have chosen for this chapter – Robert Lowell, Adrienne Rich, Robert Creeley, Elizabeth Bishop, and John Ashbery – may not be the five poets everyone would chose to represent the possibilities of poetry from about 1955 to about 1980. Yet I think almost everyone would agree they deserve serious consideration for such a role.[1] That possible agreement is good enough for me, especially since these writers not only engage the modernists but extend their work. Lowell and Rich offer surprising ways to personalize the new realism; Creeley develops what I will call a "conative poetics" in order to transform Williams' objectivism into a mode for dealing with subjective intimacies; Bishop creates dazzling syntheses of Moore, Williams, and Stevens; and Ashbery gives Auden's performative rhetoric a deliciously Stevensian cast.

Finally I address these poets because they all in various ways fought the authority of the New Criticism, the dominant aesthetic ideology from the close of the 1940s to the close of the 1960s. In so doing they helped save modernism from a debilitating orthodoxy. The New Critics were in fact quite diverse in their particular ways of reading. Allen Tate, R. P. Warren, John Crowe Ransom, I. A. Richards, René Wellek, R. P. Blackmur, and Cleanth Brooks all had their individual voices and pre-occupations. But they also shared a sense that they were establishing in prose the significance of the modernist revolution in poetry. Their major focus as theorists was on how modernist writing might resist the authority of Enlightenment values, and hence how the metaphoric language of poetry might provide an alternative to the confident reductive lucidity of scientific discourse. Eliot had praised the metaphysical conceit for establishing "felt thought," responsive at once to the claims of flesh and the claims of spirit and so capable of healing a debilitating dissociation of sensibility. The New Critics concentrated on showing discursively how poetry possessed the necessary power to accomplish that task by transforming opinion into felt thought, fact into sacrament which offered outward and natural signs of inward and spiritual grace.[2]

Because they saw their work as fomenting a cultural revolution, the New Critics presented themselves as teachers dedicated to showing how the close reading of poetry might affect readers' sense of the world beyond the text. They had surprising success – primarily because the expansion of the American universities after World War II changed the conditions of literary instruction. This expansion created audiences for the most part without the linguistic and historical knowledge to perform satisfying contextual or biographical or comparative acts of criticism. So these audiences eagerly embraced New Critical critiques of intentional, pathetic, and moralistic fallacies, and were delighted that all they needed to do was to close read the poem by paying careful attention to the verbal patterns that emerged on the page. Close reading was after all the only way to respond to the complexity of poetic discourse without turning it into what Ransom called "Platonism," the trust in the shapes for experience delivered by our abstract ideas. Here then was finally a framework capable of putting to cultural work modernism's cult of complexity and its constructivist concern that the poem establish an expressive objectivity whereby it actually enacted what it asserted. Archibald MacLeish's "a poem should not mean / but be" became the mantra of generations of English majors.

Teaching students to read well did not, however, correlate with teaching them to think well about poetry. The New Critics were conservative theorists, unwilling or unable to give modernism its due as an effort to alter radically how people imagined a secular world charged with mystery and dynamic intensity. These critics appreciated how the poets demanded complexity in order to engage urban experience and to foster integrative powers capable of resisting the secular intellect. And they valued impersonality as a means of breaking free from practical interests and focusing on contemplative acts. But their emphasis on metaphor constituted a problematic way of recuperating the force of modernist poetry, primarily because it confused ends with means and was fully responsive only to later Eliot. The New Critics relegated the power of poetry to metaphoric speech without doing a good job of specifying the place of metaphor in the overall action carried out by individual poems. For them the role of metaphor was the point; whereas for most of the modernists metaphor was one of the elements composing a distinctive experience in language (as well as a distinctive experience *of* language). These critics never saw how metaphor (and felt thought) could result from the new realism's emphasis on sensation, just as their formalist understanding of impersonality could not connect aspects of structure to Eliot's psychological claims about the cultural consequences of relying on personality. Indeed, these critics tried to avoid every aspect of psychology, as if their resistance to psychoanalysis sufficed for that domain of experience.

We shall see that each of the five poets I've chosen makes a dramatic point of engaging some of these limitations. For each managed eventually to read modernism against the prevailing grain, primarily by returning to specific modernists in order to recuperate imaginative strengths that might give their own work a distinctive focus.

I

Robert Lowell was at one time a poster boy for the New Critics. Born in 1917 of a relatively underprivileged branch of the patrician Lowell family of Boston, he spent two years at Harvard in the family tradition, but transferred to Kenyon College where he could study with John Crowe Ransom, the best philosophical mind among the New Critics. Later he studied with Brooks and became close friends with Tate, both of whom converted to Catholicism. Lowell took that conversion so seriously that he became a conscientious objector to World War II on religious grounds and was imprisoned for his beliefs. The poems he wrote as a Catholic, like "The Quaker Graveyard in Nantucket," were celebrated for their intensity and provocative complexity. But his career took a radical turn with *Life Studies* in 1959. There he announced "Life changed to landscape,"[3] and the symbolic structures of Rome had been supplanted by the intricacies of Parisian cultural commerce. In reaction to that cultural shift, these new poems completely rejected the meditative impersonality that had characterized Lowell's work. Instead they pursued a confessional mode devoted to capturing the unique timbre and feel of an individual life, with all its vices and imperfections. After about ten years of that, Lowell settled on a notebook style in which he turned the sonnet into a topical form capable of rendering the twists and turns tracking the private impressions of an intensely public man.

I want to concentrate here on Lowell's confessional work and its aftermath, because that, ironically, is more closely connected to the richest moments in modernism than his self-consciously modernist early work. But it would be remiss of me not to sample the early work and to explore how it exemplifies much of the New Critical sensibility, although with an intensity unmatched by Lowell's peers. Here are the first two stanzas and the last of "Colloquy at Black Rock":

Here the jack-hammer jabs into the ocean;
My heart, you race and stagger and demand
More blood-gangs for your nigger brass percussions,
Till I, the stunned machine of your devotion,
Clanging upon this cymbal of a hand,
And rattled screw and footloose. All discussions

End in the mud-flat detritus of death.
My heart, beat faster, faster. In Black Mud
Hungarian workmen give their blood
For the martyre Stephen, who was stoned to death. . . .

Christ walks on the black water. In Black Mud
Darts the kingfisher. On Corpus Christi, heart,
Over the drum-beat of St. Stephen's choir
I hear him, Stupor Mundi, and the mud
Flies from his hunching wings and beak – my heart,
The blue kingfisher dives on you in fire.   (Lowell, CP 11)

The New Critics loved figures of the Incarnation because it provided a perfect emblem for their poetics: by suffering the degradation of taking on flesh, then by conquering death, Christ took on the power to change unstable secular signs into the stable emblems of the life of spirit. As Eliot had argued, this logic had come to its apogee in English poetry with the elaborate metaphors known as "conceits." Such figures exhibited a hunger for the details of the world combined with a faith in the imagination's capacity to transform that world's mere signs into symbols, just as Christ turned the secular reality of bread and wine into the miraculous reality of bread and blood.

Lowell's poem enacts this same logic on several interrelated levels. Consider first the form of the poem. Lowell is willing to use the same word twice to constitute a rhyme for two reasons. The repetition provides an ideal tight framework for something close to the sprung rhythm of Gerard Manley Hopkins, and so insists on the powers that transform prose into the ritual space of poetry. And the repeated rhymes highlight by contrast the few instances where the pattern is broken, perhaps to indicate how miracles occur. In the last stanza all is repetition except the surprising rhyme of "choir" with "fire" that blends the act of worship with Christ's redemptive response.

The poem's action also turns on these analogues with the Incarnation. There is a first-person speaker. But he is clearly a speaker representing the possibilities of religious faith for any agent. As he turns to his heart, he experiences it in two fundamentally opposed ways, sharpened by the metaphors. On one level the heart is a machine, driving life as the jack-hammer jabs into the ocean. But the heart is also subject to will. The speaker counts on the heart to obey his requests to beat faster and to risk destruction as he gets excited thinking about the martyrs who chose death as their means of life.

Then the poem tries to show why the martyrs might make that choice. Mud is the domain of the kingfisher, which is in turn a symbol for Christ as fisher of men. Of course, just asserting the symbol would be an empty gesture. Lowell has to establish the symbol's role in spiritual life in order to show how it can be taken to heart, so he turns to the excitement of the choir on the feast of Corpus Christi. There he can imagine hearts beating with joy in a way that also defines how agents can appreciate Christ coming into the detritus of their lives. He can then treat his own heart as not a machine but a spiritual force, brought to a pitch where he can fully embrace the kingfisher's fiery drive. The speaker becomes a complete person only when he can finally address his heart in a different way. At the end of the penultimate line he no longer orders his heart about but becomes a silent witness to what its capacity for desire makes possible. This is the moment also when he becomes fully typological, fully an example of what grace offers every person. What begins in mud ends in Dante's and Eliot's purifying fire; what begins tormented by sin and need ends with the understanding that redemption is available even for him.

Then, in 1959, with the publication of Lowell's *Life Studies*, readers were confronted with lines like these:

I doodle handlebar
mustaches on the last Russian Czar.   (Lowell, CP 171)

I keep no rank or station.
Cured, I am frizzled, stale and small.   (Lowell, CP 186)

And for their context we find settings like Lowell's stay in McLean's psychiatric hospital. This is the last stanza of "Waking in the Blue":

After a hearty New England Breakfast,
I weigh two hundred pounds
this morning. Cock of the walk,
I strut in my turtle-necked French sailor's jersey
before the metal shaving mirrors,
and see the shaky future grow familiar
in the pinched, indigenous faces
of these thoroughbred mental cases,
twice my age and half my weight.
We are all old-timers,
each of us holds a locked razor.   (Lowell, CP 184)

No wonder critics either hated the new voice or insisted that this was a crucial anti-modernist or post-modernist breakthrough. I prefer the view that it is a significant accomplishment, but I think we over-simplify Lowell's confessional mode if we see it only as opposition to modernism. For this poetry develops surprising possibilities within the two basic modernist orientations that we have been tracing, and it develops these in conjunction with the work of several other major poets of the period, especially Sylvia Plath, Frank O'Hara, Allen

Ginsberg, Adrienne Rich, and Robert Creeley. All of these poets embrace versions of the new realism Lowell found in Williams, his favorite poet, but all six also give that realism a radical twist. And that twist made it possible utterly to reverse the case for modernist impersonality, although for reasons that are very much in sympathy with modernist assessments of the dangers of the imaginary.

Put simply, these writers in different ways developed the possibility that modernist attitudes toward sensation could be extended to include how we appear to ourselves. There is no distinctive knowledge of self; there are only contingent moments of more or less charged awareness of the psyche focused on the self rather than on other aspects of the world. Therefore there is no privileged knowledge distinctive to the first person. In fact self-knowledge is much more problematic a concept than objective knowledge because there is no way to separate subjective processes and desires from what gets attributed to the object. Knowledge of self must be filtered through sensations produced by the performance of self.

Since there is no independent object for first-person consciousness, there is also no way of postulating where the imaginary ends and where some other more objective version of attributed selfhood can begin. The imaginary is not a direction of self-consciousness but an inescapable condition of first-person attributions about the self. That is why first-person attitudes seem so "natural" to the lyric, the genre where desire is so difficult to tell from description. In these poets at least, the speakers' renderings of the sensations basic to self-consciousness seem to have no outside, no secure ground for judgment beyond what the speakers project. Of course there can be efforts to turn on the self as an object rather than as a continuation of the very process of perception. But for these writers such efforts would have the vexed relation of commentary to presentation. Selves, not just poems, are more authentic if they could not mean but simply be.[4]

Consider the lines above quoted from Lowell's report on his stay at McLean's. One might think this is simple description, a return to the old realism, but notice how the sensations rendered make subtle shifts in the speaker's sense of himself line by line. The opening self-description could almost be a 200-pound J. Alfred Prufock offering an external measure of his health to ward off any further probing. Like Prufrock, the speaker's self-consciousness is pervaded by an imaginary sense of his appearance. And the ensuing sensations build a complex presence that seems to be performing several tasks at once, each logically incompatible with the others. The speaker is primarily offering a simple appeal that the audience might understand how the activity of seemingly objective description is a mode of seeking responsibility for the self, and hence a step in what he knows now will at best be a provisional cure. But a distinctive level of fantasy pervades those details. He is terrified because manic moments can occur at any time. That terror in turn seems to ground an appeal to our pity because of this shaky future, but at the same time he insists on something driving him to speech that even our pity cannot reach. Finally there is more than a hint of aggression in the poem: I have survived this and you now might have to worry about surviving me with my razor.

There is then no single point of view that can judge this speaker's condition without depriving him of his concrete ways of being present in the world, however much this creates problems for those who care about him. Speaking in general terms, we might say Lowell's first-person rendering here of an autobiographical condition reveals two features that do not permit a more comprehensive impersonal view. Those features are symbolized by the metal mirror and the locked razor. On the one hand this entire personal statement offers a desperate attempt to make an audience willing to accept a specific image of the self that speaker and readers know is by no means impartial or dis-interested. He has to grapple with the embarrassment and vulnerability of having been a psychiatric patient. He wants his audience to know that, and to know he knows that, but he also wants to paint what seems an objective picture capable of invoking pity and even respect for his having come through. However, those who have not shared that desperation probably cannot appreciate the defensive gestures involved, and those who can share it know better than to trust the speaker's account of his condition. The patient has to see himself as almost normal since he participates in the shaving ritual. Yet he looks at a metal mirror, not a glass one, and he holds a locked razor – both emblems of society's reading of the patients as still capable of doing serious harm to themselves or others.

In general then the performance of the self seems at odds with any descriptive language about the self. When the poet tries to treat subjectivity as a series of sensations, there is no objective position available not already suffused with an imaginary version of what the self wants in the process of its characterizing itself. The self as object is subsumed within the intentional stance of the maker. Cézanne and Eliot thought a new realism could separate itself from such subjective conditions. For them perception freed from habit might be considered an impersonal process: there is a logic to seeing that stands bare when sight is isolated from all personal memory and all projection into a desired future. But the poets discussed here could not be content with this dream of transpersonal transparency. Even though these poets share a modernist sense of the interplay of the eye and the mind in producing the immediacy characterizing the real, they refuse to rely on the life of the eye as their model for the life in the poem. They regard immediacy as already suffused with the kinds of ineffable desires that make interpretation necessary, and that frustrate any effort to form interpretive judgments in so crude a medium as language. There can be no adequate judgments of the self except in terms that the self provides. While we may not believe the speakers, these poets wanted us to feel we had to find ways of dealing with these presences that beggar our interpretive languages, especially our moral languages. (Ironically, in this respect at least, confessional poetry repeats New Critical beliefs in the limitations of discursive language.)

Lowell's confessional style seems to me probably the most powerful instrument for rendering this sense of the imaginary as ineffable burden. One could still tell a Lacanian story about the traps that the imagination sets by eliciting our dreams of substantial selves.[5] But one would have to tell the story somewhat differently, as if the account of the imagination's need for substance came out of the workings of the imaginary. So the intimate, pervasive, and totalizing feel of the blend of imaginary and real becomes more important than any teleological account of desires for substantial identity. Consequently impersonality cannot be a "cure" because impersonality is impossible: the putatively impersonal is simply an imaginary or rhetorical shifting to a different level of the personal. Where the old new realism would emphasize the direct rendering of sensation, Lowell's new new realism articulates the core of fantasmatic activity, giving sensations their distinctive personal feel. And where the old new realism can be seen as fundamentally epistemic in its claims to provide knowledge, this realism is committed to needs that involve demands for sympathy, with all the ambivalence produced by that oxymoronic equation of demand with what must be freely given.

"Skunk Hour" is the most intricate treatment I know of how the imaginary can pervade every aspect of efforts at self-knowledge. Then I will turn to *History*, a later volume by Lowell, to clarify how he eventually tries to foster a public dimension for what remains his confessional model of how subjects express themselves. "Skunk Hour" is the final poem in *Life Studies*, the site where the value of the stance taken during the entire book is most emphatically at stake. One would not think the stakes were very high in the poem's opening stanzas because they present their details so laconically that they raise questions about why just these details and not others were chosen to set the scene. Description clearly seems driven by factors beyond its ken:

Nautilus Island's hermit
heiress still lives through winter in her Spartan cottage;
her sheep still graze above the sea.
Her son's a bishop. Her farmer
Is first selectman in our village;
She's in her dotage.

Thirsting for
The hierarchic privacy
of Queen Victoria's century,
she buys up all
the eyesores facing her shore,
and lets them fall.

The season's ill –
we've lost our summer millionaire, . . .
A red fox stain covers blue hill.   (Lowell, CP 191–2)

One can find traditional general themes here – pre-eminently the relation of survival to the internalizing of autumnal landscape. That is why the changing of the leaves becomes something like a cry of pain. But the contingency of detail makes it clear that even in the most "objective" segments of the poem the selections are ineluctably the act of a distinctive subject, and visibly the act of a very needy one projecting onto what otherwise might be objective. Even more important is the strange energy within this overtly casual presentation. Lowell learned from Williams that a modernist realism requires careful attention to line-endings, since it is these that in effect fix the units of perception and define tensions among these units. Here end-stopped lines mostly alternate with enjambed ones, with the second stanza's short lines especially conscious of the force of transition. Then there is the delightful yet somewhat disturbing playfulness of these lines, as if the speaker had to express an amusement with himself that we find out is also a defense against going beyond the surfaces. The opening four words could be all nouns until one sorts them out. And the *i* sounds of the first two lines play beautifully against the framing *as*. Then the tightening end-rhymes of the second stanza complement the "eyesores"/"shore" internal assonance. So much energy, so little apparent cause. In this situation playfulness with surfaces is also asked to perform other kinds of psychological work. In effect there seems nothing that is quite itself, nothing that does not call out for analysis, and nothing that will stand still for such analysis.

As "Skunk Hour" shifts to the speaker's own plight, we understand better the pressures the details are under. At first glance the last stanza celebrates a level of identification that promises the speaker has learned from his suffering. Now he has developed a capacity for sympathy on which a sense of community can be built:

> I stand on top
> of our back steps and breathe the rich air
> a mother skunk with her column of kittens swills the garbage pail.
> She jabs her wedge-head in a cup
> of sour cream, drops her ostrich tail,
> and will not scare.   (Lowell, CP 192)

Lowell wants identification with the skunk to reward the sustained confessional labor of reducing the self to raw need. The skunk provides a figure for a courage that comes only by tearing away imaginary defenses so that one gets in touch with something like primary biological needs. Yet the poem cannot reach this level of being without supplementing it by purely imaginary role-playing. Identification with the skunk as victim is inseparable from the trappings of priestly authority involved in the position at the top of the stairs. So even when Lowell tries to understand the imaginary, he remains in its grip: the projection of sympathy reinforces the ego needs that get him into trouble in the first place.

I once thought it was a telling criticism of Lowell to point out that this play of imaginary desires undercuts the resolving claim to self-knowledge afforded by identification with the skunk. But now I have to admit that the contradictions are probably "intended" because they emphasize the instability of identity that undermines projections about self-knowledge. We do not just recognize symptoms, as if the psyche conformed to epistemic criteria. We both recognize and imagine symptoms, so even this process of attempted identification renders reason problematic. Analogously, an ideal of sympathy with the speaker probably has to be distinguished from an ideal of sympathy compatible with moral judgment. Lowell wants his audience to recognize the fundamentally flawed and needy presences generating most significant speech acts. Modernist impersonality would treat such speakers as personae in order to establish distance from their imaginary needs. Lowell's confessional style is the antithesis to such objectification. It dramatizes the possibility that an individual's imaginary projections are not to be judged or pitied but to be seen as the necessary precondition for constituting specific values.

Soon after writing "Skunk Hour," Lowell probably came to understand some of the limitations of his confessional style. The very reasons that it affords a rich and challenging appeal to sympathy with the singular agent make it very difficult for that agent to find any terms at all for social life. At best there would have to be endless confessions endlessly talking by one another in a reciprocal procession of guilt and shame. This sense of limitation did not lead to Lowell's repudiating the imaginary or seeking a position from which he could ironize his needs. But he eventually began to write as if there could be a partial escape from the emphasis on individual imaginings, or, better, from imaginings confined to one's projections of one's distinctive agency. *For the Union Dead, Near the Ocean,* and many of Lowell's sonnets are efforts to stage other, more interpersonal paths to treating the imaginary itself as a possible source of social value. While this route will not produce specific political agendas, it will produce the possibility of projecting a politics of shared need and shared fears. As Jay Bernstein puts it, activating the condition of "injured and injurable animals" by taking responsibility for our particular damaged positions within social life provides a basis for a mutual compassion and perhaps the only trustworthy terms for mutual recognition.[6] Perhaps it was time for politics based on heroic dreams of reason to yield to a politics based on our necessary incompleteness and therefore our shared need for help.

To demonstrate this aspect of Lowell's sense of the imaginary I want to isolate two features of his sonnets. First he seeks a more intense and immediate realism by forgoing the complex metonymic adjustments by which the segments of "Skunk Hour" cohere. Where constructive artifice had been, there emerges the possibility that the entire sonnet can be a plausible instance of connections made in the development of a single moment of thinking as the imagination strives for a focal point. This sense of presentness makes it possible to stage subject and object as inextricably linked. Pound thought the image would fuse emotional and intellectual forces in an instant of time. Lowell sees the moment as vitally present only when there is resistance to the single image, as if time could be a factor in experience by making its distinctive claims against any objectification. Awareness of this force depends upon direct capacities for sympathy in which subjectivity is almost entirely a vehicle (rather than a composing force). The appeal to sympathy exists simply in the offering of the moment to the reader – not for any kind of truth it mediates but for the sake of a mind eager to feel alive by sharing what is offered as intense process. Lowell's sonnets on writers and historical figures read as if they were photographs by Annie Leibowitz, attuned to how characters might want to be remembered while expressing their vulnerabilities.

My second feature involves the politics of this shift in focus. If I am right about Lowell's investments in the imaginary, Lowell cannot rely on arguing for political ideas. He must test the possibilities of a politics of directed sympathy. And he must accomplish this by capturing fundamental anxieties that he does not resolve but heightens so that the shared neediness becomes inescapable. "The March I" presents a good example:

Under the too white marmoreal Lincoln Memorial,
the too tall marmoreal Washington Obelisk,
gazing into the too long reflective pool,
the reddish trees, the withering autumn sky,
the remorseless, amplified harangues for peace –
lovely to lock arms, to march absurdly locked
(unlocked to keep my wet glasses from slipping)

to see the cigarette match quaking in my fingers,
then to step off like green Union Army recruits
for the first Bull Run, sped by photographers,
the notables, the girls . . . fear, glory, chaos, rout . . .
our green army staggered out on the miles-long green fields,
met by the other army, the Martian, the ape, the hero,
his new-fangled rifle, his green new steel helmet.   (Lowell, CP 545)

Why is the memorial "too white," the Obelisk "too tall," and the reflecting pool "too long"? One answer is that Washington is just that kind of city – a city off-scale. But who treats the city this way? This is a more promising question for the poem because it calls attention to the basic trait of the speaker, and those allied with him in the peace march. The demonstrators are the ones alienated enough to record the irritating features of the cityscape. And this alienation creates the possibility that these are the people who can also appreciate fully what a new community could afford were it developed by the presence of so many like-minded people. The speaker then plausibly speaks for the crowd, or experiences as the crowd experiences, especially in his sense of the vulnerability figured by the "green" army of recruits emboldened only by their alienation.

These experiences in turn are sharply intensified when we see the opposing army. For this army does not need metaphors. The "green" now is literally the color of the helmets that serve metonymically to identify the soldiers. The poem can be resolved by this one detail because that sensation, or better that collective realization, defines how the "other army" occupies the visual field without any doubts about the situation. The resulting contrast between "us" and "them" cannot provide a thematic resolution for the poem. But attention to how the sensory details compose a situation provides a mode of self-awareness about vulnerability and need that at least can create sympathetic bonds establishing a partial sense of shared experiences, needs, and interests. And, perhaps most important, the poem so hews to aspects of that experience that it does not promise more than loose bonds of sympathy. Politics can best begin in the naming of shared disillusion: that at least helps contextualize the further disillusions that will almost inevitably follow.

This sonnet manages neither to deny the imaginary, as modernism tried to, nor to succumb to its terms, as the confessional style does.

Rather it seeks to socialize the imaginary by locating shareable terms in the very tendency to pity the self. One cannot be sure that any particular person can suspend his or her concern for the "individual" story sufficiently to let such sympathy develop into a social force. It may be that this ideal only intensifies cries of victimage and makes plausible redress or address impossible. But, at its best, the ideal of mutual sympathy provides access to the kind of pragmatic reasoning that can take place entirely in social terms, without the need for epistemic validation. Rather than focus on fictions of what keeps the self unique, readers are invited to speculate on how everyone's different versions of the imaginary may reveal sufficient common threads to provide an interest in efforts to reduce general human suffering across the board. It may be possible to organize another "green" army capable of initiating small revolutions in how we imagine ourselves imagining the political domain. There is as yet no more plausible image for the social work poetry can perform.

II

Among US poets since World War II, Adrienne Rich has probably been the most important public figure, in the sense that her work and her activities made a difference in the way many Americans viewed important political and cultural issues. (Allen Ginsberg has clearly been the most visible of these poets to the general population.) But Rich's stature has made it difficult to assess her work adequately: poets are "supposed" to be difficult and withdrawn, not active participants in various political struggles. So while sensitive critics like Margaret Atwood honor Rich's emotional force, they find much of her work overly political because it often relies on slack language and somewhat strident slogans.[7] This view seems to me to involve a limited view of art. It assumes that Rich and the readers interested in her have to be told that it is not good to sloganize or let language grow slack. The critics do not ask why Rich was willing to risk such obvious critiques during the years in the 1970s when she was formulating her political positions. And they do not concern themselves with what she hoped to produce by taking such risks. That is, they assume a very conventional view of artifice and ignore qualities like those that make Walt Whitman such a powerful and engaging figure.

In order to attend to why Rich takes such risks one has to reflect on the poet's relation to rhetoric. She manifestly refuses modernist ideals of impersonality so that she can take clear personal political stances and, more important, she can utilize every resource of spoken language in order to persuade her audience to share her values. With those ends in mind, how can she not take such risks?

In many respects Rich is Lowell's opposite. He presents himself as awkwardly stumbling into truth and forging community by emphasizing the need for mutual pity. We cannot do much better as social creatures than adjust to our inadequacies:

> We are poor passing facts
> warned by that to give
> each figure in the photograph
> his living name.   (Lowell, CP 838)

Rich, on the other hand, entered the public sphere precisely because she was fed up with the expectation that women would take the sympathetic role. She wrote public poetry out of a lucid and intense anger at injustice in the domains of gender, race, and class. For her an emphasis on sympathy repeats ancient injustices while affording people dangerous and misleading opportunities to feel good about themselves. Therefore she writes a poetry engaged in the effort to change how we formulate desires and how we take responsibility for pursuing where those desires lead us:

> . . . I am choosing
> not to suffer uselessly   and not to use her
> I choose to love   this time   for once
> with all my intelligence.[8]

The negatives here provide substantial evidence of just that intelligence capable of working economically and directly to get at why choice can provide a more capacious foundation than more passive modes of sympathy.

Despite these different paths, there is a profound bond linking these poets and explaining a good deal of their power. Both Lowell and Rich realized that the poetics of impersonality had gone tragically wrong, and they both thought only a radically different poetics could address what I have to call "the spiritual climate." Suppose poetry did not fight a perhaps hopeless battle against imaginary identifications but instead cultivated the imaginary dimension of experience – for its capacity to define individuals and for its capacity to construct communities. A lyric world struggling against imaginary identifications was necessarily a world in which passion continually ran the risk of devolving into irony and integrity into solipsism. Worse, in a world that did not honor imaginary identifications, poetry had no way to address a substantial public: it could not recover the rhetorical stances capable of projecting values against which social life could be judged and at least partially corrected. Without means of sharing identifications, measure becomes only a term relevant for specific aesthetic judgments, even at a time when public life was sorely lacking in any responsibility to standards of justice and fairness.

The parallels between these poets are easy to ignore because they chose such different paths for dealing with the imaginary. For Lowell the imaginary is primarily a relation with his own psyche, a taking permission to indulge in a realism that does not deny fantasy but embraces it as fundamental to understanding individual identity. Its social dimension then is an extension of the golden rule; treat everyone as if he or she had wounds governing their efforts at self-expression. Lowell's imaginary is both a cause for sympathy and a means of eliciting that sympathy. For Rich the imaginary is an instrument for creating the identifications that forge community: the greatest influence on her style was Yeats, not Williams. Yet two reasons make it seem urgent that we acknowledge the bonds at the root of these differences. One is their shared historical situation. Lowell and Rich came eventually to share revulsion with almost every aspect of New Critical values. Their criticisms went well beyond judgments about the lyric. They understood the ideological conservatism that made impersonality so attractive because so easy to contain – irony discourages adventures in shaping personality. And they understood the social cost of that ideology at a time when oppressed groups were finally using imaginary identifications to find the voices necessary to proclaim rights and specify injustices.

The second reason for linking Rich with Lowell is more closely connected with the choices determining the specific shapes of their poems. It is obvious and important that they rejected impersonality because the entire apparatus of third-person attitudes toward the self simply could not get into contact with how individuals are motivated or how they might enter into social relations. Efforts at realistic description can provide powerful instruments for characterizing situations and actions because they seek terms capable of making objective and shareable judgments. But they rarely capture what cannot be seen, like how the individual makes investments in the manner of the doing or in the various consequences made possible by the action. So both poets felt that the only way to embody distinctively first-person concerns was to express the shape of the desires one felt as distinctively one's own, even if they were laden with fantasy. More important, at least for Rich, these imaginary identifications were also fundamental to assertions about public identities. Many of our most powerful desires and fantasies have public dimensions: we want something for ourselves because we want something that we can feel we share with others. So a poetry responsive to conditions of individual desire might provide access to shared iden-tifications that, if we could acknowledge that social dimension, might elicit at least modest incarnations of a will to change. Rich saw a social world which confined the opportunities for significant individuation to a particular gender and a particular class, so it seemed worth taking the risks of striving for an effective rhetoric helping to make readers identify with roles capable of altering those conditions.

Adrienne Rich was born in 1929 into a bookish middle-class family living in Baltimore. Her first book, *A Change of World*, was pub-lished in 1951, the same year she graduated from Radcliffe. To read W. H. Auden's introduction to this volume (his selection for the Yale Younger Poets series) is to understand why Rich was soon to embrace the cause of feminism and to skewer male assumptions about superiority. Auden clearly respects her craft and her honesty. But it seems he cannot not condescend to her. His introduction is predicated on the idea that modernism is gone: the time is over, when twenty "men . . . were driven to find a new style which could cope with major changes in our civilization."[9] Why not then select a poet like Rich, "who is, I understand, twenty-one years old, displays a modesty not so common at that age, . . . and a love for her medium, a determination to ensure that whatever she writes shall, at least, not be shoddily made"? His strongest praise is that Rich's modesty does not allow her to lie, an important value for Auden. Her honesty helps her to present emotions that "are not peculiar to Miss Rich but are among the typ-ical experiences of our time; they are none the less for that uniquely felt by her." But when he turns to particulars, the condescending tone resumes: "Poems are analogous to persons; the poems a reader will encounter in this book are neatly and modestly dressed, . . . respect their elders but are not cowed by them, and do not tell fibs; that, for a first volume, is a good deal" (Rich, PP 278–9).

Rich's third book *Snapshots of a Daughter in Law* (1963) begins explicitly to repudiate every gesture of superiority that his culture allowed Auden's "Preface," a repudiation that would become more pronouncedly revolutionary in *Diving into the Wreck* (1971) and *The Will to Change* (1973). These volumes were followed by a decade of speeches and essays about the feminist revolution, all filling out the vision of social change that comprise the poems of *The Dream of a Common Language* (1978) and *A Wild Patience Has Taken Me This Far* (1981). There have followed in recent years several remarkable volumes like *An Atlas of the Difficult World* (1991), *Fox: Poems, 1998–2000* (2001), and *The School among the Ruins: Poems, 2000–2004* (2004) that are at once more personal and more metaphysical. She becomes less adamant about choosing her life and allows a good deal more vulnerability and fear, especially in relation to solitude and mortality.

I will confine myself to how Rich's art cultivates the dimensions of the imaginary resisted by those twenty revolutionary modernist men. Auden was not wrong about the apparent modesty of that first book. But within the formal and spiritual constraints of New Critical expectations, there is also an intricacy and tough-minded distance from distance, a revolutionary in the making that should have both pleased and troubled Auden. Consider "An Unsaid Word":

> She who has power to call her man
> From that estranged intensity
> Where his mind forages alone,
> Yet keeps her peace and leaves him free,
> And when his thoughts to her return
> Stands where he left her, still his own,
> Knows this the hardest thing to learn.   (FD 5)

This is clearly highly disciplined, formally crafted work, especially noteworthy for the way the single sentence holds the twists and turns of the syntax. This poem seems committed to extending this self-discipline so that she can accept the needs of the man to attempt this lonely form of self-possession. So this poem pursues a form of power over herself that can honor the heroic fantasies of her man – an ideal that now involves most readers in questioning the very ideology that appears to underlie the poem's strengths. It is hard not to notice that where the man is self-absorbed, she tries to get beyond the limitations of that stance. And even in 1950 the references to property (even if reciprocal – he is her man; she "his own") must at least be read as markers of tension, even if overcome by the ideal of being dutiful. Finally there is the brilliant last line. We cannot ignore the speaker's desire to overcome resentment at the man's self-centeredness because such a stance is necessary to his sense of identity. As bourgeois thinking in the fifties would have it, the speaker refers to the "hardest thing to learn" as a measure of the nobility available from the overcoming of difficulty – hence the single sentence as a figure of will and discipline. Yet the poem also invites a simpler and more psychological reading of "hardest thing."

This lesson is the hardest thing to learn because it is simply *contra naturam* (as Pound put it). This sense of accomplishment in submission requires sharply distinct gender roles that also reinforce the ideal of seeking identity through the "lessons" one can learn. In this reading, the poem is one sentence in order to stress barely contained rage – at the situation the man puts her in and at the poetics fostering the ideology that such control is a good thing.

Fewer than ten years later, Rich's "Snapshots of a Daughter-in-Law" would celebrate relegating those versions of nobility to ancient history:

> Sigh no more, ladies
> > Time is male
> and in his cups drinks to the fair.
> Bemused by gallantry, we hear
> our mediocrities over-praised,
> indolence read as abnegation,
> slattern thought styled intuition . . .   (FD 38)

Nobility and power no longer reside in the ability to master silence. The art of poetry can accommodate direct political concerns by concisely and precisely dissecting how women are treated by even well-meaning men. If the poet can render how women internalize male authority, she can also clear the way for finding imaginary versions of female identity that can provide alternative models of selfhood. Rather than depend on male gallantry, the poem turns to eroticized versions of how women can foster imaginative versions of their own distinctive powers. And it makes those powers "palpable" by the economy of phrase as well as the gorgeous control over rhythm and intricate sound patterning (especially in "her fine blades making the air wince"):

>   Well,
> she's long about her coming, who must be
> more merciless to herself than history.
> Her mind full to the wind, I see her plunge
> breasted and glancing through the currents,
> taking the light upon her
> at least as beautiful as any boy
> or helicopter,
>   poised, still coming,
> her fine blades making the air wince
>
> but her cargo
> no promise then:
> delivered
>   palpable
>   ours.   (FD 38–9)

Poetry by women need not protect itself with irony or modesty of indirection. But how can poetry be at once merciless and indulgent to the imaginary? Rich thought Lowell's realism provided one key because he defined how poetry told the "truth" in a distinctive way. The relevant sense of "truth" is not the scientific ideal of an assertion valuable because it is verified by qualified impersonal observers. Rather "truth" is personal, something which is tried on the pulses, with the power to shape a person's sense of possibility (see Rich, PP 259–63). Consider "Delta," a poem that might serve as a recasting of "An Unsaid Word":

> If you have taken this rubble for my past
> raking through it for fragments you could sell
> know that I long ago moved on
> deeper into the heart of the matter
>
> If you think you can grasp me, think again:
> my story flows in more than one direction
> a delta springing from the riverbed
> with its five fingers spread   (Rich, PP 13)

Unlike the earlier poem, this one is intensely public; its form of compression relies less on the virtues of private reflection than on condensing overt rhetorical gestures into two charged stanzas. Rich probably does not use rhyme in the first stanza because she wants the tension between casual discourse and the intensification produced by rhymes tightening the final figure. More important, the contrast between stanzas also becomes a contrast between attitudes. The first stanza dwells on the auditor for the first two lines, as if the poem had to be clear on the dangers of treating the speaker in terms of appearances that can then be used in the service of the auditor's interests. In contrast, the second stanza stages the dialectical force of second-person address as a kind of negative springboard into claiming very different kind of identifications – not with the rubble but with the multiple possibilities of the delta. Now identity is not a matter of what another can find but of how the self can forge identifications. And now the entire domain of figurative speech changes. The figure of the delta is not primarily descriptive, bound not to what she has done but to an identity that she thinks possible because she understands how spread fingers actually feel.

This intimacy nicely contrasts with the somewhat canned expression "the heart of the matter," by which the speaker first abstractly posits her freedom. What in the first stanza is abstract and clichéd gives way to evidence of an inner life not available if one relies only on observation. One has to rely on imagination – both to understand how this metaphor of the delta takes hold and to apply the sense of potential that it asserts. As Rich would put it in a poem almost con-temporaneous with this one, a dynamic figure of speech can "be the map" enabling one to "recognize that poetry / isn't revolution but a way of knowing / why it must come." Poetry can make palpable the revolutionary's sense of beginning where "the material and the dream can join" (Rich, PP 136).

Finding out how the material and the dream can join becomes for Rich the task of lyric poetry. Demonstrations of woman's independence had increasingly to merge with realizations of possible communities that could be forged out of such freedom. Hence her next two volumes, *The Dream of a Common Language: Poems, 1974–1977* and *A Wild Patience Has Taken Me This Far: Poems, 1978–1981*.[10] Both volumes are grounded in fundamental paradoxes, as if freedom for women consisted in part in their capacity to forge new combinations from an old cultural grammar. In the case of *The Dream of a Common Language*, the paradox involves integrating the apparently private space of dream with what had become a widespread philosophical interest in how common language forms expectations and expressive abilities that establish vital cultural life. By relying on both private and public realms, Rich could keep central a concern for where the common language originates and how fragile it is. Where the philosophers influenced by the later work of Wittgenstein emphasized how the grammar of the common language functions to train us to share expectations and uses, Rich dwelled on the possibility of projected identifications that enabled agents to use the full powers of "we": in short Rich wants not just the elaborate use of the rhetorical spirit but also the presence of that spirit made conscious of its fundamental drive to forge community.

In my view Rich's most interesting poem for creating that "we" is "Phantasia for Elvira Shatayev." Her search for possible idealization reaches out to the spirit of the Russian leader of a team of woman mountain climbers, all of whom died in August 1974. The poem begins with Shatayev's point of view in retrospect as she reflects on what the women gained by their labor:

> . . . For months   for years   each one of us
> had felt her own *yes*   growing in her . . .
> What we were to learn   was simply   what we had
> up here   as out of all words   that *yes*   gathered
> its forces   fused itself   and only just in time   (FD 226)

Beginning after the event allows a poignant sense of time. We arrive both after the inevitable disaster and before that disaster is known – at a time then when Shatayev can still present their dreams as a form of pregnancy. Beginning with the end allows us a strange perspective on the growing "yes" within that seeks other life with which to bond.

Then the speaker turns to address her husband. After having her acknowledge his love and asking him to appreciate their accomplishment, Rich turns everything she has learned from Yeats' fierce individualism to collective purposes. Rich has to meet the challenge that the poem not merely assert community but find in the present active resources to make the audience actually bond while honoring the space for individual choice. She responds by figuratively bringing the pregnancy to term as the elements of a collective person take form. That form is most visible when the women are buried, because Rich imagines Shatayev imagining going on

> into the unfinished   the unbegun
> the possible
> Every cell's core of heat   pulsed out of us
> into the thin air   of the universe . . .
> this mountain   which has taken   the imprint of our minds
> through changes elemental and minute
> as those we underwent
> to bring each other here
> choosing ourselves   each other   and this life   (FD 227)

Ultimately this poem repeats the logic of incarnation in quite secular terms: having risked everything and lost her life, this exemplary woman can establish a distinctive power of love that can transcend death. That is why Rich in conclusion offers Shatayev's diary, as if only after her death were known could we take fully seriously her claims about love:

> In the diary I wrote*: Now we are ready*
> *and each of us knows it I have never loved*
> *like this   I have never seen*
> *my own forces so taken up and shared*
> *and given back . . .*
>
> *We know now we have always been in danger*
> *down in our separateness*
> *and now up here together   but till now*
> *we had not touched our strength*
>
> In the diary torn from my fingers I had written:
> *What does love mean*
> *what does it mean   "to survive"*
> *A cable of blue fire ropes our bodies*
> *burning together in the snow   We will not live*
> *to settle for less   We have dreamed of this*
> *all of our lives*   (FD 227)

The modernist in me is disappointed by these lines. Certainly there are no clever conceits or even sharp formulations, and "burning" seems a melodramatic term for the passion that gives the women life in their death. But the modernist in me may have a lot to learn. Two aspects in this poem establish a powerful alternative not only to modernism's critiques of rhetoric but also to modernism's insistence on its versions of Keats' dictum to load every rift with ore. First there is the simple elemental clarity by which Rich connects the "we" of intense community to how life takes force from the encounter with death. Then there is the intelligence and skill leading Rich to rely so heavily on "this," as a means of defining what ultimately constitutes the community of women. The "this" here has a dazzlingly intricate set of referents – to the challenge, to the death, to the fact that they have not lived to settle for less, to what the shared deaths create, and to what the poem becomes in its gathering all those charged situations. The "this" grounds the "we," so that the reader realizes that these two terms are inextricably aligned: the fuller one appreciates the resonance of one, the better the position one is in to experience the power of the other. Making the last sentence of the poem a series of monosyllables creates the sense that the women can return to the simple elements with which the poem began. But now the elements are transformed by the weight of the dreams they can bear, without any need to change the direct simplicity of Shatayev's concrete experiences. The material and the dream take on communal shape, making it appear that rhetoric itself perhaps can realize no finer ideal.

III

Critics rarely read Robert Creeley in relation to Lowell and Rich because he relies on a quite different tradition, descending from Williams through the Objectivists to Charles Olson and his descendants. It is certainly to these figures we must look for the dialogues shaping Creeley's choices as a poet. But if we ask more generally why he is so insistent on engaging his private life in his poetry, comparisons to confessional poetry clearly become appropriate. Creeley shared with Lowell and Rich the sense that any poetry making a significant claim on realism would have to include in its ken the ways in which the imaginary is fostered as a distinguishing mark of the individual. However, he then turns confessional poetry on its head because he does not pursue the imaginary as a set of images for the self. Rather he wants quite a different level of the person. He wants to express the sensory level at which the imaginary takes hold, the level at which the fundamental drive to individuation takes place.

The best way to characterize the effort at individuation in Creeley's poetry is probably to begin with its sharpest philosophical formulation. For that we have to go back 350 years, to the seventeenth-century Dutch philosopher Baruch Spinoza who developed the idea of a conative drive. Conatus is defined as the drive that "as far as it can, and as far as it is in itself, . . . endeavors to persist in its own being." In one sense, this is radical individualism: the fundamental impulse in all animate beings is the desire to express the self by imposing its power of activity on an environment. But Spinoza's view is far more elemental than the views that in our culture have been developed by ego-psychology. The goal of expression is not self-knowledge as a concept or image; expressing the self consists simply in an awareness of how "the body's power of activity is increased or diminished, assisted or checked, together with the ideas of these affections."[11] Conativity is the felt power to find reflexive satisfaction within one's capacity to control the physical and imaginative space a being occupies.

From a Spinozan point of view, confessional poetry seeks the self on the wrong level – on the level of the imaginary self rather than on the level where the force underlying the imaginary might be traced. Creeley could make a similar distinction because his Williams was very different from Lowell's. More precisely, Creeley could make the break from confessional poetry because he wanted to do very different things with Williams' heritage. We might say that what primarily appealed to Lowell in Williams was the old realism in his work, the sense of concrete detail and the distrust of abstraction. What appealed to Creeley was the effort at immediacy, the sense that reality is a matter of sensations as they cohere and take sufficiently intense forms to resist mere fantasy. Creeley turns Williams' romance with objects into a romance with elemental subjective drives too subtle and varied to capture in images. His basic goal is to render the transition from inchoateness to the shapes language can give to experience.[12] The result is an intimate and intricate bond between possibilities of identification and appreciation of the resources for engaging expressive energies that poetry affords. Poetry's powers of wording become inseparable from the psyche's powers to work itself through complicated emotional itineraries without withdrawing in fear or in laziness from the modes of embodiment language affords. The ego seeks not knowledge about itself but the intensification of its sense of itself within an expressive medium.

These commitments on Creeley's part seem always to have shaped his published work. Unlike most of his peers (but like Ashbery and O'Hara), he never submitted to the authority of New Criticism. Perhaps it was largely because his father's early death left Creeley so restless that he never settled down for much formal education. He did attend Harvard but never graduated. His first stint was broken by a year with the American Field Service in India and Burma; his second by a move to Cape Cod, then to a farm in New Hampshire, then to Majorca before he was invited in 1954 to join Charles Olson, then the Provost of Black Mountain College. There would be many more moves, although Creeley did settle into a poetics allied with Olson's. But where Olson was projective, relying on quasi-mythic backdrops and on a heroic poetry of the breath, Creeley was quietly intense, developing his minimalist versions of a poetics of process. In 1966 he began teaching at SUNY Buffalo, a position he maintained till about 2002. His most influential books were published early in his career – *For Love: Poems, 1950–1960* (1962) and *Words* (1965) – because those were his most intense and anguished. But he has continued to produce a very high level of work up to the present, much of it collected in *Just in Time: Poems, 1984–1994* (2001) and *If I Were Writing This* (2003).

A good rule for a literary critic is, whenever he or she is tempted to invoke a philosopher, to compensate by paying careful attention to at least two poems. To demonstrate how Creeley focuses on conative energy, and to begin speculating on how these commitments lead to a distinctive response to the themes I have been developing, I will begin with "Joy":[13]

I could look at
an empty hole for hours
thinking it will
get something in it,
will collect
things. There is
an infinite emptiness
placed there.[14]

I am struck, first, by the courage, or folly, involved in stripping the site of poetry to such elemental relations. What drama there is has to be based simply on how the reflective process finds words for its relation to emptiness. Achieving satisfaction or momentary plenitude as a subject does not demand any particular narrative or image; nor does it rely upon what might be considered any kind of uplifting vision. It requires only getting a productive feel for the difference between the emptiness that becomes a source of anxiety and an "infinite emptiness" somehow occupying its allotted place.[15]

Actually there is considerable drama in this poem, but only if we are willing to read it on the level of delicate shifts in sensibility. Initially looking and thinking are set against the empty hole, as if the domain of consciousness were completely different from the domain of objects. Looking and thinking seem entirely activities of the individual subject, and the empty hole becomes an inert figure standing outside as object. But the slight shift from "I could" to "There is" seems to me to bring with it a substantial change in affective possibilities. The poem moves from the subjunctive and the subjective to the impersonal or transpersonal. So the speaking consciousness need not just project into the world correlates of its own emptiness. Instead its own activities can be aligned with space rather than time. Then the emptiness is not just encountered as other but is inhabited as significant modification of the subject's situation.

Creeley's breath lineation defines just what kind of significance that placement is, and just what kind of poet he is as he rises to the challenge of making every mark count. Almost every line ends with a pronounced incompleteness, hovering between a predicate expression and some possible object. I take the pauses as indices of anxiety, each expressing an urgency to see emptiness somehow filled and each frustrated by a beyond to the order of things that produces the feeling of emptiness. But negotiating emptiness here also dramatizes on the most intimate levels how it might feel to experience the satisfactions that occur when intentional dispositions hook on to what they seek. Each moment stages possibilities for a sense of arrival – not as a large dramatic realization but as a simple intensifying of the mind's capacity to find places for its energies.

There is no top of the stairs from which one can transform emptiness into a fullness by seeing it as some kind of step in a dialectical process. Instead the emptiness simply becomes a basic condition of experience admitting of more than one framing perspective. Then change is not a melodramatic production number. Experiences do not have latent substance. They appear as surrounded by possibilities of going on. So the speaker can modify his investments simply by shifting how he stands toward his own acts of figuration. Because in this case he begins with emptiness as alien and imposed, he can emphasize the subtle but crucial shift involved in coming to understand how the emptiness can seem placed, and therefore how we can find his own place in the scene. Forging a sense of presence is not a heroic act, and not the result of any sequential process. The sense of placement just takes an adjustment in learning to accept what self-consciousness can do to alter how we adapt to elemental conditions.

Now I want to exhibit some of the work Creeley's conative poetics can accomplish when he turns to other, more "substantial" situations. This is best done by continuing to compare his characteristic moves to those employed by confessional poetry because he seeks the same kind of intimacy and singularity, but by radically different lyric strategies. Being able to speak as an "I" simply depends on being able to ward off all those frameworks for which it is appropriate to speak of the "I" as an "it." Creeley's "Introduction" to *Words* is probably his clearest statement of this position:

> Things continue, but my sense is that I have at best, simply taken place with that fact. . . . So it is that what I feel, in the world, is the one thing I know myself to be, for that instant. I will never know myself otherwise. Intentions are the variability of all these feelings, moments of that possibility. How can I ever assume that they come to this or that substance? (Creeley, CP 261)

Similarly the basic ambition driving his poems is not for the self to gather itself in heroic expressive acts but to feel itself able to make all the turns and twists necessary to stay connected with where thought and speech might lead it. Feelings are registered less as elements of narrative constructs than as constant tonal shifts and quick adjustments to what the changing situation seems to demand.

Imagine turning from *The Waste Land* or "Skunk Hour" to Creeley's "A Song":

I had wanted a quiet testament
and I had wanted, among other things,
    a song.
        That was to be
of a like monotony.
               (A grace
Simply. Very very quiet.
                    A murmur of some lost
thrush, though I have never seen one.

    Which was you then. Sitting
and so at peace, so very much now this same quiet

    A song.

And of you the sign now, surely, of a gross
    Perpetuity
                (which is not reluctant, or if it is
it is no longer important.

    A song.

    Which one sings, if he sings it, with care.   (Creeley, CP 112)

The speaker wants ("among other things") a song that expresses a simple quiet, but there turns out to be nothing stable, nothing at peace in this call for quiet because the "I" seems so divided. And the speaker is also afraid that this quiet will bring a loss of these "other things" and impose a monotonous conventionality on his relationship. So the poem tries to engage this duplicity at its source and come to some resolution.

Initially this project seems to fail because the speaker's effort at lucidity in relation to song only generates constant self-mockery, with incomplete parentheses as reminders that the desire for song seems to impose either fantasy or conventionality on the particularity he wants to praise. Creeley nonetheless works his way out of this dilemma by making what undoes conventional song generate an even more powerful alternative lyric space. With that space also comes an alternative notion of the subjectivity that lyric can establish. In this case the poem mobilizes three senses of "care" and asks us to imagine a world, and a mode of subjectivity, responsive at once to all three, and to the work language does in making these aspects possible. Care can be the means of establishing and maintaining intimacy with another person, but care also has to take the form of a self-defensive scrutiny wary of appearing to be a fool or being manipulated as a fool. And throughout both conditions, care has to be a process of preserving one's intimacy with the language one speaks. If "care" in either of the first two senses stops, one risks no longer being an agent within language because the language itself seems to assert its control.

Each time the poet expresses his desire for song that expresses "care" in the first sense, "care" in the second sense seems to force him to reject the words that come to satisfy this desire. Even the dream of quiet is haunted by romantic figures of the thrush, so that he has to admit his own distance from his figures (a distance presented literally in the poem as its lines move to the right). But this frustration seems inseparable from the hope that he can fight his way through to what might actually give satisfying expression to his desire. At least a glimpse of that satisfaction finally emerges with the shift to the final line, "Which one sings, if he sings it, with care." For here it seems that the speaker has turned away from attempting to find figures of speech for desire so that he can instead directly appreciate the qualities that the song must possess, whatever the content. This move then is sanctioned by the final reference to "care" as, apparently, the word the entire poem has been looking for, because it has been exploring states that engage its various meanings. Now it seems as if the speaker manages to locate something at the core of his desire for song that has not been destroyed by the failures of expression.

Finding the full word enables the poem to turn from the unhappy "I" in the past tense who haunts the opening lines to the impersonal "one" in the present tense at the conclusion. This may seem a minor matter of grammar, but I think the capacity to make this shift manifests an important imaginative breakthrough for the poetry of the 1960s. Confessional writing tried to reward its needy speakers with various kinds of elaborate images with which they could ultimately identify because of the intensity the poem has channeled. Think of Lowell's skunk or Plath's colossus. Creeley's speaker seems rewarded for his struggle only by the less than sublime possibility of transforming the needy "I" into the objective "one" upon whom the speaker can reflect. Yet, in a world pervaded by the need for constant self-mockery, there may be no greater reward than establishing this ability to see oneself in fundamentally functional terms that absorb the felt singularity of the "I." The subject can be an object to itself without lamenting its distance because the poem finds a vehicle of expression that need not apologize for itself. Creeley's poem seems to assert that the most fundamental satisfaction for the lyric is less in what it says than in the sudden realization that the speaking has found linguistic means to bring that momentary peace. Creeley's poems are acts in the full sense because they embody a quest to find a mode of expression that can come to terms with disturbances setting the mind in motion. The poem embodies the struggle of the speaker to become "one" who can speak these words with care.

I could go on looking at Creeley's poems for hours, but shall content myself with two more. The first strikes me as Creeley's sharpest formulation of his differences from his contemporaries. Then I will focus on a poem that is probably Creeley's clearest effort to honor the Objectivist spirit of Williams while keeping his distinctive voicing.

"The Rain" constitutes a compelling struggle to find the words that might relieve a painful sense of inadequacy:

All night the sound had
    come back again
and again falls
    this quiet, persistent rain.

What am I to myself
    that must be remembered,
insisted upon
    so often? Is it

that never the ease,
    even the hardness,
of rain falling
    will have for me

something other than this,
    something not so insistent –
Am I to be locked in this
    final uneasiness.

Love, if you love me,
    lie next to me.
Be for me, like rain,
    the getting out

of the tiredness, the fatuousness, the semi-
    lust of intentional indifference.
Be wet,
    With a decent happiness.   (Creeley, CP 207)

We find poetry pursuing a form of resolution quite distinct from the imaginary satisfactions sought by confessional poetry, and indeed by most lyric work since Romanticism. For the speaker here does not try to develop any kind of synthetic image that either provides a picture of his own powers or manages to have some description take on numinous force. In fact there is no generalized quest at all. The poet seeks only a quite specific concrete sense that there is an alternative, even a momentary one, to this condition of pressing uneasiness from which he suffers. He pursues the possibility that he can identify with a way of speaking able to provide testimony for why his love seems to matter.

The test of this testimony takes two basic forms. First he takes on the task of making the woman sustain a symbolic transformation of the rain without relying on any system of belief. The poem measures what the woman means for him by first postulating a language heavy with the alienated distancing abstractness of Latinate discourse. Then, against that contrastive background, her sensuality can be fully appreciated because of the direct language it calls for. Whatever "decent happiness" can be, it must be able to incorporate these clipped constants: the monosyllabic can be heroic in a world lost in the multi-syllabic. Then we can provisionally believe that what transforms the rain is not just some idea of sexual pleasure but this specific way of attuning the registers of language to the satisfactions that the physical can provide in every domain. And we can believe in this love without having to postulate any abstractions about love in general.

Creeley's poem "Something" can even adjust for the piety creeping into my prose. It demonstrates concretely how his insistent self-consciousness positions his poetry to realize on very intimate levels what may be distinctive to other lives and to our relations with them.

The poem's realism in not in the picture it presents but in the process of recognition it establishes:

> I approach with such
> a careful tremor, always
> I feel the finally foolish
>
> question of how it is,
> then, supposed to be felt,
> and by whom. I remember
>
> once in a rented room on
> 27th street, the woman I loved
> then, literally, after we
>
> had made love on the large
> bed sitting across from
> a basin with two faucets, she
>
> had to pee but was nervous,
> embarrassed I suppose I
> would watch her who had but
>
> a moment ago been completely
> open to me, naked, on
> the same bed. Squatting, her
>
> head reflected in the mirror,
> and the hair dark there, the
> full of her face, the shoulders,
>
> sat spread-legged, turned on
> one faucet and shyly pissed. What
> love might learn from such a sight.   (Creeley, CP 281)

Creeley's poems typically present rather daunting tasks for their women because he brings such intense self-consciousness to the situations. In this case I think the uneasiness is primarily about sex, but also about encountering other aspects of the lover's nakedness. Let us call these other aspects "the encounter with the embarrassable body." Then one can see why there is much to learn from the sight of the woman shyly pissing in this hotel room. For she manages to handle the embarrassing situation without evading it, but also without insisting defensively on her nobility or on her right to honor her necessities in whatever way she feels necessary. This woman makes her embarrassment and shyness part of the emotional theater (or, to be more precise, Creeley projects these traits upon her the better to stage his own effort to honor them). She offers the shyness and embarrassment as qualifiers of her response to necessity, and by not lying or evading or ennobling the situation she makes it profoundly intimate. She can trust him to understand, and perhaps she can trust him to share the self-delight in what she manages to do within the protective cover of her own shyness.

Yet the woman's action in itself does not exhaust what this sight has to teach. The poet has to bring his investments to bear so that we feel what is involved in learning to appreciate the woman's action. The first thing love learns from such a sight is how being in love motivates one to pay attention. The woman's body and situation elicit a careful and unsentimental tracing, as if Degas were painting these lovers in the style of his portraits of bathing women. So rendered, the details suffice. The lovers take on intensity because there is no effort to make either character more appealing to the other than the scene will allow. (Love is never having to say you are compensating for the details.) That attention enables the shyness to become an expressive aspect of the woman's presence. Shyness does not have to be suppressed. Fully investing in where one is, then sharing that acceptance without an idealization of acceptance, may be the richest embodiment of love we can imagine.

But how can the poem embody that investment without depending on the idea that one should make such investments? How can it resist being nourishment for the generalizing moralist? This is where Creeley's lineation plays an important semantic role that both complements the assertions and provides an actual, temporal experience of shifts in attention that also involve shifts in valuation, without relying on abstract norms. First, the line-endings enhance the painterly qualities because they insist that, despite the flat description, this vision of the scene depends very much on the specific investments composing it. The obvious care for the placement of words and sound effects carries the poem's rendering of a parallel conative effort of the speaker to feel his own place in the scene. In fact the energy within the lines seems to be what builds to the final exclamation. The exclamation does not come from outside the poem as commentary or moral but from within as a gathering and release of the energies that the woman's gesture elicits. Here the lover performs the ultimate sonneteer's action – he raises his love to the status of exemplar, and at the same time he revels in the strangeness of this route to exemplarity.

Perhaps only poetry can make shyness exemplary. For the woman's power is inseparable from the reticent particularity of what remain highly expressive details. She matters because she manages to keep a resonant humanity within a scene that usually produces only embarrassment. And the poetry matters as a mode of caring in which antieloquence takes on its own expressive register. Shyness pervades the scene, and love is what can both elicit and register that form of human presence.

IV

Elizabeth Bishop turned her shy reticence into one of the most important bodies of poetry in the twentieth century. She envied Lowell, her very good friend, his fluent and unembarrassed first person, but knew that her strengths lay elsewhere, mostly in her ability to share Wallace Stevens' and Marianne Moore's ways of making the processes of imagination inhabit the most forbidding of apparently objective structures.

Bishop was born in 1911 in Worcester, Massachusetts. Her father died when she was eight months old and her mother went into a mental institution soon after, so she grew up both in the Worcester area and in Nova Scotia with her mother's family. After graduating from Vassar, she traveled and wrote, producing her first book, *North and South*, in 1946. She moved to Brazil in 1951 and lived there for fifteen years with Lota de Macedo Soares, who committed suicide in 1967. Her first two books, *North and South* and *A Cold Spring* (1955), combined Moore's subtle discursive distance with apparently cold scenic presentations dense with subtle metaphoric feelings. Then with the move to Brazil her poetry loosened up, becoming more personal, more topical, and more politically engaged. Finally *Geography III* (1976) presents many of her best poems, from the intensely personal and psychological "In the Waiting Room" to the intricate reflective narratives "The Moose" and "Five Flights Up," to "One Art," probably the best sestina in English.

Like Lowell, Bishop had a somewhat vexed relationship with New Critical values. Her first two books accepted the impersonal meditative style that these critics favored, and the poems at least flirted with a sacramental logic binding perception to symbolic resonance. Yet impersonality for her was less an ironic position than a means of emphasizing the powers of language to produce cogent analogies for subjective states without invoking the first person. Both Moore and Stevens would have been delighted with my first example, the title poem from *A Cold Spring*, because of its ability to activate the imagination without letting it become absorbed in imaginary roles. I will then show how the opening sequence in *Questions of Travel* exemplifies another shift in handling identification with enormous consequences for modernism. Here Bishop establishes a mandarin version of what would in large part constitute post-modernism in poetry. Rather than ask Lowell's question – "Who am I as the world besets me in various ways?" – she uses the role of tourist to focus instead on the question "Where am I standing?" Her poems then become explorations of location – of angle and relative distance. That mode of questioning allows others – other people and the entire world of nature – a significant and mobile existence. The self does not measure situations by the binary oppositions between resistance to the will or complicity with it; rather, everything becomes a matter of degree and position. The other has as much reality as the self, but in a different place changing at different rates. So Bishop may be the first white American major poet fully aware of what we all were to learn about the de-centering of the West and the limitations of the oppositions on which its imaginary world was founded.

"A Cold Spring" invites comparison with Williams' "By the Road to the Contagious Hospital":

A cold spring:
the violet was flawed on the lawn.
For two weeks or more the trees hesitated;
the little leaves waited,
carefully indicating their characteristics.
Finally a grave green dusk
settled over your big and aimless hills.
One day, in a chill white blast of sunshine,
on the side of one a calf was born.
The mother stopped lowing . . .[16]

Williams' text had been carefully constructivist, its verbless introductory fifteen lines echoing the winter environment. So I imagine Williams and his constructivist peers hating Bishop's poem. They would have to admit the sound-play is masterful. The vowel patterning evokes so much energy that the particulars seem eager to enter the world of discourse. But these poets probably could not have stomached the poem's reliance on the pathetic fallacy – for them the depths of sentimentality was reading human traits into non-human entities. And that lack of rigor seems matched by the poem seeming far too leisurely as it switches details and explores aspects of the scene. There is not enough concentrated energy.

Yet "A Cold Spring" seems too sly and too intelligent to be dismissed for what it does not do. It is more prudent to concentrate on what it does accomplish. Notice for example that this is not the usual pathetic fallacy evoking human states in describing nature. This pathetic fallacy is part of direct address – so we have either to imagine it as illicit metaphorizing on a grand scale or to see it as wittily extending the domain of terms appropriate for direct address, perhaps because these terms establish an intimacy with the scene that the poet will pursue. And the sound patterns like "flawed on the lawn" do not seek Poundian architectural effects. Rather they offer indulgent and witty reminders of how materialist this consciousness must become fully to appreciate spring. Finally, the casual handling of direct address suggests a range of attitudes possible toward spring that makes Williams' absolute contrast between the deadness of late winter and the quickening of spring seem somewhat melodramatic. Bishop too is interested in how spring quickens the world. But that quickening does not replace deadness. Rather than emphasize sudden change, Bishop concentrates on a kind of ripening, made visible by the speaker's willingness to try out various intimate modes of address.

The beginning of spring makes its appearance by working different transformations in a range of locations:

Four deer practiced leaping over your fences.
   The infant oak-leaves swung through the sober oak.
Song-sparrows were wound up for the summer,
   and in the maple the complementary cardinal
cracked a whip and the sleeper awoke,
   stretching miles of green limbs from the south. (Bishop, CP 55)

Bishop makes the eye move carefully through different registers of vision – close-up with the leaves and the single cow, but at a distance in time and space as it observes the trees and the "grave green dusk." Each verb refuses quite to be naturalized, as if the excess brought by language had to be part of the scene. Bishop does not rely on Stevens' "as," but she works out a similar principle of equivalence between words and world that makes feelings as important as perceptions. These lines do not impose strict binaries between the quick and the dead. That would be easy self-congratulation for the one identifying with the living. Instead Bishop's sense of poetry requires the discipline in author and reader to delight in the small differences making can proliferate.

The most important difference from Williams' poem occurs in the ways the poets handle their concluding stanzas. Williams' poem celebrates spring by relying on two compositional analogues for spring's power to quicken. The last stanza exaggerates enjambment in order to make palpable the poem's own concerns for the rootedness that its sequence provides. And these last lines offer almost a revel of verbs, as if the richest way to appreciate spring is to concentrate on feelings that contrast winter's heaping of actionless detail against this closing sense of spring's almost detail-less pleasure in activity. For Williams the imagination does not have to stage the agent because it suffices to develop analogies between our feelings for language and our feelings for the quickening of spring. But Bishop refuses even this analogical use of binary oppositions. Rather than having the general situation produce an intensified sense of vitality, she ties each verb to a specific kind of activity as a warmer day takes hold.

Then she allows herself a synthetic crescendo:

> Now, in the evening,
>   a new moon comes.
> The hills grow softer. Tufts of long grass show
>   where each cow-flap lies. . . .
> Now, from the thick grass, the fireflies
>   begin to rise:
> up, then down, then up again:
>   lit on the ascending flight,
> drifting simultaneously to the same height,
>   – exactly like the bubbles in champagne.

    – Later on they rise much higher.
    And your shadowy pastures will be able to offer
  these particular glowing tributes
    every evening now throughout the summer.   (Bishop, CP 55–6)

Where Williams is content to celebrate establishing verbal equivalents for this stark contrast producing the new sense of "now," Bishop wants to bring out the complexity of the moment. She wants not only the force of the "now" but a sense of the variety of expression "now" brings to the landscape we are imaginatively inhabiting. The first "now" parallels the moon as a source of light, albeit light for the active imagination as it deploys itself to participate in what the scene makes available. The second "now" stretches this sense of participation so that the poem can move from the life of the eye to a sense of metaphoric identification with the effects of the fireflies' flight as its height varies with the season. Even the "bubbles of champagne" do not refer us to the artist-composer's will but serve to extend the space where the series of perceptions is taking place (deliciously inverting Mallarmé's "Salut").

Then there is the spectacular final "now." In one sense it is more quiet than the others because it is buried within the last line rather than starting both a line and a sentence. Here the dramatic priority is given to the second-person address that Bishop wants us to see as earned by all the intimate attention that the poem gives the scene. Yet this final "now" exceeds the others in power because this one carries the burden of consciously establishing the intimacy on which the poem has been trading. This "now" matters because it has come to include the future, and therefore it has extended the range of emotional attachments available for the speaker: the speaker sees now and sees in the "now" how the pastures will offer the same life throughout the summer.

The sentence bearing this final "now" is very simple: these tributes will take place "every evening now throughout the summer." Yet what it contains and synthesizes is extraordinarily intricate. This casual expression brings together three quite different aspects of potential investments in how time unfolds – *as* the promise of repeated pleasure, *as* the intensification of the present moment now also distributed into those repetitions, and *as* a capacious projection of the general sense of emergence available throughout the summer. This "now" quickens not just our sense of the contrast with winter but our sense of the contrast with any sense of time incapable of blending intensity and promise. That quickening is not without its shadowy other comprised by feelings of imminent loss that are the converse of every moment of renewal. (It is, after all, "A Cold Spring.") But because here spring includes this temporal expansiveness, it allows projections in which that dark other becomes itself a stage enabling us the better to appreciate the expected recurrences. This is an otherness that does not require the image of the heroic ego to rise up in resistance. Adding the ego would only detract from the fullness of this state. And adding the ego might also transform the awareness that summer too has its contingency into nothing but lament. By avoiding the first person for the second, Bishop manages to have all the intensity of subjectivity with none of the melodrama of personality.

This is as good as impersonality gets as a mode of affirmation, or almost as good, since "The Bight" and "At the Fishhouses" are probably even greater poems. Yet Bishop was not content. She wanted a somewhat more personal style that directly engaged contemporary experience, perhaps in dialogue with what Lowell was developing. But she was too much the aristocrat, too self-protected and wary to allow herself full confessional intensity. And she was too good a critic not to see that this confessional poetics was likely to produce "more and more anguish and less and less poetry."[17] Luckily, about this time she moved to Brazil, and life supplemented imagination. She found the perfect situation for being personal and being intensely self-aware and self-protective at the same time: she could have her poetry emphasize the role of tourist. This would allow her poetry to bring to persons the same sense of specificity she had brought to her scenes, and she could build respect for differences into a value scheme that challenged many of the hierarchies the New Criticism stood for. Bishop would never become a Marxist – that would be for her an unseemly bid for approval and a dangerous reallocation of authority for people who might not be ready for it. But she could find in the guise of tourist a way of emphasizing the distinctness of unique cultural contexts that could no longer be kept aligned by a single dominant power, political or conceptual.

Questions of Travel has two parts, an eleven-poem section, "Brazil," dealing with the need to adjust to differences in culture and geography, and then a section, "Elsewhere," devoted to travel in time and the weight of mortality. I want simply to characterize the voice established by the first two poems in "Brazil" and to illustrate how that voice opens for Bishop a world where the differences produced by the attentive imagination take on social force. This is the opening of "Santos," the first poem of the volume (repeated from *A Cold Spring* where it had been the concluding poem):

Here is a coast; here is a harbor;
here, after a meager diet of horizon, is some scenery;
impractically shaped and – who knows – self-pitying mountains,
sad and harsh beneath their frivolous greenery

with a little church on top of one. And warehouses,
some of them painted a feeble pink, or blue,
and some tall, uncertain palms. Oh! Tourist,
is this how this country is going to answer you

and your immodest demands for a different world,
and a better life and complete comprehension
of both at last and immediately,
after eighteen days of suspension.

Finish your breakfast. The tender is coming,
a strange and ancient craft, flying a strange and brilliant rag.
So that's the flag. I never saw it before.
I somehow never thought of there *being* a flag,   (Bishop, CP 89)

I love how the poem casts the role of tourist as being positioned between self-consciousness and self-indulgence. The opening reads as if it were a response to the imperative "begin again." Each particular is named, but the naming utterly lacks precision. After all, how can the tourist do anything more than identify generic elements, even while attempting to get the emotional atmosphere right? No wonder that the speaker turns on herself, painfully aware of the gulf between powerful ambitions and reduced reality. Yet, as the speaker reins herself in, the tender emerges as a distinctively different particular – close enough for her to think about her seeing, and surprising enough to make the seeing a significant adventure. It takes disillusion with the big possibilities in order to begin the project of attending to the small details that can create permanent and productive unsettlement. Now the tourist is ready to see, and not just to repeat what fantasy had projected.

"Santos" ends with the line, "we are driving to the interior," a promise that Bishop was to explore on several levels. But the most comprehensive sense of what the interior offers occurs in the very next poem, as an introduction to the challenges posed by quite particular cases in the subsequent poems.[18] "Brazil, January 1, 1502" engages the experience of the original Portuguese settlers, from the point of view of the contemporary tourist sufficiently self-aware to recognize fully, perhaps for the first time, the psychodynamics of those who thought it was their right to conquer what did not fit their schema:

> Januaries, Nature greets our eyes
> exactly as she must have greeted theirs:
> every square inch filling in with foliage –
> big leaves, little leaves, and giant leaves,
> blue, blue-green, and olive . . .   (Bishop, CP 91)

There follow ten more lines describing the foliage: the tourist of "Santos" has learned to see. The second stanza turns to the sky, then the rocks "attacked above / by scaling-ladder vines, oblique and neat," finally to focus on the lizards who

> scarcely breathe; all eyes
> are on the smaller female one, back-to,
> her wicked tail straight up and over,
> red as a red-hot wire.   (Bishop, CP 92)

Landscape can go no further. Self-consciousness comes, and with it the comparison with the Christian invaders, alien from this nature and from the culture that inhabits it:

> Just so the Christians, hard as nails,
> tiny as nails, and glinting,
> in creaking armor, came and found it all,
> not unfamiliar:
> no lover's walks, no bowers,
> no cherries to be picked, no lute music,
> but corresponding, nevertheless,
> to an old dream of wealth and luxury
> already out of style when they left home –
> wealth, plus a brand-new pleasure.

Directly after Mass, humming perhaps
L'Homme armé or some such tune,
they ripped away into the hanging fabric,
each out to catch an Indian for himself –
those maddening little women who kept calling,
calling to each other (or had the birds waked up?)
and retreating, always retreating, behind it.   (Bishop, CP 92)

The violence first seems a surprise: even though the Christians are hard as nails, they seem like us, grappling to make sense of what is so unfamiliar that it creates confusion at every turn. But to be surprised is to ignore what the first stanza prepared. All that lushness of nature and yet no adequate language for its appreciation – such alienation will have its sexual consequences. And while we have to pity the Christians because their dreams are out of place even in their own culture, we also have to remember what expectations their culture generates: they are men after all, and violence seems both a right and a necessity.

Finally we cannot forget how the incomplete sense of familiarity suffices to make the Christians feel entitled to the women, even as the poem marvelously calls all senses of entitlement into question. Whatever that hanging fabric is (Bishop leaves it deliberately vague), ripping into it only makes more distant the objects of their desire. And with this distance comes a frightening clarity: these imperialists are all too familiar. Male destructiveness in the West is not far from tourist desires gone awry. Fueled by the imagination of wealth and sexual plenitude, and encouraged by their sense of entitlement, these men are doomed to destroy what they do not know how to possess in any other way. Yet Bishop manages by intensifying that threat also to suggest the powers of resistance possible if those who are the objects of desire can maintain their distance. The comedy of otherness is how the women find resources in retreating; the tragedy of otherness is that this retreat intensifies the naked violence of the frustrated pursuers.

V

John Ashbery's most succinct statement about New Critical poetics occurs in a review of Adrienne Rich's *Necessities of Life*.[19] He is slightly more respectful than Auden, and far more amusing. The review begins by noting that Rich at the time was a traditional poet, not a conventional one, and that "she has made progress since those schoolgirlish days when she would come home from a Bach concert worried that 'A too compassionate art is half an art'." Her development makes her "a kind of Emily Dickinson of the suburbs," but at her best she has also learned to be a "metaphysical poet" making "inner and outer reality fuse into a kind of living fabric." Praise duly given, Ashbery cannot resist making Rich into a type:

> Sometimes she does succumb to the mania for over-interpretation that plagues her contemporaries. (The technical term for this ailment is objective correlativitis. It attacks poets in their late thirties, and is especially prevalent in New England; elms are thought to be carriers.)
>
> (Rich, PP 279)

Then he adds the comment that "Everybody's hell is different, but a reader conversant with those of Burroughs, Ginsberg, and Ed Sanders, . . . is not likely to be shaken up by Miss Rich's bowling alley or reassured by the couple in the trailer." Once he has had his way with her, however, he returns to praise that reveals as much about his work as about hers:

> It is not often her way to present us with problems which we have to make an effort to take seriously, followed by their imaginary solutions. In this hard and sinewy new poetry she has mastered the art of tacking between alternative resolutions of the poem's tension and of leaving the reader at the right moment, just as meaning is dawning.
>
> (Rich, PP 280)

By Ashbery's standards this counts as direct statement – both about his contempt for the mainstream and his investment in the moment "just as meaning is dawning." I want to pursue the leads he gives here in order to develop a final version of how this generation of poets transforms modernist new realism and its ideals of impersonality. As the reader might by now expect, I find the basis of his efforts at transformation in his disdain for the poetics of "imaginary solutions." For Ashbery "solutions" occur in the domain of knowledge: they are consequences of pragmatic thinking, thinking devoted to practical or theoretical ends that are ultimately testable. Art can gravitate in that direction, as for example Rich's "An Unsaid Word" does by asking us to reflect on complex judgments. But Ashbery is more comfortable moving in the opposite direction, and for good reason. Art may be more interesting when it undoes "solutions," especially ones that depend on the imagination working as if it could be a pragmatic tool. Those powers of disruption, complication, and empuzzlement may be the basic resources of imagination when it is put in the service of art.

For Ashbery there is a basic distinction between meanings that do practical work and meanings that complicate experience, making the very desire for "solutions" seem an exercise in the wrong language game. When the imagination can be put in the service of knowledge to help compel belief, then the desire for complexity seems only evasive and nostalgic. But in domains where the gestures for claiming knowledge tend to be unconvincing, in the domain of the psyche for example, this refusal to settle for "solutions" can help us flesh out issues and not make exclusions we are likely to regret. That is why Ashbery is fascinated by the possibility that poetry can alter predominant values so that one can find resonance in moments when meaning is suspended, or just dawning because it catches for a moment some aspect of the world. Where the enigmatic can rival the epiphanic, then at least one escapes for the moment "the bog of uncertainty, otherwise known as the Slough of Despond."[20] And in escaping the sense that uncertainty is necessarily a bog, one feels anew the desire for meaning and one's capacity to enact it in the present tense – as response and responsibility, not as merely recognizing conventions. The ideal of "Fence-sitting / Raised to the level of an esthetic ideal" (Ashbery, SP 88) takes us far beyond aesthetic matters.

To pursue these possibilities of lyric, Ashbery develops a substantially different attitude toward rhetoric than any of his predecessors in American poetry. He thinks that the most serious danger in poetry is not that it will be too rhetorical but that it will not insist enough on the rhetorical theater it establishes. That opinion shares a good deal with Auden's sense of poems as performances, but Ashbery departs entirely from Auden in his view of how these performances are to be evaluated. For Ashbery the goal is not wisdom but "tacking between alternative resolutions of the poem's tension." He is more interested in the alternatives than in any "right" solution because the imagination probably works best as an instrument for entertaining options by helping the alternatives take on weight and by projecting the various selves that emerge with each possibility. The problems attributed by

Lacan to the imaginary take on force when agents fall into the trap of confusing the productive nature of the imagination with the essentially reproductive force of knowledge claims. That is, imaginary identities propose one option as a "true" version of the self, while Ashbery is interested in how the imagination establishes various selves all with a claim to fitting the situation.

On one level, then, Ashbery shares Lowell's and Rich's understanding of how imaginings are inseparable from perceptions and descriptions. But he is adamant, as adamant as his temperament can be, that such imaginings do not have to take the form of asserting personal or collective identities. That is why among contemporaries he is the keenest at distinguishing the work of imagination from the promise that particular images will bring a desired substance for the self. Rather than shore up individual projections, Ashbery envisions poetry exploring the multiple lives that one might say are embedded in the ways we project expectations onto our languages. We usually employ language practically, so we are in the habit of ignoring the many associations and implicit roles carried by our dead metaphors. Practical language is a language shorn of the sense that there are competing figures and competing paths that one might take. Yet no one path will be able to resolve the many values that language offers.

Accordingly, Ashbery is concerned less with how language mediates sensation than with what any desire to secure references for poetry will miss in the actual diction constituting the poem. Take for example how the following passage from the opening of "Scheherazade" calls attention to the play among vocabularies for landscape, for existential authenticity, for philosophical method, and for expressing care:

> An inexhaustible wardrobe has placed at the disposal
> Of each new occurrence. It can be itself now.
> Day is almost reluctant to decline
> And slowing down opens out new avenues
> That don't infringe on space but are living here with us.
> Other dreams came and left while the bank
> Of colored verbs and adjectives was shrinking from the light
> To nurse in shade their want of a method
> But most of all she loved the particles
> That transform objects of the same category
> Into particular ones, each distinct and apart
> From its own class.   (Ashbery, SP 169)

When the spirit of New England imposes nagging questions about what can possibly be at stake in this playfulness, Ashbery has available at least two responses. In part, this spirit of linguistic play is driven by simple honesty: making worlds is very different from perceiving worlds, and one major difference is the various vocabularies at the artist's disposal. A poet ought at least to acknowledge the available resources and the limitations of the games he or she is playing. At the opposite pole, one could spell out several significant virtues for this spirit of linguistic play if one were to set it against the backdrop of the substantial hells that some people face. There is, for example, the simple sense of freedom that arises when we feel our power to switch vocabularies and even the selves that depend upon them. Then one can at least avoid the brain-cramps that develop from thinking in the same position for too long. One might even suggest that such poetry expands our sense of human powers by attending to the imaginative resources that allusion and metaphor are constantly throwing off:

> There was a time when the words dug in, and you laughed and joke, accomplice
> Of all the possibilities of their journey through the night and the stars, creature
> Who looked to the abandonment of such archaic forms as these, and meanwhile
> Supported them as the tools that made you.   (Ashbery, SP 119–20)

Ashbery's responses, in short, make our moralisms wobble and our truth claims seem often anxious and narrow. Personally, I find these responses helping me take seriously the impossibility of believing in my own seriousness and the dangerous senses of urgencies such seriousness establishes. And, culturally, Ashbery's various attitudes help me come to terms with the strange blend of alienation and sense of possibility that characterizes what passes for public life in the United States (at least in whatever social classes I occupy). Ashbery combines an ability to maintain an intricate sense of reserve, modulating from irony to bare self-consciousness, with a lavish excessiveness where metaphor becomes too in love with its own productivity to sit still for self-congratulation or, worse, for self-interpretation. The result is an odd, intricate, and endlessly satisfying interplay between the demotic, the enigmatic, and the epigrammatic. Ashbery shows us that even the most ambitious poetry can embody a playfulness and a delight in the insubstantial which might carry exemplary force without seeking the sustenance of either tradition or philosophy. In a poetic culture where it seemed poetry had to be either raw or cooked, either the barbaric yawp of the confessional self or the elaborate artifice of whispered elegances and intricate ambivalences, Ashbery has developed his own version of the cry of our time – why not both? Why not let the compulsion to understand coexist with the realization of how often those efforts undo themselves, and make poetry possible in their wake?

Ashbery's path to these attitudes was a complicated one. Born in 1927 and raised in upper New York State, he went to Harvard, took an MA at Columbia, then won a Fulbright Fellowship to France, where he lived for the most part from 1955 to 1965. His first two substantial books, *Some Trees* (1956) and *The Tennis Court Oath* (1962), have a strange, flat, often dark and alienated refusal of coherence that is usually attributed to the influence of surrealism. But Ashbery has almost none of the sensuality of the French surrealists, who were concerned to entice readers to look for an unconscious working itself out in the details. Ashbery's is a surrealism of the voice, dominated by a will that thrives on letting contradictions emerge on every possible level – but for the sake of the contradictions themselves, not for what the handling might reveal about the creative state producing them.

Ashbery's subsequent work did not lose that capacity to wield distance, but his impersonality becomes one increasingly in the service of a lush contemplative imaginative life. *The Double Dream of Spring* (1970) and *Self-Portrait in a Convex Mirror* (1975) established the style that I have been and will be discussing because that vein constitutes his major work for most readers. However, one cannot overlook the extended prose meditations of *Three Poems* (1972) because of their philosophical intelligence and because they served notice that one aspect of Ashbery's imagination required the space provided by the long poem. "Litany" (1979) and *Flow Chart* (1984) were to exemplify this possibility for contemporary culture, and, true to Ashbery's sense of generative contradiction, the long poems were to intensify his fascination in later volumes like *Shadow Train* with how open he could keep quite closed forms like the sonnet and the sestina. His most recent book of poetry is *Chinese Whispers* (2002), which contains several powerful meditations on mortality.

I want to concentrate here on making good my claims for Ashbery by tracking how he extends and transforms the poetics of both Stevens and Auden. From Auden Ashbery adapts the wry performative mode that relies on the humility of the poet to check the tendency to identify with the power of imagination. By that route both Auden and Ashbery anchor responsibility in how the will attaches to processes of imagining rather than to shoring up particular images. Then from Stevens he borrows a sense of the lusciousness of imagination, stressing how that power offers an intricate, fluid world capable of substantial satisfactions that are not available when the mind is occupied by questions about truth and by the roles such questions dictate. Yet Ashbery's abstraction is very different from Stevens' – not toward some collective self but toward some endlessly permuting process of imaginary identification far too fleeting and insubstantial to sustain any claim for enduring personal substance. Stevens speaks of the idea of the hero; Ashbery of the "idea of the spectacle."[21] But Stevens starts him on his way of treating poetry as a means of living within the imaginary's full panoply of social roles while seeing how those roles themselves can be no more than something like the material of a puppet theater. Where the Lacanian imaginary cannot be separated from the desire and need for something like a full armoring of our defenses, the imaginary in Ashbery becomes something closer to a Victoria's Secrets fashion show run at double time. We are no more free in Ashbery's world, but we are a lot less bound to specific obsessive scenarios and all the modes of oppression of self and other that they entail. And that unboundedness can be the locus of intricate pleasures and strange moments of connection between lives that have few other grounds for community or intimacy.

Perhaps the major problem with Ashbery's work during the 1960s and 1970s was that critics found it easier to indulge in abstract praise like the discourse I have been presenting than to attend in detail to how the tension between the imagination and imaginary operates within particular poems. I cannot right the balance here but I can at least address it by turning to three representative lyric moments in his work from this period. The first, from "Pyrography" shows him remaking Bishop's pastoral images, but in ways that have less to do with landscape than with an "idea of spectacle":

But the variable cloudiness is pouring it on,
Flooding back to you like the meaning of a joke.
The land wasn't immediately appealing; we built it
Partly over with fake ruins, in the image of ourselves:
An arch that terminates in mid-keystone, a crumbling stone pier
For laundresses, an open-air theater, never completed
And only partially designed. How are we to inhabit
This space from which the fourth wall is invariably missing,
As in a stage set or dollhouse, except by staying as we are
In lost profile, facing the stars, with dozens of as yet
Unrealized projects, and a strict sense
Of time running out, of evening presenting
The tactfully folded-over bill.   (Ashbery, SP 212–13)

Here the use of figurative language explicitly transforms landscape into theater. And doing that radically changes how the speaker comes to understand his own place in this transformative process.

First there is the acute self-consciousness of seeing the self not as searching for truth but as producer of what gets claimed for nature. Then the more important shift emerges: this self-consciousness is in no way paralyzed by its awareness of the ironic situation. Instead, reducing the self to mere image intensifies the poem by calling attention to the play of metaphor as the relevant active agency. Because there is no need for even the illusion of illusionism here, the speaker released from responsibility to a fantasized reality might as well enjoy the pull of the metaphors composing this theatrical situation. The self is not asked to fight rhetoric in the name of authenticity but to recast the spirit of rhetoric so it becomes aligned with the service of pleasure and freedom. That process begins with a fluid merger between the objective situation of clouds "Flooding back to you" and the subtle subjective feelings that occur when we get the meaning of a joke. Then the poem returns to elaborating the scene, only to see self-reflexively how what seems an open-air theater in nature becomes in culture a proscenium stage. As nature recedes, the self can take responsibility for the intricate pleasures of finding itself both speaking and spoken for by what enables it to emerge at all.

That degree of self-consciousness allows the passage one more self-reflexive twist. Precisely because there is no fourth wall to the sense of self, there emerges the possibility that the "we" of the poem is itself something more than a rhetorical gesture. Where confession had been,

Ashbery has the act of speaking submit itself to the figural possibilities within the language so that to hear the speaker is also to hear how the speaker's identity merges into roles and desires that have inescapably public dimensions. What makes us transpersonal does not produce a Stevensian sublimity but tends toward a demotic orgy. Multiple possible identities in effect take over whatever tune seems to be sustaining the effort to make language perform some desired task. What makes us subjects also undoes any possibility of our becoming just one subject.

But that sense of the psyche proves so mobile it cannot rest content with being a subject. So the poem forces time to enter, and that entrance forces Ashbery to his final metaphoric triumph. As the conclusion approaches, the language gets most ominous and most public: "Time running out" is the sentiment that religion (and cinema) use at their most melodramatic moments. But Ashbery manages to find in the "tactfully folded-over bill" a return to the concrete domestic order that does not deny the power of endings but sets it in a new key evocative of pleasure. The closing phrase revels in the possibility that the spirit can still play with fire and switch levels of consciousness at will, even if it cannot deny the facts of our mortality. The spirit of rhetoric trumps the spirit of modern philosophy – not quite canceling its dark vision but placing it in a context of ongoingness exemplified by the sense that invention is always available if one can stop fretting over matters of identity. (I must add that "always available" does not mean "always effective." One does not want to win that much of a victory over melancholy.)

One does not want to win that much of a victory over melancholy because melancholy too is central to how humans construct the world, and therefore is basic also to other fundamental emotions it passes into – from joy or relief on the one hand to the tragic turning of melancholy about loss into taking responsibility for loss. Elaborating this fascination with transitions is obviously the domain of the long poem, or at least poems longer than I can handle comfortably here, because the poems have to allow the space for the many shadings that the imagination enacts and imposes. Still I think we would be selling Ashbery short if we did not track the working of an entire poem stressing such transitions, so I have chosen "Ut Pictura Poesis," as expansive a fairly short poem as one is likely to find:

You can't say it that way any more.
Bothered about beauty you have to
Come out into the open, into a clearing,
And rest. Certainly whatever funny happens to you
Is OK. To demand more of this would be strange
Of you, you who have so many lovers,
People who look up to you and are willing
To do things for you, but you think
It's not right, that if they really knew you . . .
So much for self-analysis. Now,
About what to put in your poem painting:
Flowers are always nice, particularly delphinium.
Names of boys you once knew and their sleds,
Skyrockets are good – do they still exist?
There are a lot of other things of the same quality
As those I've mentioned. Now one must
Find a few important words, and a lot of low-keyed
Dull-sounding ones. She approached me
About buying her desk. Suddenly the street was
Bananas and the clangor of Japanese instruments.
Humdrum testaments were scattered around. His head
Locked into mine. We were a seesaw. Something
Ought to be written about how this affects
You when you write poetry:
The extreme austerity of an almost empty mind
Colliding with the lush Rousseau-like foliage of its desire to communicate
Something between breaths, if only for the sake
Of others and their desire to understand you and desert you
For other centers of communication, so that understanding
May begin, and in doing so be undone.

(Ashbery, SP 235; ellipses original)

In this poem the basic tension may be between the condition of address, of being singled out so that one can be told what to do if one wants to pursue beauty, and the freedoms the text finds by which to interpret and satisfy those demands. If we are to make poetry, we have to at least know what it might be like to view our desires and activities from the outside. But it may be impossible to view ourselves entirely from the outside. The "you" that is the object of demand inevitably also approaches the "you" who has some claim to sympathy and so exists in a world where fantasized identification belies any possibility of objectivity. Hence the reference to lovers and then the gesture of identification with the idea of a real "you." So by simply raising the issue of address the poem leads us into a situation where the roles of "I" and "you" are not quite clear, yet remain intriguingly intricate as affect modulates between self-projection and anxiety.

It seems as if the poem takes a clear direction when the voice of demand tries to become helpful with advice about what goes into our poem-painting. Now perhaps the poem can be treated entirely as a rhetorical construct subject to authorial control. But the poem instantly turns to irony, as if asking what should go into a poem also requires the poet to establish a means of escape from responsibility. At the least, he must defeat the possibility of taking such questions seriously. Yet the helpful voice is not wrong; it is only irrelevant because we realize the immense gulf between what can be said in general about poems and the particulars that actually constitute their possible hold on an audience. All the efforts to provide contents that might be approved by some public sense of self seem unable to escape the self-disgust that comes from feeling one is trapped in cliché.

Even though "Ut Pictura Poesis" captures an interesting dilemma, I suspect that few readers would think its opening section is great poetry. However, the opening does manage to set the stage for Ashbery's distinctive gifts because the situation does not admit a resolution. Instead the situation elicits a sense of continuing process in which thinking turns this way and that as it offers opportunities to explore our investments in various aspects of what I think of as a dialectic of call and response. As in Stevens and Bishop, the imagination is continually at war with the imaginary and its efforts to fix images worthy of desire. In this case the poem quickly turns against its emphasis on artifice. It switches to concrete yet shadowy details and memories, in part because the speaker cannot deny the pull of those particulars even when he is self-conscious about the rhetorical situation.

On one level the poem retains its ironic attitude – certainly one is no closer to an adequate theory of poetry after the comment about affect than one was being told about the importance of low-keyed words. But now irony seems to open into a strange generosity. The poem veers sharply away from what can be controlled into the rush of concerns and fantasies that are entirely discontinuous and so perhaps have equal claims to enter the space of composition. And once the urgency of the particulars enters, the poem cannot rest in what seems an effort to restore control by again generalizing about what writing involves. The poem does utter another imperative in response to these particulars: "Something / Ought to be written about how this affects / You when you write poetry." That, however, generates an almost complete transformation in the prevailing style and tone. Rather than writing "*about* how this affects you when you write poetry," the poem suddenly becomes gorgeous poetry in its own right. The only feasible responses to questions about poetry have fully to utilize the resources of that art.

Wary self-consciousness suddenly blossoms into both a diction and a syntax that celebrates how poetry can draw on linguistic resources. Now the poem can turn away from what comes to seem a ridiculous prosaic confidence that writing can directly follow from or be accounted for by the analytic mode. The speaking position is no longer caught in anxious searching but relaxes into the flow of an expansive rhetoric – just listen to the contrast with the opening lines provided by the sound play of "The extreme austerity of an almost empty mind." As in the best of Stevens, poetry celebrates its distinctive linguistic powers by becoming supremely clear and elegantly sensuous statement. Then Ashbery pushes this sense of permission even further in the next line, literally composing the "Rousseau-like foliage" of a desire to communicate. The rhetoric of landscape leads to a sense that the psyche itself finds in landscape a fundamental resource for expression. Here, as often in Ashbery, romantic talk about harmony between man and nature is not a description of an actual situation but an account of shared processes sufficient to appreciate what a "Rousseau-like foliage" might feel like.

But irony will not be so easily dismissed. The poem cannot rest in this lyrical exuberance because it has to see the exuberance also from the outside, if only because that perspective is probably necessary for realizing an inside deployed within it. So, rather than revel in an irony that can handle the imaginary by keeping it in its place, Ashbery elaborates an irony that composes its own place. Poetry lies ultimately not in what presents positive answers to our questions but in the relation between beginning and undoing that keeps us constantly attuned to the play of desire pervading our language. In our culture we cannot not seek understanding, just as we cannot not somewhat share the anxieties about poetry that open this text. But we also cannot not distrust everything that goes into our efforts to understand, including the effort to make sense of our distrust. Rather than treat such antinomies as grounds for self-indulgent pathos, Ashbery projects an attitude that accepts and even endorses this relationship between doing and undoing.[22] At the very least such poetry brings to the fore all the resources of language the psyche can muster as its contribution to this endless process.

Close reading, however, will not in itself explain Ashbery's enormous influence on poetry in the last two decades of the twentieth century. One has to expand one's account to deal with how his distinctive style takes on cultural agency. To illustrate this process I propose a thought experiment. Imagine how we would have to alter our basic vocabulary for poetry if we made Ashbery our exemplar. And reflect on the fact that this would not prove especially difficult, much less difficult than it would with any other contemporary. The linguistic families surrounding the predicates "true" and "good" would encounter destitute times. "Beauty" might not fare much better. Clearly "uncertain" and "enigmatic" would become central. Yet those terms by themselves would be only descriptive. They would not sufficiently characterize desire and hence they would not provide an adequate language for the motives governing whatever "causes" the determination of a style.

We would come closer to characterizing the sense of motive informing this style if we emphasized how so much of the poetry seems in service of the "now," of sense always on a border between appearing and disappearing. Poetry for Ashbery is the art that makes the importance of "now" in writing visible and lasting, primarily by staging the force of that sense of presence against various elements that threaten it, like "certitude." But at the same time we have to admit that in intensifying our sense of presence, Ashbery's poetry also provides a temporality quite different from our ordinary lives, since we tend to emphasize either the past or the future selves that occupy our imaginary projections.

Ashbery's "now" is related to modernist ideals of presence, but it decidedly cannot be fully identified with modernist poetry. His is a distinctively late-twentieth-century attitude towards such presence because he does not find it in any content of consciousness. He pursues neither the real as a world of objects nor the real as a domain of immediate sensations. Rather his "now" involves an intriguing synthesis of the spirit of the new realism with the return to rhetoric inaugurated by Auden and Stevens.

Consider the last stanza of "As We Know":

The light that was shadowed then
Was seen to be our lives
Everything about us that love might wish to examine
Then put away for a certain length of time, until
The whole is to be reviewed, and we turned
Toward each other; to each other.
The way we had come was all we could see
And it crept up on us, embarrassed
That was so much to tell now, really now.   (Ashbery, SP 259)

I love the way the public voice of Whitman's "tell" here becomes suffused by the private satisfaction possible only when a lover's discourse
surprises itself into full self-consciousness of what the connection
entails. And I love even more the way that there is an abstraction to
the intimate speaking that allows for generalization despite the specific
address. The first "now" acknowledges both urgency and surprise, a
felicitous combination. Here the speaker recognizes and accepts his
own satisfactions in what he is telling. Then "really now" functions as
an intensifier, a mark that self-consciousness need not distance itself
from the urgency but can embrace it because the intensifier indicates
how compelling that state is. "Really now" in effect opens onto something more grand and more mysterious than the speaker can control.
Yet he can will the adventure that this loss of defenses will involve.
Because the state involves telling, the private ecstasy carries over
into the public world. What the lovers share, the poem can echo.
After all, we are not talking about anything objective, or anything
distinctly subjective for that matter. We are talking about a "now"
that completely fuses subject and object in a moment definable to
self-consciousness.

One might say that this attitude toward the rhetoric within poetry
repeats Denise Levertov's ideal, "every step an arrival."[23] But there are
two differences from Levertov that betoken a new dispensation, one
that we are only now beginning to work through. First, there is no
transcendental ground for Ashbery's sense of constant arrival. One
does not arrive anywhere that can be distinctively sought or even distinctively praised. "Now" is a pure celebration of process – not quite
for its own sake but for the intelligence and luck that manage to keep
interest engaged as we move. Second, and more important, there is

for Ashbery a constant sense that every arrival is also a departure. "Now" is inseparable from "then," fullness from an impinging emptiness. For Ashbery the "now" calls forth both joy and melancholy – exhilaration because it frees us from what has gone stale, and melancholy because that freedom is inseparable from an awareness of utter contingency, from the sense that one is left "the ex-president / of the event" (Ashbery, SP 208). "Now" is the site where all our images seem to enter the dump together, but in ways that make the transition from scene to dump itself the locus for a parallel fusion between melancholy and exhilaration.

And "now" is the point at which this book must leave its objects. Ashbery's "now" fulfills one dream that a realism can be correlated with a means of providing intense subjective states without the theatricalizing of terms whereby the subjects might become objects of their own desire. But Ashbery's "now" also marks what may be the end of an era. The ideal of telling really now, and telling how the "now" comes about may have become somewhat anachronistic because of its fascination with subjectivity and with what remain the intricacies of its expressive acts. Many of our best younger poets now seem driven by a quite different imperative – not to tell so much as to explain, and not to make the "now" vital but to speculate on its relation to "before" and to "after." Under the pressure of contemporary politics, it may have become necessary that they worry about questions of causality and responsibility on a collective scale. It may be a time in which the subject of speaking has to recede and the object of analysis come to the fore even of our lyrical projections.

Notes

1 Introduction:
The Art of Twentieth-Century
American Poetry: An Overview

1 Marjorie Perloff, *21st-Century Modernism: The New Poetics*, Oxford: Blackwell, 2002, p. 200.
2 Christopher MacGowan, *Twentieth-Century American Poetry*, Oxford: Blackwell, 2004.
3 "Introduction," in Yeats (ed.), *The Oxford Book of Modern Verse*, Oxford: Clarendon Press, 1936, p. xxvii.
4 Ian F. A. Bell. *Critic as Scientist: The Modernist Poetics of Ezra Pound*, London: Methuen, 1981.
5 T. S. Eliot, *The Inventions of the March Hare: Poems 1909–1917*, ed. Christopher Ricks, New York: Harcourt, Brace, 1996, p. 409.
6 Jean-Paul Sartre, *Being and Nothingness*, trans. Hazel E. Barnes, New York: Washington Square Press, 1993.
7 My project entails reconsidering first-generation modernist work that in the past decade has been severely criticized for its conservative politics and elitist distance from common experience. I think what the art makes visible can be adapted for a very different politics, if we grant that common experience need not create an effective sense of community because it is at least as likely to manifest the habitual blindness of the communities responsible for the social problems in question. Under those conditions we desperately need uncommon experience that might shake people into recasting their basic psychological investments. For a concrete example of such blindness at work in efforts to establish critical positions on the modernists, see my critique of Douglas Mao's essay, "How to do Things with Modernism" (*Wallace Stevens Journal*, 26 (Fall 2002): 160–80), in my

"The Fate of the Imaginary in Modern American Poetry," *American Literary History*, 17 (2005): 70–94.

8 T. S. Eliot, *Selected Essays*, New York: Harcourt Brace, 1950, p. 7.

2 The New Realism in Modernist Poetry: Pound and Williams

1 In *Selected Prose, 1909–1965: Ezra Pound*, ed. William Cookson, New York: New Directions, 1973, p. 102. (Hereafter Pound, SP.)

2 Ernest Fenollosa, "The Chinese Written Character as a Medium for Poetry," in Karl Shapiro (ed.), *Prose Keys to Modern Poetry*, New York: Harper & Row, 1962, p. 142. (Hereafter CWC.)

3 William Carlos Williams, *The Embodiment of Knowledge*, ed. Ron Loewinsohn, New York: New Directions, 1974, p. 27. (Hereafter EK.)

4 I have to include my *Painterly Abstraction in Modernist American Poetry* (New York: Cambridge University Press, 1989) as one of the works that emphasized modernist formal innovation without a sufficient sense of how those innovations were motivated by writers' efforts to engage what they saw as a new realism.

5 I have already cited Ian Bell because his concerns closely intersect with mine. Other important works on modernist writing and contemporary science include Stephen Kern, *The Culture of Time and Space 1880–1918* (Cambridge, Mass.: Harvard University Press, 2003); Lisa Steinman, *Made in America: Science, Technology, and American Modernist Poets* (New Haven: Yale University Press, 1987), and Daniel Albright, *Quantum Poetics: Yeats, Pound, Eliot and the Science of Modernism* (New York: Cambridge University Press, 1977).

6 See Bell, *Critic as Scientist*, pp. 95–103, who is quite critical of Bergson for his suspicious attitude toward science as a necessarily spatializing discourse.

7 Henri Bergson, *Matter and Memory*, trans. N. M. Paul and W. S. Palmer, Cambridge: Zone Books, 1990, p. 28. (Hereafter MM.)

8 Henri Bergson, *Time and Free Will*, trans. F. L. Pogson, Mineola, NY: Dover Publications, 2001, pp. 132–3. (Hereafter TFW.)

9 Pound's essays on Arnaut Daniel and on Calvacanti in *Literary Essays* show how thoroughly his playing the role of scholar in verse forms enabled him to create new ideals of rhythm. There is probably still no better attack on the limitations of iambic pentameter, in contrast to song cadence, as a model for verse in English.

10 Ezra Pound, *Personae: Collected Shorter Poems of Ezra Pound*, London: Faber & Faber, 1952, p. 17. (Hereafter P.)

11   All the citations in this paragraph are from CWC 151. Pound edited the essay but said he only reshaped a few sentences.

12   Ezra Pound, *Literary Essays of Ezra Pound*, ed. T. S. Eliot, London: Faber & Faber, 1960, p. 4. (Hereafter LE.)

13   The best critical account I know of the power and the limitations of realism as a mode of representation is offered by Philip Weinstein, *Unknowing: The Work of Modernist Fiction*, Ithaca: Cornell University Press, chs. 2 and 3.

14   As we shall see, ultimately Pound thought poetry must be held to a higher standard: "Poetry is a centaur. The thinking, word arranging, clarifying faculty must move and leap with the energizing, sentient musical faculties. . . . I dare say there are very good marksmen who just can't shoot from a horse. . . . As the man, as his mind, becomes a heavier and heavier machine, a constantly more complicated structure, it requires a constantly greater voltage of emotional energy to set it in harmonious motion" (LE 52). The luminous details in poetry must not only be precise, they must also be rendered so as to elicit and reward a dynamic sense of movement. In such movement the image fully becomes an intellectual and emotional complex because it dramatically exists both in the space of description and in the time of musical structure.

15   Pound often insists on the parallels between art and science because the task of both is to give true reports of how things are (LE 41–3). This epistemic standard runs the risk of a dangerously authoritarian framework, since such a claim about art seems to assume that the observer is in a position to know enough about a constant human nature to distinguish accurate from inaccurate art. The knowledge claim seems inseparable from his eventual fascination with fascist power. But at least until the 1930s Pound fused this realism with individualism by insisting that the artist reports directly on "his nature," the "nature of his ideal of the perfect," and of the force with which he believes good and evil exist (LE 43; see also Pound, SP 200). The truth in art is not determined by principle or representation but by the energy that one feels embedded in the particular act of witnessing.

16   In fact Vorticist theory was for the most part much more clear on what the artists opposed than on what they were trying to do. In particular the Vorticists were most upset by a quality they called "the caressable," because that indicated the artists' interest in charming their audience by providing delightful representations that might serve as "substitutes" for honored persons or dramatic scenes (Ezra Pound, *Gaudier-Brzeska: A Memoir*, New York: New Directions, 1970, p. 97; hereafter GB).

17   Pound offers a terrific way of imagining this permanence of form in mathematical rather than transcendental terms by elaborating four kinds

of "intensities" of mathematical expression: the arithmetical, the algebraic, the geometrical, and that of analytical geometry (GB 90–2). See also Pound, SP 377 for Pound's insistence that Vorticism applies to all the arts because "The 'organizing' of the creative–inventive faculty is the thing that matters."

18 Pound has a lovely description of specific forms doing concrete work within Vorticist art in GB 137–8.

19 Developing this new psychology in turn made it possible for Pound to place his poetic theory in relation to the two dominant art movements of the previous epoch. He could show how his poetic might borrow the Impressionist "method of presentation," stressing the artist's hand and the fragmentary nature of the psyche without succumbing to Futurism's tendency to be merely an "accelerated Impressionism." The Vorticists need not succumb because they also incorporated what was most productive in symbolist art – the feeling that art is not just a matter of receiving sensations but "as directing a certain fluid force against circumstance" (GB 89). Such resistance to mere circumstance could establish the relation among images as "permanent metaphor," even for one denied the belief in a permanent transcendental world (GB 82–5). The reference established by any one image is less important than the way the images function in tandem as assorted pigments in the service of a complex composition (GB 86).

20 I cannot resist pointing out that my discussion of Canto 2 in *Painterly Abstraction in Modernist American poetry* elaborates how motifs of sensation and witnessing function in this new poetic economy.

21 Herschel Chipp (ed.), *Theories of Modern Art*, Berkeley: University of California Press, 1968, p. 22.

22 Ibid., p. 20.

23 I want again to invoke my *Painterly Abstraction*, where I elaborate this point about mass to argue that many of Cézanne's landscapes painted in the 1890s deny the force of gravity. Gravity is an inference not given in the immediate act of looking. This denial in turn links to a fourth feature in this still-life that would prove central in the transition from the new realism to Cubism. Notice how this painting requires us to recognize at least two perspectives, one from above that yields all the information about the fruit in the dishes, and one below that minimally captures the seductive curves and shadows created by the tablecloths. Scholars now see this as evidence of Cézanne's awareness that ideas and memories can complicate vision. At times we do not see isolated objects only from one perspective but we think visually so that the object takes on memories affording different perspectives all synthesized and struggling for domination in the moment realized.

24 Meyer Schapiro, "The Apples of Cézanne: An Essay on the Meaning of Still-Life," in Schapiro, *Modern Art: 19th and 20th Centuries: Selected Papers*, New York: George Braziller, 1979, p. 25.

25 See, e.g., Williams' concise statement in EK 162–3.

26 William Carlos Williams, *Selected Essays of William Carlos Williams*, New York: Random House, 1954, p. 71. (Hereafter Williams, SE).

27 William Carlos Williams, *Imaginations: Five Experimental Prose Pieces*, ed. Webster Schott. New York: New Directions, 1970, p. 302.

28 William Carlos Williams, *The Collected Poems of William Carlos Williams*, vol. 1, ed. A. Walton Litz and Christopher MacGowan, New York: New Directions, 1991, p. 198. (Hereafter Williams, CP.)

29 This accomplishment is especially important now, "after" deconstruction, since that movement emphasized the importance of putting the rhetorical and the descriptive in conflict with each other.

30 The editors of his *Collected Poems* note that Williams said he was recalling an experience in Germany in 1909, but the context of his work and his commitment to the American scene suggest that we treat this tree as repatriated.

31 In my *Particulars of Rapture* (Ithaca: Cornell University Press, 2003), pp. 232–6, I show how "To a Young Housewife," another Williams poem contemporaneous with "Spring Strains," develops in a somewhat different way a realism clearly honoring the complexities of human consciousness. This poem does not so much portray energies within a scene as it makes present a demand for processing the intricacies of a situation:

> At ten A.M. the young housewife
> moves about in negligee behind
> the wooden walls of her husband's house.
> I pass solitary in my car.
>
> Then again she comes to the curb
> to call the ice-man, fish-man, and stands
> shy, uncorseted, tucking in
> stray ends of hair, and I compare her
> to a fallen leaf.
>
> The noiseless wheels of my car
> rush with a crackling sound over
> dried leaves as I bow and pass smiling.   (CP57)

Rather than dramatic confrontation the poem stresses quiet tonal adjustment to the limitations of both the speaker's and the housewife's situations. So the rueful smile acknowledging time and distance is all the evaluation the speaker can honestly muster.

32 I have learned in conversation with Brian Glaser to make this distinction between *Spring and All* and Williams' earlier modernist but not yet fully constructivist poems.

33 I refer to six poems (8, 10, 13, 17, 24, and 25) which seem to cultivate a kind of contingency for their own sake. These poems can be seen as an important aspect of continuous beginning because such work will not be trapped by the high seriousness surrounding ideas of poetry or the typical intentions of poets. The poems simply find their own way, refusing to honor any expectations about coherence or thematic import.

34 When sensation replaces pictorial representation as the basis of the real, there becomes a problem in determining the boundaries of objects. There is no longer a distinctive *eidos* for a substance. Artists and writers handle this issue by stressing how the nature of a medium need not be simply a lens with which to see the world. It can be a stimulus for recombining sensations to create objects distinctive to a medium or mode of imagination capable of resisting habit. Think of Pound's "apparition" and "carnage."

35 Actually the last poem in *Spring and All* is a better example of Williams' emphasis on liberating words from the real in order to "affirm reality by their flight." But I have written on that poem in *Painterly Abstraction*. Moreover, the poem I have chosen here brings us closer to what Williams learns about that freedom specifically from the visual arts.

36 In *The Visual Text of William Carlos Williams* (Urbana: University of Illinois Press, 1983), Henry Sayre denies that Williams is referring to the Gris collage *Roses* because Sayre could find no reproduction printed before 1930 (pp. 41–2). But Williams could have had the collage described to him by people returning from Europe. The timing works for that collage to be the reference, so while we cannot be sure, we cannot confidently deny the possibility.

3 The Doctrine of Impersonality and Modernism's War on Rhetoric: Eliot, Loy, and Moore

1 Friedrich Nietzsche, *Beyond Good and Evil*, New York: Vintage, 1989, sect. 261.

2 Mina Loy, *The Lost Lunar Baedeker*, ed. Roger L. Conover, New York: Farrar, Straus & Giroux, 1996, p. 151. (Hereafter LLB.)

3 Hugh Kenner, *The Pound Era*, Berkeley: University of California Press, 1971, p. 136; see also pp. 130–41.

4 Eliot, *Inventions of the March Hare*, p. 17.

5   T. S. Eliot, *The Complete Poems and Plays of T. S. Eliot*, New York: Harcourt Brace, 1969, p. 17. (Hereafter Eliot, CP.)

6   T. S. Eliot, *Selected Essays*, New York: Harcourt Brace, 1950, p. 9. (Hereafter Eliot, SE.)

7   Maud Ellmann, *The Poetics of Impersonality: T. S. Eliot and Ezra Pound* (New York: Cambridge University Press, 1987), offers a good example of this line of criticism.

8   Most current Eliot criticism would not accept this claim because of his decidedly reactionary political stance. But Lacan himself was quite politically conservative, sharing with Eliot the conviction that liberalism depended on the positive assertions of mainstream nineteenth-century philosophy that had led modern culture horribly astray.

9   Nietzsche, *Beyond Good and Evil*, sect. 5.

10   William Butler Yeats, *Essays and Introductions*, New York: Collier Books, 1961, pp. 350–1. This is a good place to make the crucial distinction between the imaginary as a problematic way of reinforcing unstable subjective projects and the ideal of imagination as a modernist principle of value asked to do the work writers and poets felt could no longer be performed by reason. Yeats is almost explicit on the contrast, since imagination is defined as that which allows the self to escape from itself into the presence of beauty. Then, from I. A. Richards' *Coleridge on Imagination* (1936) to Northrop Frye's work on the Bible, the concept of imagination can be said to have dominated critics' assertions about how literary texts fostered values. Imagination provided modes of synthesis and intricate hypothetical experience which could be employed to establish what the critics called "non-discursive knowledge," capable of competing with the kinds of knowledge established by science. Analogously, imagination took on moral force because it could exemplify virtue compatible with complex experience, help establish sympathy, and bring to reflection the comprehensive forms of desire fundamental to cultural life. Correlatively, American poetry from the 1940s to the 1960s everywhere idealized the concept of imagination. Stressing imagination sanitized the imaginary and put all the emphasis on how poetry might be a mode of responding to the world rather than of absorbing the world into the self.

Important as this concept is, however, I fear we pay a substantial price if we simply stop with the contrast between imagination and the imaginary. Imagination wins too easily, and too easily becomes subsumed within both moral and epistemic frameworks that reintroduce imaginary structures while proclaiming their difference from them. By making the male imagination a mode of knowing that could compete with science, the New Criticism arrogated to itself the authority of those who assert their access to knowledge, without even providing a disciplinary basis crucial for securing a possible range of actual knowledge claims. And moral criticism's use of the imagination as a dialogical principle basic to the development of sympathetic identifications made it all too easy for critics and writers to bask in their nobility without in fact having to do anything very demanding. Both routes of idealization manage to restore the kinds of roles on which the imaginary feeds while minimalizing the theatricality the imaginary makes possible for artistic imagining. And both routes of idealization clarify the challenge facing poets like Stevens who want to restore that theatricality while distancing themselves (not always successfully) from such forms of self-congratulation.

11 W. H. Auden, *Collected Poems*, ed. Edward Mendelson, New York: Vintage, 1991, p. 540. (Hereafter Auden, CP.)

12 Jacques Lacan, The *Four Fundamental Concepts of Psycho-Analysis*, trans. Alan Sheridan, New York: W. W. Norton, 1978, p. 197. For my argument I rely primarily on Lacan's essay, "The Mirror Stage as Formative of the Function of the I," in *Ecrits: A Selection*, trans. Alan Sheridan, New York: W. W. Norton, 1977, pp. 1–7. I find the most useful commentary on Lacan, Tim Dean's *Beyond Sexuality*, Chicago: University of Chicago Press, 2000.

13 Althusser's basic statement of this idea is in his essay "Ideology as State Apparatus," in *Essays in Ideology*, London: Verso, 1984.

14 My *Painterly Abstraction in Modernist American Poetry* spends a good deal of time on this topic.

15 T. S. Eliot, *The Complete Poems and Plays of T. S. Eliot*, New York: Harcourt Brace, 1969, p. 3.

16 T. S. Eliot, "Ulysses, Order, and Myth," repr. in Frank Kermode (ed.), *Selected Prose of T. S. Eliot*, New York: Harvest, 1975, p. 178.

17 Marianne Moore, *The Complete Poems of Marianne Moore*, New York: Macmillan, Viking, 1981, p. 36. (Hereafter Moore, CP.)

4 How Modernist Poetics Failed and Efforts at Renewal: Williams, Oppen, and Hughes

1 Friedrich Nietzsche, *The Birth of Tragedy*, Mineola, NY: Dover Publications, 1995, sect. 5.

2 I develop this deliberate conflict between poetry and prose in my chapter on Williams in *Painterly Abstraction*.

3 It did not take the war in Iraq for critics like like Eric Homburger (in *American Writers and Radical Politics, 1900–39: Equivocal Commitments*, New York: Palgrave Macmillan, 1986) to recognize how poets turned from ideals of individuality in the poetry of the 1930s.

4   Wallace Stevens, *The Collected Poems of Wallace Stevens*, New York: Knopf, 1964, pp. 227–8 (ellipses original). (Hereafter Stevens, CP.)

5   Here I will engage two of Cary Nelson's books, *Repression and Recovery*, Madison: University of Wisconsin Press, 1989, and *Revolutionary Memory: Recovering the Poetry of the American Left*, Oxford: Routledge, 2003.

6   Nelson, *Repression and Recovery*, pp. 35–6.

7   Ibid., pp. 23, 61.

8   Ibid., p. 58.

9   Nelson, *Revolutionary Memory*, p. 3.

10 Lawrence Dembo, "The Objectivist Poet: Four Interviews," *Contemporary Literature*, 10 (1969): 155–219, p. 161.

11 Louis Zukofsky, *Prepositions*, Berkeley: University of California Press, 1981, p. 15. (Hereafter Prepositions.)

12 I am indebted to Rachel Blau DuPlessis and Peter Quartermain's "Introduction" to their edition of *The Objectivist Nexus: Essays in Cultural Poetics* (Tuscaloosa: University of Alabama Press, 1999) for some of this information, and to their book for much of my own formulation of this poetic.

13 Carl Rakosi was more explicit on how "sincerity" fits the heritage of impersonal poetics: The term Objectivism "conveyed a meaning which was, in fact, my objective: to present objects in their most essential reality, to make of each poem an object . . . meaning, by this, obviously, the opposite of a subject; the opposite, that is, of all forms of personal vagueness" (quoted in DuPlessis and Quartermain (eds.), *Objectivist Nexus*, p. 10; ellipses original).

14 Lawrence Dembo, "Oppen in his Poems," in Burton Hatlen (ed.), *George Oppen, Man and Poet*, Orono, Me.: National Poetry Foundation, 1981, p. 212.

15 Peter Nichols, "On Being Ethical: Reflections on George Oppen," in DuPlessis and Quartermain (eds.), *Objectivist Nexus*, p. 252.

16 My appreciation of Nichols on Oppen does not entail agreeing with his basic claim that high modernism pursued the opposite ideal in which "the self's relation to the other is generally construed as one of domination and is characterized by discontinuity and separateness" (ibid., p. 242). This claim fails to distinguish what the writers felt they had to describe from what they desired. Eliot in particular despised a mythos of domination, but he saw it everywhere.

17 See Burton Hatlen's excellent reading of this passage, "A Poetics of Marginality and Resistance: The Objectivist Poets in Context," in DuPlessis and Quartermain (eds.), *Objectivist Nexus*, pp. 38–9.

18 I am quoting from the "Introduction" to DuPlessis and Quartermain (eds.), *Objectivist Nexus*, p. 13, where the editors cite a letter from Zukofsky to the editor of *Poetry* defending Objectivist work from the charge of

political elitism and emphasizing how the poems seek to realize "complex linguistic 'inter-relation'."

19 Ibid., pp. 11–12.

20 Dembo, "Oppen in his Poems," p. 161.

21 George Oppen, _New Collected Poems_, ed. Michael Davidson, New York: New Directions, 2002, pp. 357–8. (Hereafter NCP.)

22 John Shoptaw, "Lyric Incorporated: The Serial Object of George Oppen and Langston Hughes," _Sagetrieb_, 12 (1993): 108. This essay is important because it shows how the Objectivists share a good deal with the version of realism Langston Hughes would later develop.

23 There is a somewhat different reading of this poem in my book _The Particulars of Rapture_.

24 My treatment of this poem is based on a reading I published in DuPlessis and Quartermain (eds.), _Objectivist Nexus_.

25 Langston Hughes, _The Collected Poems of Langston Hughes_, ed. Arnold Rampersad and David Roessel, New York: Knopf, 1994, p. 32. (Hereafter Hughes, CP.)

26 The situation of this poem proves a superb example of what Jean-François Lyotard would theorize as the "differend," the statement of complaint that cannot be heard as legitimate by those in power (Jean-François Lyotard, _The Differend_, Minneapolis: University of Minnesota Press, 1988).

5 The Return to Rhetoric in Modernist Poetry: Stevens and Auden

1 Stevens, CP 279.

2 My essay "Intentionality as Sensuality in _Harmonium_," _Wallace Stevens Journal_, 27 (2003): 163–72, explores the playful impersonality of the opening group of poems in this volume.

3 W. S. Merwin, _The Lice_, New York: Atheneum, 1967, p. 25.

4 Wallace Stevens, _The Necessary Angel_, New York: Random House, 1951, p. 35.

5 I have elaborated this argument about Whitman in my essay, "Spectacular Anti-Spectacle: Ecstasy and Nationality in Whitman and his Heirs," _American Literary History_, 11 (Spring 1999): 34–62.

6 See especially my _Painterly Abstraction_, ch. 1, and "The Pound/Stevens Era," _Wallace Stevens Journal_, 26.2 (Fall 2002): 228–50.

7 Stevens, _Necessary Angel_, pp. 25, 35–6.

8 Poetry about this "sharing" must be abstract because it has to be constructed by the feeling for imaginative activity rather than by specific images bound to memories that allow the poetry only an evocative function.

9   Mao is responding to Marjorie Perloff's "Pound/Stevens: Whose Era?" (*New Literary History*, 13 (1982): 495–514) in the *Wallace Stevens Journal* 26.2 (Fall 2002), an issue devoted to a twenty-year retrospect on that essay.

10 I am indebted to John Fuller, *W. H. Auden: A Commentary* (Princeton: Princeton University Press, 1998) for this publishing information (p. 88) and much else.

11 W. H. Auden, *The Complete Works of W. H. Auden: Prose*, vol. 2: *1939–1948*, ed. Edward Mendelson, Princeton: Princeton University Press, 2002, p. 48.

12 See W. H. Auden, *The Dyer's Hand and Other Essays*, New York: Random House, 1962, pp. 67–70. (Hereafter DH.)

13 Each key term here is carefully defined by Auden. A crowd consists of "members whose only relation is mathematical; they can only be counted." A society consists of members "united in a specific manner into a whole with a characteristic mode of behavior which is different from the modes of behavior of its component members in isolation." Finally, a community is comprised of members united by "a common love of something other than themselves" (DH 63–4). The poet produces relations among words that draw them into a distinct common mode of behavior so that the potential for identification with a "community" can be realized. The loves that form communities involve self-conscious commitment, whereas societies are "submembers of the total system of nature" (DH 64) and so do not depend on individual wills.

14 Rainer Emig, *W. H. Auden: Towards a Postmodern Poetics* (New York: Palgrave Macmillan, 2000) is quite good on how Auden rejects modernism, but Emig seems forced to the argument that Auden must then be postmodern. The broad themes by which Emig characterizes Auden's postmodernity seem to me not fundamental to why Auden's work has an impact on readers.

6 Modernist Dilemmas and Early Post-Modernist Responses

1   There are obvious alternatives, but I have said all I have to say about Frank O'Hara and Sylvia Plath, and I do not know how to say anything interesting about James Merrill and Allen Ginsberg – Merrill because I cannot crack his mandarin distance and Ginsberg because I cannot sufficiently respond to his awesome and needy generosity of spirit.

2   A brief sample of New Critical claims will have to suffice to indicate the cast they gave to their poetic heritage. Allen Tate made popular the notion that poetry was a distinctive mode of discourse because it alone managed

to escape both the orientation toward description and the orientation toward personal expression. If the former is characterized by philosophy as "extensional," and the latter exhibits the indeterminacy of "intensional" language, then poetry may be the one mode that can build on the "tension" between these orientations. Poetic language is what makes one connect feeling to description where otherwise there would be mere outpouring of the psyche. Because this language creates the organic unity correlating feeling with a sense of objectivity, it tends to seek ironic (or at least reflective) distance rewarding impersonal meditation. Analogously, Cleanth Brooks praised modern poetry for its commitment to paradox that preserved the perspective of metaphysical poetry and refused to submit to Enlightenment calls for clear and distinct extensional discourse. And John Crowe Ransom, the most openly theological and politically conservative of the group, treated metaphor as the "miraculist" reconciliation between the empiricist and the idealist attitudes towards knowledge. For more on the New Critics see Murray Krieger, *The New Apologists for Poetry*, Minneapolis: University of Minnesota Press, 1956; Mark Jancovich, *The Cultural Politics of the New Criticism*, Cambridge: Cambridge University Press, 1993; and my "The New Criticism," in Julian Wolfrey (ed.), *The Edinburgh Encyclopedia of Modern Criticism and Theory*, Edinburgh: Edinburgh University Press, 2002, pp. 436–44.

3   Robert Lowell, *Collected Poems*, ed. Frank Bidart and David Gewanter, New York: Farrar, Straus & Giroux, 2003, p. 113. (Hereafter Lowell, CP.)

4   For criticism responsive to the kind of agent Lowell's confessional poetry establishes, I am most indebted to Alan Williamson, *Introspection and Contemporary Poetry*, Cambridge, Mass.: Harvard University Press, 1984. In their edition of Lowell's poetry, Frank Bidart and David Gewanter also speak of a "standard of truth which you wouldn't ordinarily have in poetry – the reader was to believe he was getting the real Robert Lowell" (Lowell, CP 1000).

5   I am painfully aware that Lacan's model of the imaginary can always swallow up any effort at impersonality or rhetoric because there is always a level on which the agent can look back and decide that his or her action was good, and the terms by which that judgment is made will involve how the agent wants to be seen. (Even God looks back on the seventh day.) Nonetheless I think there is a substantial difference between actions shaped by imaginary ends and actions that in retrospect provide pleasures in relation to our considered investments.

6   Jay Bernstein, *Adorno and the Ethics of Disillusionment*, Cambridge: Cambridge University Press, 2001, pp. 416–17; see also pp. 402–9.

7   Margaret Atwood, "Review of *Diving into the Wreck*," *New York Times Book Review* (Dec. 30, 1973), repr. in *Adrienne Rich's Poetry and Prose*, 2nd edn,

sel. and ed. Barbara Charlesworth Gelpi and Albert Gelpi, New York: W. W. Norton, 1993, pp. 280–2.

8   Adrienne Rich, *The Fact of a Doorframe: Poems Selected and New 1950–1984*, New York: W. W. Norton, 1984, p. 229. (Hereafter FD.)

9   Adrienne Rich, *Adrienne Rich's Poetry and Prose*, 2nd edn, sel. and ed. Barbara Charlesworth Gelpi and Albert Gelpi, New York: W. W. Norton, 1993, p. 278. (Hereafter Rich, PP.)

10   Rich's cleanest statement on the use of the past to forge communities of women is "Heroines" in *A Wild Patience Has Taken Me This Far*. The poem ends:

> how can I give you
> all your due
> take courage from your courage
> honor your exact
> legacy as it is
> recognizing
> as well
> that it is not enough?   (FD 295)

11   This and the previous statement quoted from Baruch Spinoza, *The Ethics and Selected Letters*, trans. Samuel Shirley, Indianapolis: Hackett Publishing, 1982, pp. 109, 104.

12   Heather McHugh, "Love and Frangibility: An Appreciation of Robert Creeley" (*American Poetry Review* (May–June 1997): 9–16), is superb on the "perscendent" rather than "transcendent" self in Creeley, who climbs "not beyond but through the material world, the better to see, and hear it, through and through. At their best Creeley's poems move with a rhetorical care capable of palpably reminding us how mind finds its own forms in language" (p. 16).

13   I take my reading of this poem from my book *The Particulars of Rapture*, pp. 135–6, where I use it to make a much more elaborate argument for the importance of Spinoza.

14   Robert Creeley, *The Collected Poems of Robert Creeley 1945–1975*, Berkeley: University of California Press, 1982, p. 350. (Hereafter Creeley, CP.)

15   For Creeley on the interplay of subjective and objective see *A Quick Graph: Collected Notes and Essays*, ed. Donald Allen, San Francisco: Four Seasons Foundation, 1970, pp. 18–19.

16   Elizabeth Bishop, *The Complete Poems 1927–1979*, New York: Farrar, Straus & Giroux, 1983, p. 55. (Hereafter Bishop, CP.)

17   Letter to Anne Stevenson, Oct. 24, 1967, cited in Brett Millier, *Elizabeth Bishop: Life and the Memory of It*, Berkeley: University of California Press, 1993, p. 361.

18 David Kalstone, in *Five Temperaments* (Oxford: Oxford University Press, 1977), develops a plausible plot for the "Brazil" section of this volume.

19 John Ashbery, "Tradition and Talent," *New York Herald Tribune Book Week* (Sept. 4, 1966), repr. in Rich, pp. 279–80.

20 John Ashbery, *Selected Poems*, New York: Viking, 1985, p. 319. (Hereafter Ashbery, SP.)

21 John Ashbery, *Three Poems*, New York: Viking, 1972, p. 118.

22 See also the conclusion to Ashbery's "As One Put Drunk into the Packet Boat":

> The summer demands and takes away too much, But night, the reserved, the reticent, gives more than it takes.   (Ashbery, SP 164)

23 Denise Levertov, *The Jacob's Ladder*, New York: New Directions, 1961, p. 73.

Works Cited

Allbright, Daniel. *Quantum Poetics: Yeats, Pound, Eliot and the Science of Modernism.* New York: Cambridge University Press, 1977.

Althusser, Louis. *Essays on Ideology.* London: Verso, 1984.

Altieri, Charles. "The Fate of the Imaginary in Modern American Poetry." *American Literary History,* 17 (2005): 70–94.

——. "Intentionality as Sensuality in *Harmonium.*" *Wallace Stevens Journal,* 27 (2003): 163–72.

——. "The New Criticism." In Julian Wolfrey (ed.), *The Edinburgh Encyclopedia of Modern Criticism and Theory.* Edinburgh: Edinburgh University Press, 2002, pp. 436–44.

——. *Painterly Abstraction in Modernist American Poetry: The Contemporaneity of Modernism.* New York: Cambridge University Press, 1989.

——. *The Particulars of Rapture.* Ithaca: Cornell University Press, 2003.

——. "The Pound/Stevens Era." *Wallace Stevens Journal,* 26.2 (Fall 2002): 228–50.

——. "Spectacular Anti-Spectacle: Ecstasy and Nationality in Whitman and his Heirs." *American Literary History,* 11 (Spring 1999): 34–62.

Ashbery, John. *Chinese Whispers.* New York: Farrar, Straus & Giroux, 2002.

——. *Selected Poems.* New York: Viking, 1985.

——. *Three Poems.* New York: Viking, 1972.

——. "Tradition and Talent." *York Herald Tribune Book Week* (Sept. 4, 1966). Repr. in *Adrienne Rich's Poetry and Prose,* 2nd edn, sel. and ed. Barbara Charlesworth Gelpi and Albert Gelpi. New York: W. W. Norton, 1993, pp. 279–80.

Atwood, Margaret. "Review of *Diving into the Wreck.*" *New York Times Book Review* (Dec. 30, 1973). Repr. in *Adrienne Rich's Poetry and Prose,* 2nd edn, sel. and ed. Barbara Charlesworth Gelpi and Albert Gelpi. New York: W. W. Norton, 1993, pp. 280–2.

Auden, W. H. *Collected Poems*, ed. Edward Mendelson. New York: Vintage, 1991.

——. *The Complete Works of W. H. Auden: Prose*, vol. 2: *1939–1948*, ed. Edward Mendelson. Princeton: Princeton University Press, 2002.

——. *The Dyer's Hand and Other Essays*. New York: Random House, 1962.

Bell, Ian F. A. *Critic as Scientist: The Modernist Poetics of Ezra Pound*. London: Methuen, 1981.

Bergson, Henri. *Matter and Memory*, trans. N. M. Paul and W. S. Palmer. Cambridge: Zone Books, 1990.

——. *Time and Free Will*, trans. F. L. Pogson. Mineola, NY: Dover Publications, 2001.

Bernstein, Jay. *Adorno and the Ethics of Disillusionment*. Cambridge: Cambridge University Press, 2001.

Bishop, Elizabeth. *The Complete Poems 1927–1979*. New York: Farrar, Straus & Giroux, 1983.

Brooks, Cleanth. The *Well-Wrought Urn*. New York: Harvest, 1956.

Chipp, Herschel (ed.). *Theories of Modern Art*. Berkeley: University of California Press, 1968.

Clark, T. J. *Farewell to an Idea*. New Haven: Yale University Press, 1999.

Crary, Jonathan. *Suspension of Perception: Attention, Spectacle, and Modern Culture*. Cambridge, Mass.: MIT Press, 1999.

——. *Techniques of the Observer: On Vision and Modernity in the Nineteenth Century*. Cambridge, Mass.: MIT Press, 1990.

Creeley, Robert. *The Collected Poems of Robert Creeley 1945–1975*. Berkeley: University of California Press, 1982.

——. *If I Were Writing This*. New York: New Directions, 2003.

——. *Just in Time: Poems, 1984–1994*. New York: New Directions, 2001.

——. *A Quick Graph: Collected Notes and Essays*, ed. Donald Allen. San Francisco: Four Seasons Foundation, 1970.

Dean, Tim. *Beyond Sexuality*. Chicago: University of Chicago Press, 2000.

Dembo, Lawrence. "The Objectivist Poet: Four Interviews." *Contemporary Literature*, 10 (1969): 155–219.

——. "Oppen in his Poems." In Burton Hatlen (ed.), *George Oppen, Man and Poet*. Orono, Me.: National Poetry Foundation, 1981.

DuPlessis, Rachel Blau, and Quartermain, Peter (eds.). *The Objectivist Nexus: Essays in Cultural Poetics*. Tuscaloosa: University of Alabama Press, 1999.

Eliot, T. S. *The Complete Poems and Plays of T. S. Eliot*. New York: Harcourt Brace, 1969.

——. *The Inventions of the March Hare: Poems 1909–1917*, ed. Christopher Ricks. New York: Harcourt, Brace, 1996.

——. *Selected Essays*. New York: Harcourt Brace, 1950.

——. "Ulysses, Order, and Myth." Repr. in Frank Kermode (ed.), *Selected Prose of T. S. Eliot*. New York: Harvest, 1975.

Ellmann, Maud. *The Poetics of Impersonality: T. S. Eliot and Ezra Pound*. New York: Cambridge University Press, 1987.

Emig, Rainer. *W. H. Auden: Towards a Postmodern Poetics*. New York: Palgrave Macmillan, 2000.

Fenollosa, Ernest. "The Chinese Written Character as a Medium for Poetry." In Karl Shapiro (ed.), *Prose Keys to Modern Poetry*. New York: Harper & Row, 1962.

Frye, Northrop. *The Great Code*. New York: Harvest, 2002.

Fuller, John. *W. H. Auden: A Commentary*. Princeton: Princeton University Press, 1998.

Hatlen, Burton. "A Poetics of Marginality and Resistance: The Objectivist Poets in Context." In Rachel Blau DuPlessis and Peter Quartermain (eds.), *The Objectivist Nexus: Essays in Cultural Poetics*. Tuscaloosa: University of Alabama Press, 1999, pp. 37–55.

Homburger, Eric. *American Writers and Radical Politics, 1900–39: Equivocal Commitments*. New York: Palgrave Macmillan, 1986.

Hughes, Langston, *The Collected Poems of Langston Hughes*, ed. Arnold Rampersad and David Roessel. New York: Knopf, 1994.

Jancovich, Mark. *The Cultural Politics of the New Criticism*. Cambridge: Cambridge University Press, 1993.

Kalstone, David. *Five Temperaments*. Oxford: Oxford University Press, 1977.

Kenner, Hugh. *The Pound Era*. Berkeley: University of California Press, 1971.

Kern, Stephen. *The Culture of Time and Space 1880–1918*. Cambridge, Mass.: Harvard University Press, 2003.

Krieger, Murray. *The New Apologists for Poetry*. Minneapolis: University of Minnesota Press, 1956.

Lacan, Jacques. *Ecrits: A Selection*, trans. Alan Sheridan. New York: W. W. Norton, 1977.

——. *The Four Fundamental Concepts of Psycho-Analysis*, trans. Alan Sheridan. New York: W. W. Norton, 1978.

Levertov, Denise. *The Jacob's Ladder*. New York: New Directions, 1961.

Lowell, Robert. *Collected Poems*, ed. Frank Bidart and David Gewanter. New York: Farrar, Straus & Giroux, 2003.

Loy, Mina. *The Lost Lunar Baedeker*, ed. Roger L. Conover. New York: Farrar, Straus & Giroux, 1996.

Lyotard, Jean-François. *The Differend*. Minneapolis: University of Minnesota Press, 1988.

MacGowan, Christopher. *Twentieth-Century American Poetry*. Oxford: Blackwell, 2004.

McHugh, Heather. "Love and Frangibility: An Appreciation of Robert Creeley." *American Poetry Review* (May–June 1997): 9–16.

Mao, Douglas. "How to do Things with Modernism." *Wallace Stevens Journal,* 26 (Fall 2002): 160–80.

Merwin, W. S. *The Lice.* New York: Atheneum, 1967.

Millier, Brett. *Elizabeth Bishop: Life and the Memory of It.* Berkeley: University of California Press, 1993.

Moore, Marianne. *The Complete Poems of Marianne Moore.* New York: Macmillan, Viking, 1981.

Nelson. Cary. *Repression and Recovery.* Madison: University of Wisconsin Press, 1989.

——. *Revolutionary Memory: Recovering the Poetry of the American Left.* Oxford: Routledge, 2003.

Nichols, Peter. "On Being Ethical: Reflections on George Oppen." In Rachel Blau DuPlessis and Peter Quartermain (eds.), *The Objectivist Nexus: Essays in Cultural Poetics.* Tuscaloosa: University of Alabama Press, 1999, pp. 240–56.

Nietzsche, Friedrich. *Beyond Good and Evil.* New York: Vintage, 1989.

——. *The Birth of Tragedy.* Mineola, NY: Dover Publications, 1995.

Oppen, George. *New Collected Poems,* ed. Michael Davidson. New York: New Directions, 2002.

Perloff, Marjorie. "Pound/Stevens: Whose Era?" *New Literary History,* 13 (1982): 495–514.

——. *21st-Century Modernism: The New Poetics.* Oxford: Blackwell, 2002.

Pound, Ezra. *Gaudier-Brzeska: A Memoir.* New York: New Directions, 1970.

——. *Literary Essays of Ezra Pound,* ed. T. S. Eliot. London: Faber & Faber, 1960.

——. *Personae: Collected Shorter Poems of Ezra Pound.* London: Faber & Faber, 1952.

——. *Selected Prose, 1909–1965: Ezra Pound,* ed. William Cookson. New York: New Directions, 1973.

Ransom, John Crowe. *The World's Body.* Baton Rouge: Louisiana State University Press, 1968.

Rich, Adrienne. *Adrienne Rich's Poetry and Prose,* 2nd edn, sel. and ed. Barbara Charlesworth Gelpi and Albert Gelpi. New York: W. W. Norton, 1993.

——. *The Fact of a Doorframe: Poems Selected and New 1950–1984.* New York: W. W. Norton, 1984.

——. *Fox: Poems, 1998–2000.* New York: W. W. Norton, 2001.

——. *The School among the Ruins: Poems, 2000–2004.* New York: W. W. Norton, 2004.

Richards, I. A. *Coleridge on Imagination.* Oxford: Routledge, 2001.

Sartre, Jean-Paul. *Being and Nothingness,* trans. Hazel E. Barnes. New York: Washington Square Press, 1993.

Sayre, Henry. *The Visual Text of William Carlos Williams.* Urbana: University of Illinois Press, 1983.

Schapiro, Meyer. "The Apples of Cézanne: An Essay on the Meaning of Still-Life." In Schapiro, *Modern Art: 19th and 20th Centuries: Selected Papers*. New York: George Braziller, 1979, pp. 1–38.

Shoptaw, John. "Lyric Incorporated: The Serial Object of George Oppen and Langston Hughes." *Sagetrieb*, 12 (1993): 108.

Spinoza, Baruch. *The Ethics and Selected Letters*, trans. Samuel Shirley. Indianapolis: Hackett Publishing, 1982.

Steinman, Lisa. *Made in America: Science, Technology, and American Modernist Poets*. New Haven: Yale University Press, 1987.

Stevens, Wallace. *The Collected Poems of Wallace Stevens*. New York: Knopf, 1964.

——. *The Necessary Angel*. New York: Random House, 1951.

Tate, Allen. *Essays of Four Decades*. New York: William Morrow & Co., 1968.

Watten, Barrett. *The Constructivist Moment: From Material Text to Cultural Poetics*. Middletown, Conn.: Wesleyan University Press, 2003.

Weinstein, Philip. *Unknowing: The Work of Modernist Fiction*. Ithaca: Cornell University Press, 2005.

Whitehead, Alfred North. *Science in the Modern World*. New York: Macmillan, 1926.

Williams, William Carlos. *The Collected Poems of William Carlos Williams*, 2 vols., ed. A. Walton Litz and Christopher MacGowan. New York: New Directions, 1986, 1988.

——. *The Embodiment of Knowledge*, ed. Ron Loewinsohn. New York: New Directions, 1974.

——. *Imaginations: Five Experimental Prose Pieces*, ed. Webster Schott. New York: New Directions, 1970.

——. *Selected Essays of William Carlos Williams*. New York: Random House, 1954.

Williamson, Alan. *Introspection and Contemporary Poetry*. Cambridge, Mass.: Harvard University Press, 1984.

Yeats, William Butler. *Essays and Introductions*. New York: Collier Books, 1961.

——. "Introduction." In Yeats (ed.), *The Oxford Book of Modern Verse*, Oxford: Clarendon Press, 1936.

Zukofsky, Louis. *Prepositions*. Berkeley: University of California Press, 1981.

Further Reading

Books on General Topics

Altieri, Charles. *Self and Sensibility in Contemporary American Poetry*. Cambridge: Cambridge University Press, 1984.

Breslin, James. *From Modern to Contemporary: American Poetry 1945–1965*. Chicago: University of Chicago Press, 1984.

Broe, Mary Lynn, and Scott, Bonnie Kime (eds.). *The Gender of Modernism*. Bloomington and Indianapolis: Indiana University Press, 1990.

Brogan, Jacqueline. *Part of the Climate: American Cubist Poetry*. Berkeley: University of California Press, 1991.

Costello, Bonnie. *Shifting Ground: Reinventing Landscape in Modern American Poetry*. Cambridge, Mass.: Harvard University Press, 2003.

Critchley, Simon. *Things Merely Are: Philosophy in the Poetry of Wallace Stevens*. New York: Routledge, 2005.

Davidson, Michael. *Ghostlier Demarcations*. Berkeley: University of California Press, 1997.

——. *The San Francisco Renaissance: Poetics and Community at Mid-Century*. Cambridge: Cambridge University Press, 1991.

Diggory, Terence, and Miller, Stephen (eds.). *The Scene of My Selves: New Work on New York School Poets*. Orono, Me.: National Poetry Foundation; distr. by University Press of New England, 2001.

DuPlessis, Rachel. *Genders, Races, and Religious Cultures in Modern American Poetry 1908–1934*. Cambridge: Cambridge University Press, 2001.

Ellmann, Richard, and Fiedelson, Charles (eds.). *The Modern Tradition*. Oxford: Oxford University Press, 1965.

Gardner, Thomas. *Regions of Unlikeness*. Lincoln: University of Nebraska Press, 1999.

Gregory, Elizabeth. *Quotation and Modern American Poetry*. College Station: Texas A&M University Press, 1996.

Haralson, Eric, and Hollander, John (eds.). *Encyclopedia of American Poetry: The Twentieth Century.* Chicago: Fitzroy Dearborn, 2001.

Hutchinson, George. *The Harlem Renaissance in Black and White.* Cambridge, Mass.: Harvard University Press, 1995.

Kolocotroni, Vassiliki, et al. *Modernism: An Anthology of Sources and Documents.* Edinburgh: Edinburgh University Press, 1994.

Lentricchia, Frank. *Modernist Quartet.* New York: Cambridge University Press, 1994.

Levenson, Michael. *A Genealogy of Modernism.* Cambridge: Cambridge University Press, 1984.

Longenbach, James. *Modern Poetry after Modernism.* Oxford: Oxford University Press, 1997.

——. *Modernist Poetics of History: Pound, Eliot, and the Sense of the Past.* Princeton: Princeton University Press, 1987.

——. *Stone Cottage: Pound, Yeats, and Modernism.* Oxford: Oxford University Press, 1988.

Miller, Brett, and Parini, Jay (eds.). *Columbia History of American Poetry.* New York: Columbia University Press, 1993.

Molesworth, Charles. *The Fierce Embrace: A Study of Contemporary American Poetry.* Columbia: University of Missouri Press, 1979.

Morrison, Paul. *The Poetics of Fascism: Ezra Pound, T. S. Eliot, Paul de Man.* Oxford: Oxford University Press, 1996.

Nichols, Peter. *Modernisms.* New York: Palgrave Macmillan, 1995.

Nielsen, Aldon. *Reading Race in American Poetry.* Champaign: University of Illinois Press, 2000.

Perkins, David. *A History of Modern Poetry.* Cambridge, Mass.: Harvard University Press, 1976.

Perloff, Marjorie. *The Dance of the Intellect: Studies in the Poetry of the Pound Tradition.* Cambridge: Cambridge University Press, 1985.

——. *The Poetics of Indeterminacy.* Evanston, Ill.: Northwestern University Press, 2000.

——. *Radical Artifice.* Chicago: University of Chicago Press, 1994.

Roberts, Neil (ed.). *A Companion to Twentieth-Century Poetry.* Oxford: Blackwell, 2001.

Sherry, Vincent. *The Great War and the Language of Modernism.* New York: Oxford University Press, 2003.

Stitt, Peter. *Uncertainty and Plenitude.* Iowa City: University of Iowa Press, 1997.

Von Hallberg, Robert. *American Poetry and Culture, 1945–1980.* Cambridge, Mass.: Harvard University Press, 1988.

Watson, Steven. *The Birth of the Beat Generation: Visionaries, Rebels, and Hipsters, 1944–1960.* New York: Pantheon, 1998.

Books on Individual Poets

John Ashbery

Ashbery, John. *Other Traditions.* Cambridge, Mass.: Harvard University Press, 2000.

——. *Reported Sightings: Art Chronicles 1957–1987,* ed. David Bergman. Cambridge, Mass.: Harvard University Press, 1991.

Kelly, Lionel. *Poetry and the Sense of Panic: Critical Essays on Elizabeth Bishop and John Ashbery.* Amsterdam: Rodopi, 2000.

Packard, William (ed.). *The Poet's Craft: Interviews from the New York Quarterly.* St. Paul: Paragon House, 1986.

Richie, Eugene (ed.). *Selected Prose: John Ashbery.* Ann Arbor: University of Michigan Press, 2004.

Schultz, Susan (ed.). *The Tribe of John: Ashbery and Contemporary Poetry.* Tuscaloosa: University of Alabama Press, 1995.

Shoptaw, John. *On the Outside Looking Out.* Cambridge, Mass.: Harvard University Press, 1994.

W. H. Auden

Bozroth, Richard. *Auden's Game of Knowledge: Poetry and the Meanings of Homosexuality.* New York: Columbia University Press, 2001.

Bucknell, Katherine, and Jenkins, Nicholas (eds.). *The Language of Learning and the Language of Love: Uncollected Writing, New Interpretations/W. H. Auden.* New York: Oxford University Press, 1994.

Callan, Edward. *Auden: A Carnival of the Intellect.* Oxford: Oxford University Press, 1983.

Haffenden, John (ed.). *W. H. Auden: The Critical Heritage.* Oxford: Routledge, 1983.

Mendelson, Edward. *Early Auden.* New York: Farrar, Straus & Giroux, 1981.

——. *Later Auden.* New York: Farrar, Straus & Giroux, 1999.

—— (ed.). *Plays and Other Dramatic Writings by W. H. Auden, 1928–1938.* London: Faber & Faber, 1988.

Smith, Stan. *W. H. Auden.* Oxford: Blackwell, 1985.

Elizabeth Bishop

Bishop, Elizabeth. *Elizabeth Bishop: The Collected Prose.* New York: Farrar, Straus & Giroux, 1984.

Costello, Bonnie. *Elizabeth Bishop: Questions of Mastery.* Cambridge, Mass.: Harvard University Press, 1991.

McCabe, Susan. *Elizabeth Bishop: Her Poetics of Loss.* University Park: Pennsylvania State University Press, 1994.

Monteiro, George (ed.). *Conversations with Elizabeth Bishop*. Jackson: University Press of Mississippi, 1996.

Schweik, Susan. *A Gulf So Deeply Cut: American Women Poets and the Second World War*. Madison: University of Wisconsin Press, 1991.

Stevenson, Anne. *Five Looks at Elizabeth Bishop*. London: Bellew, 1998.

Travisano, Thomas. *Elizabeth Bishop: Her Artistic Development*. Charlottesville: University Press of Virginia, 1988.

Robert Creeley

Creeley, Robert. *The Collected Essays of Robert Creeley*. Berkeley: University of California Press, 1989.

———. *The Collected Prose of Robert Creeley*. New York: Marion Boyars, 1984.

———. *Contexts of Poetry: Interviews, 1961–1971*. San Francisco: Four Seasons Foundation, 1973.

Faas, Ekbert. *Robert Creeley: A Biography*. Hanover, NH: University Press of New England, 2001.

Olson, Charles, and Creeley, Robert. *Charles Olson and Robert Creeley: The Complete Correspondence*, ed. George Butterick. Santa Barbara: Black Sparrow Press, 1987.

Terrell, Carroll F. *Robert Creeley: The Poet's Workshop*. Lebanon, NH: University Press of New England, 1984.

Wilson, John (ed.). *Robert Creeley's Life and Work: A Sense of Increment*. Ann Arbor: University of Michigan Press, 1988.

T. S. Eliot

Ackroyd, Peter. *T. S. Eliot: A Life*. New York: Simon & Schuster, 1984.

Bagchee, Shyamal (ed.). *T. S. Eliot, A Voice Descanting: Centenary Essays*. New York: Palgrave Macmillan, 1990.

Brooker, Jewel Spears. *Mastery and Escape: T. S. Eliot and the Dialectic of Modernism*. Amherst: University of Massachusetts Press, 1994.

——— (ed.). *T. S. Eliot and Our Turning World*. New York: Palgrave Macmillan, 2001.

Bush, Ronald (ed.). *T. S. Eliot: The Modernist in History*. Cambridge: Cambridge University Press, 1991.

Davidson, Harriet. *T. S. Eliot*. London and New York: Longman, 1999.

Eliot, T. S. *The Letters of T. S. Eliot*, vol. 1: *1898–1922*, ed. Valerie Eliot. San Diego: Harcourt, 1988.

———. *Selected Prose of T. S. Eliot*, ed. Frank Kermode. New York: Harvest, 1975.

Eliot, Valerie (ed.). *Waste Land: A Facsimile & Transcript of the Original Drafts, Including the Annotations of Ezra Pound*. San Diego: Harcourt, 1971.

Gardner, Helen. *The Composition of 'Four Quartets.'* London: Faber, 1978.

Gordon, Lyndall. *T. S. Eliot: An Imperfect Life*. New York: W. W. Norton, 1998.

Grant, Michael (ed.). *T. S. Eliot: The Critical Heritage*. Oxford: Routledge, 1982.

Laity, Cassandra, and Gish, Nancy K. (eds.). *Gender, Desire, and Sexuality in T. S. Eliot*. Cambridge: Cambridge University Press, 2004.

Moody, David. *Thomas Stearns Eliot, Poet*. Cambridge: Cambridge University Press, 1979.

—— (ed.). *The Cambridge Companion to T. S. Eliot*. Cambridge: Cambridge University Press, 1994.

North, Michael (ed.). *The Norton Critical Edition of 'The Waste Land.'* New York: W. W. Norton, 2001.

Pollard, Charles W. *New World Modernisms: T. S. Eliot, Derek Walcott, and Kamau Brathwaite*. Charlottesville: University Press of Virginia, 2004.

Schuchard, Ronald. *Eliot's Dark Angel: Intersections of Life and Art*. Oxford: Oxford University Press, 1999.

Smith, Grover. *T. S. Eliot's Poetry and Plays: A Study in Sources and Meanings*. Chicago: University of Chicago Press, 1956.

Langston Hughes

Appiah, Anthony, and Gates, Henry Louis, Jr. (eds.). *Langston Hughes: Critical Perspectives Past and Present*. New York: Amistad, 1993.

Hughes, Langston. *The Collected Works of Langston Hughes*, 16 vols., ed. Arnold Rampersad. Columbia: University of Missouri Press, 2001.

Miller, R. Baxter. *The Art and Imagination of Langston Hughes*. Lexington: University Press of Kentucky, 1989.

Rampersad, Arnold. *The Life of Langston Hughes*. Oxford: Oxford University Press, 2002.

Tracy, Steven C. *Langston Hughes and the Blues*. Champaign: University of Illinois Press, 2001.

—— (ed.). *A Historical Guide to Langston Hughes*. New York: Oxford University Press, 2004.

Trotman, C. James (ed.). *Langston Hughes: The Man and his Continuing Influence*. New York: Garland, 1995.

Robert Lowell

Axelrod, Steven. *The Critical Response to Robert Lowell*. Westport, Conn.: Greenwood, 1999.

Bell, Vereen. *Robert Lowell: Nihilist as Hero*. Cambridge, Mass.: Harvard University Press, 1983.

Doreski, William. *Robert Lowell's Shifting Colors: The Poetics of the Public and the Personal.* Athens: Ohio University Press, 1999.

Lowell, Robert. *The Collected Prose,* ed. Robert Giroux. New York: Farrar, Straus & Giroux, 1990.

——. *Robert Lowell: Interviews and Memoirs,* ed. Jeffrey Meyers. Ann Arbor: University of Michigan Press, 1988.

Perloff, Marjorie. *The Poetic Art of Robert Lowell.* Ithaca: Cornell University Press, 1973.

Travisano, Thomas. *Midcentury Quartet: Bishop, Lowell, Jarrell, Berryman, and the Making of a Postmodern Aesthetic.* Charlottesville: University Press of Virginia, 1999.

Williamson, Alan. *Pity the Monsters: The Political Vision of Robert Lowell.* New Haven: Yale University Press, 1974.

Mina Loy

Burke, Carolyn. *Becoming Modern: The Life of Mina Loy.* New York: Farrar, Straus & Giroux, 1996.

Miller, Tyrus. *Late Modernism.* Berkeley: University of California Press, 1999.

Shreiber, Maeera, and Tuma, Keith (eds.). *Mina Loy: Woman and Poet.* Lebanon, NH: University Press of New England, 1998.

Marianne Moore

Costello, Bonnie. *Marianne Moore: Imaginary Possessions.* Cambridge, Mass.: Harvard University Press, 1981.

Gregory, Elizabeth. *The Critical Response to Marianne Moore.* Westport, Conn.: Praeger, 2003.

Heuving, Jeanne. *Omissions are Not Accidents: Gender in the Art of Marianne Moore.* Detroit: Wayne State University Press, 1992.

Joyce, Elizabeth. *Cultural Critique and Abstraction: Marianne Moore and the Avant-Garde.* Lewisburg, Pa.: Bucknell University Press, 1998.

Miller, Cristanne. *Marianne Moore: Questions of Authority.* Cambridge, Mass.: Harvard University Press, 1995.

Molesworth, Charles. *Marianne Moore: A Literary Life.* Boston: Northeastern University Press, 1990.

Moore, Marianne. *The Poems of Marianne Moore,* ed. Grace Schulman. New York: Viking, 2003.

——. *The Selected Letters of Marianne Moore,* gen. ed. Bonnie Costello. New York: Knopf, 1997.

Schulze, Robin. *Becoming Marianne Moore: The Early Poems, 1907–1924.* Berkeley: University of California Press, 2002.

———. *The Web of Friendship: Marianne Moore and Wallace Stevens*. Ann Arbor: University of Michigan Press, 1996.

Slatin, John. *The Savage's Romance*. University Park: Pennsylvania State University Press, 1986.

Willis, Patricia. *Marianne Moore: Woman and Poet*. Lebanon, NH: University Press of New England, 1990.

George Oppen

Hatlen, Burton. *George Oppen, Man and Poet*. Lebanon, NH: University Press of New England, 1981.

Oppen, George. *The Selected Letters of George Oppen*, ed. Rachel Blau DuPlessis. Durham, NC: Duke University Press, 1990.

Ezra Pound

Brooke-Rose, Christine. *A ZBC of Ezra Pound*. Berkeley: University of California Press, 1971.

Davie, Donald. *Ezra Pound: Poet as Sculptor*. Oxford: Oxford University Press, 1964.

Dilligan, Robert, et al. *A Concordance to Ezra Pound's Cantos*. New York: Garland, 1981.

Froula, Christine. *A Guide to Ezra Pound's Selected Poems*. New York: New Directions, 1983.

Nadel, Ira B. *Ezra Pound: A Literary Life*. New York: Palgrave Macmillan, 2004.

Pound, Ezra. *Poems and Translations/Ezra Pound*, ed. Richard Sieburth. New York: Library of America, 2003.

——— and Lewis, Wyndham. *Pound/Lewis: The Letters of Ezra Pound and Wyndham Lewis*, ed. Timothy Materer. New York: New Directions, 1985.

——— and Shakespeare, Dorothy. *Ezra Pound and Dorothy Shakespeare: Their Letters, 1909–1914*, ed. A. Walton Litz and Omar Pound. New York: New Directions, 1984.

——— and Williams, William Carlos. *Pound/Williams: Selected Letters of Ezra Pound and William Carlos Williams*, ed. Hugh Whitemeyer. New York: New Directions, 1996.

Ruthven, K. K. *A Guide to Ezra Pound's Personae*. Berkeley: University of California Press, 1969.

Sherry, Vincent. *Ezra Pound, Wyndham Lewis, and Radical Modernism*. Oxford: Oxford University Press, 1993.

Terrell, Carroll F. *A Companion to the Cantos of Ezra Pound*, 2 vols. Berkeley: University of California Press, 1980, 1984.

Wilhelm, James. *The American Roots of Ezra Pound*. Reading: Garnet, 1985.

———. *Ezra Pound in London and Paris*. University Park: Pennsylvania State University Press, 1990.

———. *Ezra Pound: The Tragic Years*. University Park: Pennsylvania State University Press, 1994.

Adrienne Rich

Dickie, Margaret. *Stein, Bishop, and Rich: Lyrics of Love, War, and Place*. Chapel Hill: University of North Carolina Press, 1997.

Ostriker, Alicia. *Writing Like a Woman*. Ann Arbor: University of Michigan Press, 1983.

Prins, Yopie, and Shreiber, Maeera (eds.). *Dwelling in Possibility: Women Poets and Critics on Poetry*. Ithaca: Cornell University Press, 1997.

Rich, Adrienne. *Blood, Bread, and Poetry: Selected Prose, 1979–1985*. New York: W. W. Norton, 1994.

———. *Collected Early Poems, 1950–1970*. New York: W. W. Norton, 1993.

———. *Of Woman Born: Motherhood as Experience and Institution*. New York: W. W. Norton, 1995.

———. *On Lies, Secrets, and Silence: Selected Prose, 1966–1978*. New York: W. W. Norton, 1995.

———. *What is Found There: Notebooks on Poetry and Politics*. New York: W. W. Norton, 2003.

Templeton, Alice. *The Dream and the Dialogue: Adrienne Rich's Feminist Poetics*. Knoxville: University of Tennessee Press, 1995.

Yorke, Liz. *Adrienne Rich: Passion, Politics and the Body*. Thousand Oaks, Calif.: Sage, 1998.

Wallace Stevens

Berger, Charles. *Forms of Farewell: The Late Poetry of Wallace Stevens*. Madison: University of Wisconsin Press, 1985.

Cleghorn, Angus. *Wallace Stevens' Poetics: The Neglected Rhetoric*. New York: Palgrave Macmillan, 2001.

Filreis, Alan. *Wallace Stevens and the Actual World*. Princeton: Princeton University Press, 1991.

——— et al. *Modernism from Right to Left: Wallace Stevens, the Thirties, and Literary Radicalism*. Cambridge: Cambridge University Press, 1994.

Gelpi, Albert (ed.). *Wallace Stevens: The Poetics of Modernism*. Cambridge: Cambridge University Press, 1985.

Jenkins, Lee. *Wallace Stevens: Rage for Order*. Brighton: Sussex Academic Press, 2000.

Richardson, Joan. *Wallace Stevens: The Early Years, 1879–1923*. New York: Beech Tree Books, 1986.

——. *Wallace Stevens: The Later Years, 1923–1955*. New York: Beech Tree Books, 1988.

Riddel, Joseph. *The Clairvoyant Eye: The Poetry and Poetics of Wallace Stevens*. Baton Rouge: Louisiana State University Press, 1991.

Sharpe, Tony. *Wallace Stevens: A Literary Life*. New York: Palgrave Macmillan, 2000.

Stevens, Wallace. *Letters of Wallace Stevens*, ed. Holly Stevens. Berkeley: University of California Press, 1996.

——. *Stevens: Collected Poetry and Prose*, ed. Frank Kermode and Joan Richardson. New York: Library of America, 1997.

Vendler, Helen. *On Extended Wings: Wallace Stevens' Longer Poems*. Cambridge, Mass.: Harvard University Press, 1969.

William Carlos Williams

Ahearn, Barry. *William Carlos Williams and Alterity: The Early Poetry*. Cambridge: Cambridge University Press, 1994.

Axelrod, Steven, and Deese, Helen (eds.). *Critical Essays on William Carlos Williams*. Boston: G. K. Hall, 1995.

Bleck, John. *Writing the Radical Center: William Carlos Williams, John Dewey, and American Cultural Politics*. Albany: State University of New York Press, 2001.

Bremen, Brian. *William Carlos Williams and the Diagnostics of Culture*. Oxford: Oxford University Press, 1993.

Breslin, James. *William Carlos Williams: An American Artist*. Chicago: University of Chicago Press, 1970.

Doyle, Charles (ed.). *William Carlos Williams: The Critical Heritage*. Oxford: Routledge, 1980.

Halter, Peter. *The Revolution in the Visual Arts and the Poetry of William Carlos Williams*. Cambridge: Cambridge University Press, 1994.

Mariani, Paul. *William Carlos Williams: A New World Naked*. New York: Norton, 1981.

Rapp, Carl. *William Carlos Williams and Romantic Idealism*. Hanover, NH: University Press of New England for Brown University Press, 1984.

Riddel, Joseph. *The Inverted Bell*. Baton Rouge: Louisiana State University Press, 1974.

Williams, William Carlos. *A Recognizable Image: William Carlos Williams on Art and Artists*, ed. Bram Dijkstra. New York: New Directions, 1978.

——. *The Selected Letters of William Carlos Williams*, ed. John Thirlwall. New York: New Directions, 1985.

Index

Made in the USA
Lexington, KY
10 December 2012